Uncharted Depths
Descent Narratives in English and French
Children's Literature

LEGENDA

LEGENDA, founded in 1995 by the European Humanities Research Centre of the University of Oxford, is now a joint imprint of the Modern Humanities Research Association and Routledge. Titles range from medieval texts to contemporary cinema and form a widely comparative view of the modern humanities, including works on Arabic, Catalan, English, French, German, Greek, Italian, Portuguese, Russian, Spanish, and Yiddish literature. An Editorial Board of distinguished academic specialists works in collaboration with leading scholarly bodies such as the Society for French Studies and the British Comparative Literature Association.

MHRA

The Modern Humanities Research Association (MHRA) encourages and promotes advanced study and research in the field of the modern humanities, especially modern European languages and literature, including English, and also cinema. It also aims to break down the barriers between scholars working in different disciplines and to maintain the unity of humanistic scholarship in the face of increasing specialization. The Association fulfils this purpose primarily through the publication of journals, bibliographies, monographs and other aids to research.

Routledge
Taylor & Francis Group

LONDON AND NEW YORK

Routledge is a global publisher of academic books, journals and online resources in the humanities and social sciences. Founded in 1836, it has published many of the greatest thinkers and scholars of the last hundred years, including Adorno, Einstein, Russell, Popper, Wittgenstein, Jung, Bohm, Hayek, McLuhan, Marcuse and Sartre. Today Routledge is one of the world's leading academic publishers in the Humanities and Social Sciences. It publishes thousands of books and journals each year, serving scholars, instructors, and professional communities worldwide.

www.routledge.com

Uncharted Depths

Descent Narratives in English and French Children's Literature

KIERA VACLAVIK

LEGENDA

Modern Humanities Research Association and Routledge

2010

First published 2010

Published by the
Modern Humanities Research Association and Routledge
2 Park Square, Milton Park, Abingdon, Oxon OX14 4RN
711 Third Avenue, New York, NY 10017, USA

LEGENDA is an imprint of the
Modern Humanities Research Association and Routledge

Routledge is an imprint of the Taylor & Francis Group, an informa business

© Modern Humanities Research Association and Taylor & Francis 2010

ISBN 978-1-906540-39-5 (hbk)

CONTENTS

FOR THOMAS LUCIEN BURNS

ACKNOWLEDGEMENTS

I am indebted to many individuals at a number of institutions for their contributions to the various stages of this project: Rachel Falconer and David McCallum at the University of Sheffield; Adrian Armstrong, Hilary Owen, Jonathan Hensher, Barbara Lebrun and above all Penny Brown at the University of Manchester; and finally Will McMorran and all of my other colleagues in the School of Languages, Linguistics and Film at Queen Mary, University of London. For invaluable practical assistance, encouragement and support, I should also like to thank Charles Forsdick, Timothy Unwin, René Paul, Graham Nelson, Richard Correll, my father, the Buck and Burns families, Stéphane Calmé-Magnan, Nicole Armaingaud and Agnieszka Gratza.

Part of Chapter 1 appeared in a different form in my 'Jules Verne écrivain... de jeunesse: The Case of *Voyage au centre de la terre*', *Australian Journal of French Studies*, 42 (2005), 276–83; part of Chapter 2 in my 'Death for Beginners: Nineteenth-Century Katabatic Narratives for Young Readers', in *Birth and Death in Nineteenth-Century French Culture*, ed. by Nigel Harkness, Lisa Downing, Sonya Stephens and Timothy Unwin (Amsterdam/New York: Rodopi, 2007), pp. 127–38; and part of Chapter 3 in my 'The descent to the underworld retold and regendered in Philip Pullman's *The Amber Spyglass*', *The Journal of Children's Literature Studies*, 5 (2008) 37–56. I am grateful to the editors for their guidance in the writing of these articles.

LIST OF ABBREVIATIONS

Paradis	Antoine de La Sale, *Le Paradis de La Reine Sibylle*
Télémaque	François de Fénelon, *Aventures de Télémaque*
Triumphs	William Hayley, *The Triumphs of Temper*
Voyage	Jules Verne, *Voyage au Centre de la Terre*
Wonderland	Lewis Carroll, *Alice's Adventures in Wonderland*
Princess	George MacDonald, *The Princess and the Goblin*

TRANSLATIONS USED

HOMER, *The Odyssey*, trans. by Robert Fagles (London: Penguin, 2001)

VIRGIL, *The Aeneid*, trans. by David West (London: Penguin, 2001)

DANTE, *The Inferno*, trans. by Robert Pinsky (London: Dent, 1997)

FRANÇOIS DE FÉNELON, *Telemachus, son of Ulysses*, ed. and trans. by Patrick Riley (Cambridge: CUP, 1994)

STÉPHANIE DE GENLIS, *Tales of the Castle: or, Stories of Instruction and Delight*, trans. by Thomas Holcroft, 5 vols (London: Robinson, 1785)

JULES VERNE, *Journey to the Centre of the Earth*, trans. by William Butcher, 3rd edn (Oxford/New York: OUP, 1992)

HECTOR MALOT, *No Relations*, trans. by May Laffan, 3 vols (London: Bentley, 1880)

GEORGE SAND, 'Fairy Dust: A Story for Children', [no trans.] *The Strand Magazine*, 11 (1891), 536–43

GÉRARD GENETTE, *Palimpsests: Literature in the Second Degree*, trans. by Channa Newman and Claude Doubinsky (Lincoln/London: University of Nebraska Press, 1997)

Unless stated in the notes, all other translations into English are my own.

INTRODUCTION

> [...] you have to laugh at the claim — made by others first, but repeated by Pullman [...] — that he has rewritten *Paradise Lost*. Not every story of rebellion against authority is Miltonic. Or, to take another example, *Ulysses* is a rewriting of the *Odyssey*, Judith Kerr's *Mog Goes to the Vee, Eee, Tee* (also the story of a departure from, and then a return to, home) is not.[1]

Dina Rabinovitch's withering remarks concerning Philip Pullman's immensely successful and critically acclaimed *His Dark Materials* trilogy raise a number of issues about the status of children's literature and its position in the cultural arena. Rabinovitch effectively carves out two distinct fields with *Paradise Lost*, *Ulysses*, and the *Odyssey* set against and above *His Dark Materials* and *Mog*. For this journalist, bringing works from the two realms into conjunction is utterly absurd. Children's literature emerges here as both different from, and inferior to, adult literature. There is of course nothing new in this relegation of children's literature to the margins. Described in 1994 as being 'invisible in the literary world', it has traditionally been defined by what it lacks with respect to adult literature and has been associated with limitation, in terms of both subject matter and form.[2] At the same time, its frequently overt didacticism links it with a utilitarianism long deemed to be diametrically opposed to the creative.[3] As Rabinovitch's comments suggest, children's literature continues to be regarded by many as the poor relation of the literary establishment.

Yet alongside, and as part of, a more general interrogation of literary and cultural boundaries, there has been a great deal of interest in children's literature in recent years, both within the academy and beyond.[4] Thus, for example, Peter Hunt rejects outright the marginalization of children's literature, evoking the immense power of children's books, and their educational, social, cultural and commercial importance.[5] Although their outlooks are so divergent, Hunt, like Rabinovitch, regards children's literature as being utterly unlike adult literature:

> The texts themselves have evolved very differently; the authors of them have seen themselves in different roles; their motivations have been different; their relationship with their audience is different; their relationship with their subject-matter, their style, their narrative modes are different.[6]

For Hunt, then, children's books are different from, but not inferior to, those written for adults, and he advocates their removal from 'the literary hierarchy', and their treatment 'as a separate group of texts, without reference (at least in principle) to literature as it is known and misunderstood'.[7]

But an exclusive focus on children's literature runs the risk of its ghettoization, and Hunt himself concedes that children's literature 'does not exist separately' or 'in a vacuum'.[8] The fact that adults produce, market, buy, and often consume works of children's literature itself argues against any radical separation of the two fields. Although distinct in many ways, adult and children's literature nevertheless frequently share common features, such as, for example — and as Rabinovitch's comments suggest — overarching story patterns. More than three decades ago, James Steel Smith stressed the 'special characteristics of form that distinguish children's literature and adult literature from each other' but also pointed to a number of common features shared by all literary works, irrespective of audience.[9] Calling into question both Aristotelian and Cartesian logic, children's literature is at once different from, and similar to, adult literature.

Bringing the two realms into conjunction is, then, by no means as ludicrous as Rabinovitch's comments would suggest. Indeed, it is an extremely important undertaking. Only by examining children's literature in relation to adult literature is it possible for speculation concerning the similarities and differences between the two to be concretized. Any endeavour to understand children's literature more fully, rather than merely attribute value and establish literary pecking orders, must be wide-ranging. As Margery Hourihan argues, its import and impact 'cannot be properly appreciated unless it is explored in the broader cultural context'.[10] Nor is children's literature the sole beneficiary of such an approach: Deborah Cogan Thacker has recently shown that both fields can be better understood by being brought together rather than kept apart.[11]

The examination of story patterns apparent in both adult and children's literature, such as the *nostos* alluded to by Rabinovitch, can reveal important things about the stories we have told and continue to tell ourselves and the power of specific forms of narrative. Such an endeavour can also provide valuable insights into processes of transmission and acculturation, and the ways in which readers develop familiarity with literary conventions. The connections between Pullman and Milton therefore clearly merit serious attention rather than scoffing dismissal. Nor is *Paradise Lost* the only canonical text of Western literature with which the *His Dark Materials* trilogy can be fruitfully related on the basis of shared story pattern. As part of their rebellion against authority, Pullman's hero and heroine embark upon a particular form of journey undertaken not only by Odysseus, but also by Aeneas and Dante the pilgrim.

Due to the subterranean situation of its destination, the journey in question was known to the ancient Greeks as *katabasis*. It is defined by Raymond J. Clark as 'a Journey of the Dead made by a living person in the flesh who returns to our world to tell the tale'.[12] The relationships between the three katabatic narratives which occur in the eleventh book of the *Odyssey*, the sixth book of the *Aeneid*, and the first part of the *Divina Commedia* have been examined in considerable detail by a number of critics.[13] Closely concerned with the crossing of the ultimate border between life and death, this world and the next, the katabatic narrative has itself crossed not only temporal but also geographical, linguistic, theological and cultural boundaries. As H. W. Stubbs has observed: 'The story of the Hero who descends to the Underworld is as successful on BBC television as it was in Sumerian cuneiform.'[14] The continuation of this highly compelling form of narrative in the modern period, despite seismic changes concerning the very concept of the underworld, has also been widely remarked and studied. Critics have identified a vast range of modern manifestations of katabasis, especially in English and French literature and, adopting a wide range of critical perspectives, have undertaken frequently detailed examinations of the relationships between these narratives and their classical and medieval predecessors.

Several critics have focused on the nineteenth century, which has been presented by both Wendy Lesser and Rosalind Williams as the quintessential age of the underground.[15] Even if belief in the land of the dead as a physical place situated beneath the surface began to wane from the second half of the century onwards, it was also a period in which, with its mines, metro lines, railway tunnels and archaeological sites, the actual physical underground gained huge importance, becoming more visible and accessible than ever before.[16] A range of predominantly canonical Romantic, realist and *fin-de-siècle* nineteenth-century texts have been examined in studies on katabasis and/or underground locales by Lesser and Williams, as well as Lyle Thomas Williams, Walter Strauss and David L. Pike.[17] The studies by Lesser and Pike also include twentieth-century texts, while various modern and postmodern works of the period are examined by critics such as Evans Lansing Smith, Rachel Falconer, Bent Sørensen, and (in an earlier publication) Pike.[18] The presence of katabasis in non-literary productions has also been explored: painting and a range of films including Westerns, *Apocalypse Now* and the *Matrix* trilogy have all formed the object of detailed examinations from this perspective.[19] Scientific rather than artistic pursuits have also been identified as forms of katabasis: Williams argues that the 'common plotline' of nineteenth-century geology, palaeontology, anthropology and archaeology is the 'descent into the underworld in quest of truth.'[20]

The various texts in which katabasis has been identified do not necessarily involve a chthonic locale, physical descent or even any form of physical displacement. The 'underworld' can be situated on the surface of the external world: with reference to classical literature, Clark writes that 'many stories of Journeys into the Unknown seem to have been cast into a kind of catabatic framework', and he points to Jason's quest *across* the sea in search of the Golden Fleece or Theseus's journey *into* the Labyrinth as versions of katabasis.[21] Both Williams and Lesser show how nineteenth-century interest in what was commonly regarded as the social underground of the working classes took the form of the traditional katabatic journey.[22] The 'underworld' can also be situated within the protagonist: in the work of Rachel Falconer, for example, katabasis is 'interpreted more metaphorically, as not necessarily meaning [...] a descent underground [...], but rather a general geographical traversal accompanied by the psychological suffering and purification of the protagonist.'[23]

It has, moreover, been argued that katabasis is not only a journey undertaken by protagonists *within* narratives, but is also performed by the two key actors involved in the production of textual meaning: the writer and the reader. Evans Lansing Smith argues that the katabasis, or in his preferred terminology, the *nekyia*, is 'the myth readers live by'; every reader is a katabatic traveller who journeys 'into the underworld' of the text where the truth, the meaning they seek, 'lies buried'.[24]

Moreover, for Smith, 'the *nekyia* is an image of *poesis*, and the underworld a topos, or 'place of invention".[25] This view is shared by the writer Margaret Atwood who, in her revealingly titled collection of essays, *Negotiating with the Dead: A Writer on Writing*, argues that:

> not just some, but *all* writing of the narrative kind, and perhaps all writing, is motivated, deep down, by a fear of and fascination with mortality — by a desire to make the risky trip to the Underworld, and to bring something or someone back from the dead.[26]

From this perspective, all literary works — regardless of context, form, content or audience — have a katabatic dimension. A still vast and varied network of katabatic texts emerges even in the critical literature adopting a narrower, less metaphorical, or more protagonist-centred approach.

But however wide-ranging and extensive the body of works examined to date, it is by no means exhaustive. Pullman's *The Amber Spyglass*, the final volume of the *His Dark Materials* trilogy, is in fact only one of the latest works of children's literature which incorporates katabasis. Deliberately undertaken physical journeys into and back from an underground locale are apparent in a significant number of often highly celebrated works for young readers, and undergrounds as backdrops, other forms of subterranean journey, and more metaphorical forms of katabasis, are present in many more.[27] Yet relatively few works of children's literature are discussed in critical studies focusing on katabasis.[28] That katabatic children's literature has gone largely unregistered by the critical radar suggests that Rabinovitch is by no means alone in her reluctance to bring works of children's literature into conjunction with foundational, canonical texts and to allow the former to encroach upon the hallowed territory of the latter.[29]

This study aims to extend and enhance our understanding of katabasis, as well as the intersections between adult and children's literature more generally, by examining the relationships between works of children's literature incorporating this form of narrative and the *Odyssey*, the *Aeneid* and the *Inferno*. A corpus of eleven texts will receive detailed examination: Antoine de La Sale's *Le Paradis de La Reine Sibylle* (1437); François de Fénelon's *Aventures de Télémaque* (1699); William Hayley's *The Triumphs of Temper* (1781); Stéphanie de Genlis's *Alphonse et Dalinde, ou La féerie de l'art et de la nature* (1784); Jules Verne's *Voyage au Centre de la Terre* (1864); Lewis Carroll's *Alice's Adventures in Wonderland* (1865); George MacDonald's *The Golden Key* (1867) and *The Princess and the Goblin* (1872); George Sand's 'La Fée Poussière' (1875); Hector Malot's *Sans Famille* (1878), and finally Henry Rider Haggard's *King Solomon's Mines* (1885).[30] The focus on works in English and French, the two national literatures which have received most attention in critical work on katabasis to date, is designed to best complement and build on existing scholarship. Moreover, the children's literature of each country exerted a considerable influence on that of the other, and frequent exchanges of material occurred between the two. Seven of the eleven texts under consideration in this study were indeed rapidly translated and widely known on the other side of the Channel.[31] The majority of the works date from the second half of the nineteenth century — a period which, as we have seen, has received considerable attention in critical studies of katabasis, and which, moreover, is widely regarded as having witnessed the first full emergence of children's book publishing as a result of a range of economic, demographic, technological and cultural factors.[32] But what Townsend refers to as the 'prehistory' of children's literature is both substantial and important: prior to the nineteenth-century Golden Age, books were written for a young audience, and, even further back, for specific young aristocrats.[33] Moreover, children of a certain class or in specific parts of society read books in the pre-nineteenth-century period, appropriating a number of works never produced specifically for them. If children's literature by no means sprang fully formed into existence in the mid-nineteenth century, nor was it only at this point that works for young readers suddenly began to incorporate katabasis. As the texts by La Sale, Fénelon, Hayley and Genlis demonstrate, the presence of katabatic narratives was already a long-standing tradition in children's literature by the nineteenth century.

Children's literature is an extremely broad church and this is reflected in the diversity of the present corpus. These texts fit within the category of children's literature in quite different ways. Certain works (*Télémaque*, *Alice*) were originally written exclusively for specific young individuals (the duc de Bourgogne and Alice Liddell); others for a broader, anonymous public (e.g. *Princess*); and several were produced both with specific individuals and a more general, primarily young, readership in mind (e.g. *Sans Famille*, 'La Fée Poussière', *The Golden Key*).[34] Whereas several texts were written exclusively or principally for a young audience (*Alphonse et Dalinde*, *Sans Famille*), others clearly targeted a multi-generational readership (*Voyage*, *King Solomon's Mines*).[35] Indeed, two of the texts were not initially conceived for a young audience at all but can, nevertheless, be regarded as works of children's literature due to their subsequent handling and reception. *Paradis* was originally written for the thirty-year-old Agnès de Bourgogne, but was subsequently incorporated into *La Salade* (*c.* 1440), 'une sorte de manuel pédagogique' [a sort of pedagogical handbook] produced for La Sale's young ward, Jean de Calabre.[36] Hayley's *Triumphs* was 'intended principally' for the 'perusal' of a female though not specifically juvenile audience (xii). But this deliberately and overtly didactic text was widely read by young readers, and indeed it appears to have been this particular readership which was largely responsible for the work's phenomenal success.[37]

As this suggests, certain texts emerge from localized didactic contexts and/or respond to precise, clearly formulated pedagogical agendas. This is particularly true of the French texts to be considered here, and La Sale, Fénelon, Genlis and Sand were all engaged in pedagogical activities at the time the texts were produced.[38] The remaining works by Verne and Malot were both begun under the direction of the editor, Pierre-Jules Hetzel, whose didactic aims were reiterated time and again and are abundantly clear in the title of his celebrated *Magasin d'Education et de Récréation*. But as the *Magasin*'s title also suggests, these works were at the same time intended to entertain, each of the writers firmly believing that the most effective manner of delivering lessons was by means of amusement and diversion.[39] For the English writers whose texts are included in this corpus, the emphasis was reversed. With the exception of Hayley, these authors were much less didactically motivated than their French counterparts, the texts arising less from a desire to deliver lessons and transmit information than to entertain, amuse and stimulate the imagination of their young readers. Nevertheless, just as the French texts involve entertainment, so too do the English works inevitably involve various forms of edification since, as Margaret Meek has pointed out, 'all children's literature is inescapably didactic'.[40]

Nor is it only with respect to their contexts of production and targeted audiences that the corpus is eclectic. Works of prose dominate, but poetry is also present with Hayley's six-canto verse epic. Two of the principal genres of children's literature are represented: *Paradis*, *Télémaque*, *Alphonse et Dalinde*, *Voyage*, *Sans Famille* and *King Solomon's Mines* can all be grouped within the adventure genre which is in many ways the direct descendant of the epic form; while *Triumphs*, *Wonderland*, *The Golden Key*, *Princess* and 'La Fée Poussière' are forms of fantasy or fairy tale. In terms of their length, texts such as *Paradis* and 'La Fée Poussière' are highly condensed and succinct, digestible in a single sitting, while others, such as *Voyage* and *King Solomon's Mines* unfold over several hundred pages. Certain texts stand alone as discrete entities (*Triumphs*, *Sans Famille*, *King Solomon's Mines*, *Voyage*) while others are embedded within overarching works (*Alphonse et Dalinde* in *Les Veillées du château, ou Cours de morale à l'usage des enfans* and *Paradis* in *La Salade*). Two of the texts originally stood alongside other texts in multi-part collections ('La Fée Poussière' in *Les Contes d'une Grand-mère*, *The Golden Key* in *Dealings with the Fairies*), while both *Alice* and *Princess* can be seen as the first volume of a two-part work (alongside *Through the Looking Glass* (1871), and *The Princess and Curdie* (1883) respectively).

The corpus is, then, as diverse and wide-ranging as the network of adult katabatic literature which has emerged from critical studies to date. But despite their eclecticism, the texts are nevertheless united by a range of elements. Young readers constitute at the very least a significant part of their targeted or actual audience. Most of the authors of the texts to be examined here were aware that their audience would be made up, entirely or in part, of young readers perceived as having particular needs and requirements. Furthermore, the majority of the texts met with considerable, and in many cases lasting, popular success, and have also received considerable critical attention and acclaim. Several are regarded as seminal works within the field of children's literature, while authors such as Carroll and Verne in particular have achieved more general canonical status. Most importantly in the present context, each work incorporates at least one deliberately undertaken journey into and back from an underground locale.

In *Paradis*, La Sale narrates his own visit to a cave situated at the top of a mountain near Montemonaco in northern Italy before relating the journeys into and beyond the cave undertaken by other travellers. Of these, only a German knight and his squire complete a full katabasis, reaching and (at least temporarily) returning from the underground realm of the Reine Sibylle. *Télémaque*'s journey in search of Ulysse has already taken him to a range of destinations when, in book XIV, he ventures down to the land of the dead in order to ascertain his father's fate. In the third canto of the *Triumphs*, the dreaming heroine, Serena, travels into the subterranean abode of Spleen under the guidance of the fairy of benign Temper,

Sophrosyne. The eponymous hero of Genlis's *Alphonse et Dalinde* embarks on a wide-ranging journey undertaken to win the hand of Dalinde, and during a visit to Tenerife he ventures into an underground domain, and, in the company of his mentor, Thélismar, later visits a Swedish silver mine. (In later editions of the *Veillées*, Alphonse and Thélismar also visit Fingal's cave on the island of Staffa). In *Voyage*, Axel and his uncle, Professor Lidenbrock, discover an encrypted account of an earlier journey to the depths, and set out for Iceland, where the Sneffels peak provides access to the underground. After extensive subterranean travels they eventually return to the surface via the chimney of the Stromboli volcano in Sicily. Carroll's sleepy (indeed sleeping) Alice leaves her sister behind on the riverbank and sets out in pursuit of the White Rabbit who leads her into a rabbit hole, down a well and so into Wonderland where she meets a range of characters in various locales. In *The Golden Key*, Tangle and Mossy meet at the cottage of a mystical grandmother figure before setting out together. They pass through a great plain of shadows, but, having been separated from each other, Mossy continues his journey across land and sea while Tangle journeys down through the underground under the direction of three benign and powerful Old Men, before finally rejoining the hero. The heroine of *Princess*, Irene, is given a ring by her mystical grandmother and told that if she is ever frightened she should reach for and follow a thread attached to it. When awakened by a strange noise, Irene duly follows the thread out of the palace and into the underground, where it leads her to the hero, Curdie, who had been imprisoned by goblins. Irene frees the young miner and, continuing to follow the thread, leads him out from the underground. In 'La Fée Poussière', the narrator/ protagonist calls out to the dust fairy as she sleeps and finds herself in the grounds of a beautiful palace, from which she is led down into the very bowels of the earth. During the ascent to the surface, she witnesses a speeded-up replay of evolution before returning to the palace and finally finding herself once more at home in bed. In *Sans Famille*, Rémi has already journeyed extensively across France when he starts out again in order to keep united the members of the dispersed Acquin family who had sheltered him in Paris. His first port of call is the mining community of Varses where, due to an injury sustained by his friend, Rémi takes up the mantle of miner. His initial descent into the mine is followed by a further underground visit to the home of a learned, elderly miner, the *magister*. During his second and final descent into the mine, Rémi is trapped below ground with five other miners and some two weeks pass before they are finally rescued and return to the surface. In *King Solomon's Mines*, during an eventful visit to the fictitious South African country of Kukuanaland, the English travellers eventually undertake their katabasis in the company of the 'natives' Gagool and Foulata. They too are immured in the underground, but by descending further into the presumed former workings of the mine, eventually find their way back to the surface.

The presence of the katabatic narrative in individual works and the consequent relationship with the *Odyssey*, *Aeneid* and *Inferno* has gone unnoticed or is even categorically denied in critical work on specific texts such as *Alphonse et Dalinde*, *Sans Famille* and *King Solomon's Mines*.[41] On the other hand, it has been repeatedly registered in studies of works by MacDonald, Carroll and Verne in particular.[42]

However, even here cursory observations are rarely supplemented by detailed analysis and there has, to date, been no examination of the function or effect of the relationship between katabases for young readers and earlier versions of the narrative.[43]

This study aims to move beyond the simple identification of intertextual relationships. As certain theorists of intertextuality have made clear, texts can be related to each other in many different ways, and even relations based, as here, on shared story patterns, vary enormously. The first chapter of this study sets out to establish the precise nature of the intertextual relationships between the works for young readers involving katabasis and their classical and medieval pre-texts. Gerard Genette's differentiation in *Palimpsestes* between intertextual relationships in terms of their levels 'd'abstraction, d'implication et de globalité' [abstraction, implication and comprehensiveness] will serve to guide the discussion.[44] While the examination of scale and abstraction is predominantly text-based, the issue of implication moves the discussion out into the broader realm of authorial intention and the extent to which the katabatic narratives for young readers can be regarded as deliberate rewritings of earlier versions. This leads in turn to an examination of the availability of the intertextual relationships to the targeted young readers, as well as a consideration of their function and effect with regard to this audience, something which has been overlooked in discussions of the individual texts to date.

Drawing on the range of 'transpositions thématiques' [thematic transpositions] outlined by Genette, the study then moves on to examine, in Chapters 2 to 4, key elements of traditional katabatic narratives and their handling in works targeted at young readers.[45] As we have seen, children's literature generally is both akin to and distinct from adult literature; these chapters will seek to establish the similarities, differences and shifts in emphasis in katabatic narratives specifically. The nature of the issues involved in katabases, such as death, sin and knowledge, make it an ideal focus in evaluating traditional images of, and attitudes towards, children's literature. Katabatic narratives for young readers enable an in-depth examination of its reputation for utilitarianism, conservatism, and its association with constraint, restriction and limitation. I will aim to establish whether and in what ways the specificity of the audience targeted in these texts entails alterations in the katabatic narrative, whether particular aspects are emphasized at the expense of others, as well as the possible reasons for any such shifts. In Chapter 2, I shall examine the nature of the underground landscape and its population, and the extent to which subterranean landscapes for young readers preserve the moral and chthonic dimensions of the earlier narratives. The following chapter again considers the inhabitants of the underworld, but also the travellers and guides, from a gender perspective. Via examination of role allocation, the key traits of the principal characters, as well as interaction between protagonists, the chapter will assess the extent to which the male domination of traditional narratives is preserved or instead challenged and interrogated in katabases for young readers. The final chapter will examine whether katabases for young readers inject a didactic and moralizing dimension into the traditional narrative, and whether any ludic dimension of earlier versions is extended. The conclusion will review the continuities, departures and

Strauss, *Descent and Return: The Orphic Theme in Modern Literature* (London: OUP, 1971); Pike, *Subterranean Cities* and *Metropolis on the Styx: The Underworlds of Modern Urban Culture, 1800–2001* (Ithaca, NY: Cornell University Press, 2007).

18. Evans Lansing Smith, *Rape and Revelation: The Descent to the Underworld in Modernism* (Lanham, MD/London: University Press of America, 1990) and *The Descent to the Underworld in Literature, Painting and Film, 1895–1950* (Lewiston, NY/Lampeter: Edwin Mellen Press, 2001); Rachel Falconer, *Hell in Contemporary Literature: Western Descent Narratives since 1945* (Edinburgh: Edinburgh University Press, 2004); Bent Sørensen, 'Katabasis in Cormac McCarthy's *Blood Meridian*', *Orbis Litterarum*, 60 (2005), 16–25; David Pike, *Passage Through Hell: Modernist Descents, Medieval Underworlds* (Ithaca, NY/London: Cornell University Press, 1997).

19. Both visual art and film are addressed by Pike in *Subterranean Cities* and *Metropolis on the Styx*, and in Smith, *The Descent to the Underworld in Literature, Painting and Film*. Films are also examined by Falconer and are the main focus of John R. Harris, 'The Katabasis and the Cowboy Film: A Study in Clashing Myths', *Yearbook of Comparative and General Literature*, 47 (1993), 132–48; and Erling B. Holtsmark, 'The *Katabasis* in Modern Cinema', in *Classical Myth and Culture in the Cinema*, ed. by Martin M. Winkler (Oxford: OUP, 2001), pp. 23–50.

20. R. Williams, p. 23 Not all critics employ the term *katabasis* and its associated adjective (which is in fact a meteorological term: a 'katabatic' wind being one which is 'caused by local downward motion of cool air' (*OED*)). Lansing Smith's use of the *nekyia* has the disadvantage of overemphasizing the Homeric descent, while Lesser's 'underground adventure story', and especially Lyle Thomas Williams's 'descent-into-the-earth literature' are both rather cumbersome. Critics who do use the term include Falconer, Sørensen and Holtsmark.

21. Clark, p. 34.

22. R. Williams, Chapter 6; Lesser, Chapter 4.

23. Sørensen, p. 18.

24. Smith, *Rape and Revelation*, p. 134.

25. Smith, *Rape and Revelation*, p. 130.

26. Margaret Atwood, *Negotiating with the Dead: A Writer on Writing* (Cambridge: CUP, 2002), p. 156. See also Ruth Padel, *The Poem and the Journey* (London: Chatto and Windus, 2007) who discusses *katabasis* at some length and argues that 'the quest for words you can only learn in the dark and from the dead' is 'a vital idea for poems' (p. 45).

27. In the significant body of mining novels for young readers the underground is not, as in katabasis, an extraordinary destination for the principal protagonist (see, for example, R. M. Ballantyne, *Deep Down: A Tale of The Cornish Mines* (1869); George E. Sargent, *Down in a Mine; or, Buried Alive* (1878); G. A. Henty, *Facing Death; or, the Hero of the Vaughan Pit. A Tale of the Coal Mines* (1882); and, slightly later, two reworkings of *Germinal* for young readers, A. de Geriolles', *Sous Terre* (1909) and Augusta Latouche's *L'Enfant de la mine* (1910)). Juliana Horatia Ewing's 'Amelia and the Dwarves' (1870) and MacDonald's 'The Day Boy and the Night Girl' (1882), constitute forms of abduction narrative rather than katabasis since although the protagonists do travel down to and back from the underground, the original journeys are enforced rather than freely and deliberately undertaken. More metaphorical forms of katabasis abound. It is, for example, possible to interpret *all* adventure stories for young readers as forms of katabasis. Note the striking similarity between Clark's definition of katabasis and Richard Phillips's description of the adventure story: 'In their perilous journeys, adventurers depart violently from the world they know, but find something on the other side, survive the ordeal and return to tell the tale.' (Richard Phillips, *Mapping Men and Empire: A Geography of Adventure* (London: Routledge, 1997), p. 113.)

28. The exceptions include Lesser's chapter entitled 'The Child's Underground', Pike's discussion of *Les Indes Noires* and (less extensively) *The Wind in the Willows*, Williams's analysis of Verne, and references to various texts in Stubbs. In all but the first of these, works for young readers are incorporated without comment within the wider corpus of works studied: Verne's mining novel, *Les Indes Noires*, is, for example, studied alongside texts by Hugo and Dickens in Chapter 6 of *Notes on the Underground*. Lesser's approach is also problematic given that the texts discussed are selected on an entirely (if openly) idiosyncratic basis, and are separated from works by Carroll and Verne, which are each considered in discrete chapters.

shifts of emphasis discernible between the traditional katabatic na
works for young readers, and will also discuss a small number of w
of course, Pullman's *The Amber Spyglass*, demonstrating the contin
katabases for the young in the contemporary world.

Notes to the Introduction

1. Dina Rabinovitch, 'His bright materials', *The Guardian*, 10 December 2003
   14–15 (p. 15). The *Odyssey* alone is not, of course, the story of a *departure from* l
2. Peter Hunt, *An Introduction to Children's Literature* (Oxford: OUP, 1994), p. 7.
3. Drawing on Sartre's comments in *Qu'est-ce que la littérature?*, Arthur B. Evans c
   in which, from the mid-nineteenth century, '[a]ll literary works viewed as havi
   function to society in practical, moral, or educational terms immediately l
   (Arthur B. Evans, 'Jules Verne and the French Literary Canon', in *Jules Vei*
   Modernity, ed. by Edmund J. Smyth (Liverpool: Liverpool University Press, 200·
   18)).
4. See Charles Butler, 'Introduction', in *Teaching Children's Fiction*, ed. by
   (Basingstoke: Palgrave Macmillan, 2006), pp. 1–5 (p. 1). The existence of such
   evidence of the rise in fortunes of children's literature.
5. Peter Hunt, 'Introduction: The World of Children's Literature Studies', in *Understa*
   Literature: Key Essays from the 'International Companion Encyclopedia of Children's Lii
   Peter Hunt (London/New York: Routledge, 1999), pp. 1–14 (p. 1).
6. Peter Hunt, "Children's Literature': An Historical/Political/Theoretical Ov
   Comparison, 20 (1995), 6–13 (p. 11).
7. Hunt, *An Introduction to Children's Literature*, p. 7.
8. Hunt, *An Introduction to Children's Literature*, p. 7; Hunt, 'Introduction: The World
   Literature Studies', p. 2.
9. James Steel Smith, *A Critical Approach to Children's Literature* (New York: McGraw
   p. vii. See also, p. 6, pp. 15–20.
10. Margery Hourihan, *Deconstructing the Hero: Literary Theory and Children's Literatui*
    New York: Routledge, 1997), p. 5.
11. Deborah Cogan Thacker and Jean Webb, *Introducing Children's Literature: From Ro*
    Postmodernism (London: Routledge, 2002), p. 2.
12. Raymond J. Clark, *Catabasis: Vergil and the Wisdom-Tradition* (Amsterdam: Grüner, 1
    In a different sense, *katabasis* also refers to a military defeat.
13. In addition to Clark, see also Pierre Brunel, *L'Évocation des morts et la descente aux enfe*
    Virgile, Dante, Claudel (Paris: SEDES, 1974) and Ronald R. MacDonald, *The Buri*
    Memory: Epic Underworlds in Vergil, Dante and Milton (Amherst: University of Ma
    Press, 1987). At the beginning of book XI of the *Odyssey*, widely referred to as the
    seems that it is the dead who rise up to Odysseus rather than the hero who journeys
    the underworld. Yet the subterranean situation of the land of the dead is firmly e:
    in the course of the narrative and, even though it is impossible to establish the prec
    of departure, it is nevertheless clear that the hero has passed into this undergroun
    Odysseus's presence in the underground is reinforced by the repeated use of the det·
    'here' and 'this', indicating proximity and immersion rather than distance.
14. H. W. Stubbs, 'Underworld Themes in Modern Fiction', in *The Journey to the Other W*
    by H. R. Ellis Davidson (Cambridge: Brewer, 1975), pp. 130–49 (p. 130).
15. Wendy Lesser, *The Life Below the Ground: A Study of the Subterranean in Literature and*
    (Boston/London: Faber & Faber, 1987); Rosalind Williams, *Notes on the Underground: A*
    on Technology, Society, and the Imagination (Cambridge, MA/London: MIT Press, 1990).
16. See R. Williams, chapters 2–4; Lesser, p. 5. See also David L. Pike, *Subterranean Cities: The*
    Beneath Paris and London, 1800–1945 (Ithaca, NY/London: Cornell University Press, 2005
17. Lyle Thomas Williams, 'Journeys to the Center of the Earth: Descent and Initiation in Se
    Science Fiction' (unpublished doctoral dissertation, University of Indiana, 1983); V

29. Novelist A. S. Byatt has proved considerably more perspicacious than most critics in this regard. In both *Possession* (1991) and *The Children's Book* (2009), female protagonists produce children's stories involving descents. In the more recent text, the underground becomes almost synonymous with Golden Age children's literature.

30. Antoine de La Sale, *Le Paradis de La Reine Sibylle*, trans. by Francine Mora-Lebrun (Paris: Éditions Stock, 1983); François de Fénelon, *Aventures de Télémaque*, ed. by Jeanne-Lydie Goré (Paris: Garnier–Flammarion, 1968); William Hayley, *The Triumphs of Temper; a poem in six cantos* (London: Dodsley, 1781); Stéphanie de Genlis, *Alphonse et Dalinde, ou la féerie de l'art et de la nature, conte moral* (Orléans: Berthevin, 1797–98 [an VI]); Jules Verne, *Voyage au centre de la terre*, ed. by Jean-Pierre Goldenstein (Paris: Pocket, 1991); Lewis Carroll, *The Annotated Alice*, ed. by Martin Gardner (Harmondsworth: Penguin, 1976); George MacDonald, *The Princess and the Goblin* (London: Puffin, 1996); George MacDonald, *The Golden Key* (London/Sydney/ Toronto: Bodley Head, 1967); George Sand, 'La Fée Poussière', in *Contes d'une Grand-mère*, ed. by ed. by Béatrice Didier (Paris: Flammarion, 2004), pp. 394–405; Hector Malot, *Sans Famille*, 2 vols (Paris: Gallimard, 1997); Henry Rider Haggard, *King Solomon's Mines*, ed. by Dennis Butts (Oxford: OUP, 1998). Subsequent references are, unless otherwise indicated, to these editions and are given after quotations in the main body of the text.

31. The first of many English translations of *Télémaque* appeared in 1699 (François de Fénelon, *The Adventures of Telemachus, the Son of Odysseus*, trans. by Isaac Littlebury (London: Awnsham and Churchill, 1699)). Genlis's *Veillées* were translated into English in 1785 (Stéphanie de Genlis, *Tales of the Castle: or, Stories of Instruction and Delight*, trans. by Thomas Holcroft (London: Robinson, 1785)). The first English translation of *Voyage* appeared in 1872 (Jules Verne, *A Journey to the Centre of the Earth* [no trans.] (London: Griffith and Farran, 1872)). *Wonderland* first appeared in French translation in 1869 (Lewis Carroll, *Les Aventures d'Alice au pays des merveilles*, trans. by Henri Bué (London: Macmillan, 1869)). *Sans Famille* appeared in English translation in 1880 (Hector Malot, *No Relations*, trans. by May Laffan, 3 vols (London: Bentley, 1880)). Several of Sand's *Contes* were translated into English between 1880 and 1930, and 'La Fée Poussière' appeared in *The Strand Magazine* in 1891 (George Sand, 'Fairy Dust: A Story for Children', [no trans.] *The Strand Magazine*, 11 (1891), 536–43). Finally, *King Solomon's Mines* appeared in serial publication in the *Magasin d'Éducation et de Récréation* in 1887 under the title *Les Mines du Roi Salomon*.

32. Ganna Ottevaere-van Praag, *La Littérature pour la jeunesse en Europe occidentale (1750–1925)* (Berne: Peter Lang, 1987), p. 193; Julia Briggs and Dennis Butts, 'The Emergence of Form (1850–90)', in *Children's Literature: An Illustrated History*, ed. by Peter Hunt (Oxford/New York: OUP, 1995), pp. 130–65 (p. 130).

33. John Rowe Townsend, 'British Children's Literature: A Historical Overview', in *The International Companion Encyclopedia of Children's Literature*, ed. by Peter Hunt (London/New York: Routledge, 1996), pp. 676–87 (p. 676).

34. Sand wrote the *Contes d'une Grand-Mere*, including 'La Fée Poussière', in the first instance for her granddaughters, Aurore (b. 1866) and Gabrielle (b. 1868), but was also conscious that the stories would be published and read by both adults and children. Both Malot and MacDonald tested their works on their own children prior to publication.

35. Haggard dedicated *King Solomon's Mines* 'to all the big and little boys who read it' (n.p.); Verne was writing for the *Magasin d'Éducation et de Récréation* which, as Christian Robin has pointed out, targeted 'la famille au grand complet' (Christian Robin, 'Avant-Propos', in *Un éditeur et son siècle: Pierre-Jules Hetzel (1814–1886)*, ed. by Christian Robin (Saint-Sébastien: ACL Edition, 1988), pp. 7–11 (p. 9)).

36. Francine Mora-Lebrun, 'Postface', in La Sale, *Le Paradis de la Reine Sibylle* (Paris: Éditions Stock, 1983), pp. 129–42 (p. 129).

37. Although Hayley has been totally overlooked in historical surveys of children's literature, Alison Milbank refers to the *Triumphs*'s wide circulation 'as a suitable poem for the young', while Bishop describes its 'perennial' popularity, 'especially as a present to children calculated to improve their dispositions'. (Alison Milbank, *Dante and the Victorians* (Manchester: Manchester University Press, 1998), p. 8; Morchard Bishop, *Blake's Hayley: The Life, Works and Friendships of William Hayley* (London: Victor Gollancz, 1951), p. 132).

38. La Sale was governor to Jean de Calabre (b. 1425) from 1435; Fénelon was tutor to the heir to the throne, the duc de Bourgogne (b. 1682) between 1689 and 1699; Genlis was responsible for the education of a range of children, including, from 1782, the future king Louis-Philippe; Sand assumed the responsibility of the education of her granddaughters towards the end of her life.

39. Thus, for example, Fénelon's aim was to 'amuser Monsieur le duc de Bourgogne par ces aventures' [amuse the duc de Bourgogne with these adventures] and to 'l'instruire en l'amusant' [instruct him whilst amusing him]. (Quoted in Robert Granderoute, *Le Roman pédagogique de Fénelon à Rousseau* (Geneva/Paris: Slatkine, 1985), p. 52). Similarly, in the preface to the *Veillées*, Genlis states that feeling and imagination serve to improve the efficacy of the didactic message, and *Télémaque* is cited as an example of a work which is effective because attractive (Stéphanie de Genlis, *Les Veillées du château, ou Cours de morale à l'usage des enfans*, 2 vols (Brussels: Meline and Cans, 1842), I, pp. vii–viii).

40. Margaret Meek, 'Introduction', in *The International Companion Encyclopedia of Children's Literature*, ed. by Peter Hunt (London/New York: Routledge, 1996), pp. 1–13 (p. 11).

41. Although she makes extensive reference to katabatic texts such as *Gilgamesh* and the *Odyssey*, Margery Hourihan states that *King Solomon's Mines* employs the overarching 'hero story' structure 'without any obvious references to particular pre-texts' (Hourihan, p. 13).

42. Studies of katabasis in the individual texts include: Giorio [*sic*] Spina, 'The Influence of Dante on George MacDonald', trans. by Paul Priest, *North Wind: The Journal of the George MacDonald Society*, 9 (1990), 15–36; John Docherty, 'Dantean Allusions in Wonderland', *Jabberwocky: The Journal of the Lewis Carroll Society*, 19 (1990), 13–16; Robert Brockway, 'The *Descensus Ad Inferos* of Lewis Carroll', *Dalhousie Review*, 62 (1982), 36–43.

43. Mora-Lebrun states that 'le souvenir du 6e livre de l'*Enéide* est forcément présent, par Sibylle interposé, dans *Le Paradis*', (Mora-Lebrun, p. 134). David Meakin points to the fact that in *Voyage*, 'Verne [...] draw[s] on a common fund, a common ancestry, with shades of Homer, Virgil, Dante read and re-read' (David Meakin, 'Jules Verne's Alchemical Journey Short-Circuited', *French Studies*, 45 (1991), 152–65 (p. 157)). Neither critic expands upon these somewhat cursory observations.

44. Gérard Genette, *Palimpsestes: La Littérature au second degré* (Paris: Seuil, 1982), p. 8.

45. Genette, p. 293.

CHAPTER 1

Katabatic Intertextual Relations

In the Introduction to this study, it was argued that children's literature as a body of texts cannot be studied successfully in isolation. Indeed, following the various theories of intertextuality which have developed over the past forty years, it is impossible to fully comprehend any individual text, whether for children or adults, without reference and recourse to others. In contradistinction to New Criticism, theories of intertextuality arise from the conviction that a text 'cannot exist as a hermetic or self-sufficient whole, and so does not function as a closed system'.[1] Like man, no text is an island: 'Il n'y a pas d'œuvre individuelle. L'œuvre d'un individu est une sorte de nœude [*sic*] qui se produit à l'intérieur d'un tissu culturel' [There are no individual works. The work of an individual is a sort of knot produced within a cultural fabric].[2] Any one text 'se construit comme mosaïque de citations' [is constructed as a mosaic of quotations], and is thus held within an almost inconceivably vast textual network.[3] Relationships which may or may not be identified by the reader, can be deliberately set down by the author. But although many critics reject the legitimacy or at least the pertinence of such a view, relationships not intended by the author can also be established on the part of the reader.[4] The number of links between texts is thus infinite, and the limitlessness of intertextual relations may well seem 'bewildering', overwhelming and unworkable in practice.[5]

Yet it is possible to make some sense of the seething intertextual abyss without having to take the rather conservative and problematic step of distinguishing between 'proper' and 'fake' intertextuality, between what does and does not count. Firstly, as Andrew Weiner points out, if '[a]ll texts are intertextual, [...] some are more intertextual — at least more insistently and deliberately intertextual — than others'.[6] Equally, all texts may be intertextual, but the nature of their multiple relationships with other texts varies widely. It is, then, both possible and productive to distinguish between different forms as well as different scales or degrees of intertextuality.[7]

This is the move made by Genette in the opening pages of *Palimpsestes*. He outlines five forms of 'transtextual' relationship — *intertextualité, paratextualité, métatextualité, hypertextualité*, and *architextualité* [intertextuality, paratextuality, metatextuality, hypertextuality, architextuality] — in which increasing levels 'd'abstraction, d'implication et de globalité' [abstraction, implication and comprehensiveness] are apparent, with *intertextualité* the most concrete, explicit and atomistic, and *architextualité* the most abstract, implicit and widescale.[8] Although, as will become clear, Genette's concerns are very different from those of the present study, these three key characteristics provide the framework for a detailed exploration of the precise nature of the intertextual (or, for Genette, transtextual) relations between katabasis for young readers and earlier versions of the narrative. I will begin by considering the central issue of scale, which will involve an examination of the important *transformations quantitatives* [quantitative transformations] apparent between these works, before moving on to consider levels of abstraction.[9] The question of explicitness, to be examined next, prompts a brief investigation of authorial deliberateness and intentionality with regard to these relationships. This leads naturally to the crucial issue of readerly competence and the capacity of young readers specifically to discern these relations. Their function (whether identified or not) with respect to this particular audience will then be discussed.

Scale

For Genette, size matters. In *Palimpsestes*, he mounts an attack on Riffaterre's focus on small textual units, 'de l'ordre des micro-structures sémantico-stylistiques, à l'échelle de la phrase, du fragment, ou de texte bref, généralement poétique' [semantic-semiotic microstructures, observed at the level of a sentence, a fragment, or a short, generally poetic, text].[10] Genette is not the only critic to have underlined the intrinsic problems of the Riffaterrean approach: Owen Miller, for example, points to the way in which

> the very constrained nature of his model (the examples he gives are limited to very specific problems of the meanings of words) makes it difficult to see how it could address the larger interpretational problems which link a text like *Ulysses* to the *Odyssey* or how it would be conceivable to envisage intertextuality functioning across linguistic and cultural boundaries.[11]

Given that katabasis crosses multiple boundaries, Riffaterre's approach is clearly of limited use for the purposes of the present study. For Genette, who does indeed address the connections between Joyce and Homer, relationships between texts are not restricted to those designated under the term *intertextualité* (including *citation, plagiat* and *allusion*). His concern is instead with 'l'œuvre considerée dans sa structure d'ensemble' [the work considered as a structural whole].[12] His focus is therefore on hypertextuality, which is defined as: 'toute relation unissant un texte B (que j'appellerai *hypertexte*) à un texte antérieur A (que j'appellerai, bien sûr, *hypotexte*) sur lequel il se greffe d'une manière qui n'est pas celle du commentaire' [any relationship uniting a text B (which I shall call the *hypertext*) to an earlier text A (I shall, of course, call it the *hypotext*), upon which it is grafted in a manner which is not that of commentary].[13] More particularly, Genette is concerned with hypertextual relations in which 'la dérivation de l'hypotexte à l'hypertexte est [...] massive (toute une œuvre B dérivant de toute une œuvre A)' [the shift from hypotext to hypertext is [...] massive (an entire work B deriving from an entire work A)].[14]

It is this form of transtextual relation, wherein the entirety of a given text is reworked to produce another full text, with which Dina Rabinovitch is concerned in her discussion of Pullman's *His Dark Materials* trilogy. Hypertextual adaptations are widely apparent in the realm of children's literature, which has been described by Stephens as 'radically intertextual': '[w]hen compared with general literature, the literature produced for children contains a much larger proportion of retold stories.'[15] This can be explained in part by pure practical necessity and expediency: in the nineteenth century, insufficient specifically targeted texts existed to satisfy the demands generated by the sudden rise in literacy and development of mass education, so adaptations of adult works were a convenient solution.[16] Yet adaptation substantially predates this period and indeed Soriano argues that it is 'aussi vieille que l'humanité' [as old as humanity].[17] It serves as a highly effective means of exposing children to those things — a general type of culture, specific works of literature — felt to be valuable to their moral and social development at any given time. Both targeted adaptations which are closely modelled on the original text and rewritings which are more freely inspired by an earlier work, serve 'to initiate children into aspects of a social heritage, transmitting many of a culture's central values and assumptions and a body of shared allusions and experiences'.[18] The hypotexts of countless texts for young readers are earlier works originally targeted at a more general, adult audience and indeed entire series of texts have been produced along these lines (e.g. the *Told to the Children* series published by T. C. & E. C. Jack, the *Told Through the Ages* series by Harrap, or Dent's *Children's Illustrated Classics*). The list of domains addressed by Stephens and McCallum suggests that few canonical works have not been treated in this way:

> biblical literature and related religious stories; myths; hero stories; medieval and quasi-medieval romance; stories about Robin Hood [...]; folktales and fairy tales; oriental stories, usually linked with *The Arabian Nights*; and modern classics [including Shakespeare's plays and *Robinson Crusoe*].[19]

Over the past two hundred years, the classical and medieval katabatic pre-texts examined in this study have also been subject to such treatment in both England and France. Examples of Homeric adaptations include Charles Lamb's *Adventures of Ulysses* (1808), Charles Hanson's *The Siege of Troy and the Wanderings of Ulysses* (1887), Jeanie Lang's *Stories from the Odyssey* (1906),[20] Alfred J. Church's *The Children's Odyssey* (1907) (later translated into French),[21] or André Bonnard's *L'Odyssée Adaptée pour la jeunesse* (1948). Recent adaptations include Rosemary Sutcliff's *The Wanderings of Odysseus: The Story of the Odyssey* (1995) and Hélène Kérillis's *L'Extraordinaire Voyage d'Ulysse* (2004). In addition to *The Children's Odyssey*, Church also produced *The Children's Aeneid* (1909) and in France a certain Général L. M. published *L'Énéide racontée à mes petits enfants* (1935) thanks to which, according to the preface by François Ollier, 'les petits Français [...] recevront, sans même en apercevoir, la plus noble et la plus stimulante des leçons morales' [without even noticing, French children will receive the noblest and most stimulating moral lessons] including 'l'ardent patriotisme, la piété, le courage tenace, la modération et l'humanité' [the ardent patriotism, piety, tenacious courage, moderation and humanity] of Aeneas.[22] Recent adaptations of Virgil include Penelope Lively's *In Search of a Homeland: The Story of the Aeneid* (2001) and Marie Goudot's *Enée ou la cité promise* (2005).

Despite the fact that '[g]iving Dante to children may seem a fruitless task', his works have also been adapted for young readers.[23] Rose Emily Selfe produced targeted versions of both the second and third parts of the *Commedia*: *How Dante climbed the mountain. Sunday readings with the children from the 'Purgatorio'* (1887), and *With Dante in Paradise — readings from the 'Paradiso'* (1900). Selfe's clearly stated omission of the first part is fully approved by the Lord Bishop of Ripon in the preface to *How Dante climbed the mountain*: he states that while it is 'fit and right' to expose young readers to *Purgatory* ('to make great books part of the inheritance of childhood'), '[o]ne would not too early familiarise childhood with the weird and terrible scenes of the *Inferno*'.[24] Yet this is precisely what Mary MacGregor undertakes just over twenty years later in her *Stories from Dante told to the children* (illustrated by R. T. Rose). Over half of this text is devoted to the pilgrim's katabasis, which is, however, couched within a 'wonderful dream' (for more on this strategy see Chapter 4).[25] More recent adaptations of Dante include Blandine Deroux's *Le Pèlerinage (ou, 'La Divine Comédie' de Dante dei Aligheri racontée aux enfants)* (1975), Joseph Tusiani's *Dante's 'Divine Comedy': As Told for Young People* (2001) and John Agard and Satoshi Kitamura's *The Young Inferno* (2008).

Two of the texts of our corpus — *Télémaque* and *Triumphs* — are closely related to this process and very clearly fulfil the same function of exposing the young reader to foundational works. But rather than producing targeted adaptations of a particular adult work, Fénelon and Hayley draw on one dominant pre-text as well as a range of other earlier texts, in order to create new, independent works. Fénelon's *Télémaque* (or the *Suite du quatrième livre de l'Odysée d'Homère ou les Avantures de Télémaque fils de Ulysse*, to give it its full 1699 title) recounts the story of the Greek prince's search for his father. Fénelon draws on Virgil, Plato, Horace, Herodotus, Ovid, the Bible, as well as travel writing, fable and fairy tale. In parts of the text, certain sources acquire particular prominence. Thus, the katabasis of book XIV, where Télémaque ventures down to the land of the dead in order to ascertain his father's fate, is closely modelled on the sixth book of the *Aeneid*. Nevertheless, the Homeric epic serves as the principal, overarching pre-text of *Télémaque* as a whole. Fénelon's text fills the gap left by Telemachus's disappearance in books V–XV of the *Odyssey*, thus constituting what Genette refers to as 'une continuation *paraleptique*, chargée de combler d'éventuelles paralipses, ou ellipses latérales ('Que faisait X pendant que Y...') [a *paraleptic* continuation, designed to bridge paralipses, or lateral ellipses ('Meanwhile, back at the ranch...')].[26] But in *Télémaque*, Fénelon not only creates but recreates; the text not only fills gaps but also frequently parallels the Homeric epic, and can therefore be regarded less as a 'suite' than a 'recommencement'.[27] In addition to the katabasis of book XIV, Télémaque also encounters Calypso, travels widely, is shipwrecked, taken prisoner and faces a range of dangerous opponents. The incorporation of the *Odyssey* into *Télémaque* is widescale, the Homeric hypotext permeates the entire hypertext, and thus corresponds to the form of hypertextuality with which Genette is concerned. Several pages are indeed devoted to it in *Palimpsestes*.

Hayley's ambitious aim in the *Triumphs* was, as he states in the preface, 'to unite some touches of the sportive wildness of Ariosto, and the more serious sublime painting of Dante, with some portion of the enchanting elegance, the refined imagination, and the moral graces of Pope' (x). That the *Commedia* is Hayley's principal pre-text is signalled in a range of paratextual elements, including the arrangement of the poem in cantos, and the employment of the didactically charged lines of *Inferno* IX as epigraph:

> O voi ch'avete gl'intelleti sani
> Mirate la dottrina, che si asconde
> Sotto' il velame degli versi strani.
>
> [[...] O you whose mind is clear:
> Understand well the lesson that underlies
> The veil of these strange verses I have written.]

That the *Triumphs*, unlike *Télémaque*, are not discussed by Genette is undoubtedly due to the little-known status of Hayley's text. Moreover, although Hayley reworks the *Divina Commedia* in its entirety, the text cannot be said to properly fulfil Genette's criteria in terms of size and scale. The dreaming heroine, Serena, not only undertakes a journey through the subterranean Abode of Spleen (canto three), but also travels into the sphere of Sensibility and Temper (canto five), just as Dante the pilgrim passes through hell, purgatory and paradise. But while 'toute une œuvre A' [an entire work A] is thus drawn on, it does not occupy 'toute une œuvre B' [an entire work B], since the Dantesque episodes occupy just two of six cantos, with the other four devoted to the Pope-esque, mock-heroic trials faced by the heroine in the society of eighteenth-century London.

The katabasis is, then, just one part of their respective hypotexts which is incorporated to varying extents into the hypertexts of *Télémaque* and the *Triumphs*. In the majority of the works for young readers which make up our corpus, however, it is the katabasis alone which forms the basis of the relationship with the earlier works. In the latter, the katabasis is a specific journey within the extensive travels of the heroes. For convenience's sake we can say that one of twenty-four books of the *Odyssey*, one of twelve books of the *Aeneid*, and one of three parts of the *Divina Commedia* are devoted to the katabasis. Admittedly, then, a steady process of amplification can be discerned in terms of the proportion of the overall text which is occupied by these katabases. But however substantial the proportion, the katabasis always constitutes a single, discrete episode rather than an entire work, and as such, the relationships with which we are concerned can never correspond exactly to the form of hypertextuality focused on by Genette.

In most of the works for young readers, the katabases also constitute episodes within the surrounding narratives and, in that these episodes are relatively short, they adhere more closely to the classical than the medieval model. Analysis of the number of pages of the editions used in this study which are concerned with the katabatic narrative shows that it is *Alphonse et Dalinde* which devotes the shortest proportion of the narrative to katabasis, occupying nine pages of a total of 203. The next proportionally shortest katabasis is that of *Princess*, where the descent occupies approximately eleven of a total of 157 pages. This is followed by the katabases of *Sans Famille* (88 pages of 670), then *King Solomon's Mines* (44 pages of 315), *The Golden Key* (12 pages of 78), and finally *Paradis* (13 pages of 35). The proportion of the text occupied by the katabases whose surrounding narratives are themselves embedded in an overarching text (i.e. *Paradis*, *Alphonse et Dalinde*, and *Princess* — if taken together with *The Princess and Curdie*) is of course further reduced if the latter is taken into account, becoming fractional rather than merely episodic. Rather than 'toute une œuvre B dérivant de toute une œuvre A' [an entire work B deriving from an entire work A] the relationships between these texts for young readers and their pre-texts may instead be formulated as follows: 'toute une épisode B dérivant de toute une épisode A' [an entire episode B deriving from an entire episode A], or, more precisely, given the multiplicity of the pre-texts, 'des épisodes A' [from several episodes A].

In this corpus, there are, however, a small number of texts for young readers in which the katabasis does not form a more or less extensive episode, but instead occupies the majority of the text, its parameters thus extended even beyond those of the *Inferno* within the *Commedia*. The katabasis in *Voyage* forms almost three fifths of the work as a whole (166 pages of 190), the remainder of the text being closely concerned with the descent, in terms of preparations, motivation etc. Similarly, if the overarching framework of the *Contes* is not taken into account, the specifically katabatic part of the journey of 'La Fée Poussière' occupies the same proportion of the text as that of *Voyage* (five pages of nine). Even if *Wonderland* is taken in conjunction with *Looking Glass*, the katabasis still forms a considerable proportion — almost half — of the overall work; and if *Wonderland* is considered alone, the descent here extends its parameters to the extent that it occupies almost the entirety of the text: just the prefatory poem and three pages of 139 at the beginning and end of the text do not form part of the katabatic narrative, although, as in *Voyage*, they are closely related to it. In these three texts, therefore, the intertextual relations consist not in the incorporation of an entire text in an entire text, or an episode in an episode, but instead the amplification of an episode into the majority of the text.

The intertextual relations with which we are concerned are, thus, never as small-scale or atomistic as those upon which Riffaterre focuses. Nor however, with the exception of *Télémaque*, are they ever as extensive as the hypertextual relations with which Genette is concerned. These relationships involve the incorporation of a whole text in part of a text (*Triumphs*), part of a text in the majority of a text (*Voyage*, 'La Fée Poussière', *Wonderland*), or part of a text in part of a text (all the others). We are thus dealing with a form of transtextuality which in terms of its scale is situated midway between Riffaterrian microstructures and Genettian hypertextuality.

Abstraction and Implication

Having established that relations based on katabasis are situated midway on the scale of *globalité*, we will now consider their positioning in terms of the other features outlined by Genette. Transtextual relationships also vary in their degree of abstraction and explicitness, becoming increasingly abstract and implicit as one moves away from relations of *intertextualité* and towards those of *architextualité*. An intertextual relationship based on quotation is, thus, the most explicit and concrete, whereas an architextual relationship on the basis of genre is the most implicit and abstract. Genette is not alone in his recognition that relations between texts do not exist only on the basis of the repetition of specific signifiers in quotation and allusion. Plett, for example, differentiates between 'material (particularizing) inter-textuality' which involves the repetition of signs (the 'model case' for this form being quotation), 'structural (generalizing) intertextuality' involving the repetition of rules, and a third form which combines the first two.[28] In relationships between texts of different media, but equally applicable to texts of the same medium, Plett observes that: 'Usually it is not single signifiers which are exchanged for others but themes, motifs, scenes, or even moods of a pre-text which take shape in a different medium.'[29]

It is primarily an abstract form of textual relationship which exists between the texts under consideration in this study. A specific event, the katabasis forms (a more or less extensive) part of the story which is 'a construct and an abstraction from the set of observable signifiers which is the text, and is thus intangible in itself'.[30] The katabasis is also necessarily abstract, unrestricted to specific signifiers. No matter what the (very considerable) variations in detail, in any katabasis, a central character acts in a certain way, i.e. goes to a certain place and does certain things when he gets there. The overall event can therefore be broken down into similarly abstract elements: a central character, and usually various auxiliary characters (guides, inhabitants); a specific setting; and 'a series of mini-events and intermediary states'.[31] On a scale stretching from *intertextualité* to *architextualité*, katabatic intertextual relations are, then, clearly situated closer to the latter than the former. But given that the katabasis usually has clearly demarcated start and end points, they are nevertheless further from the architextual end of the spectrum than, say, relations based on the simple co-presence of a journey, or an underground locale. Katabatic intertextual relations are by no means as diffuse and intangible as those based on genre, and thus here again they are positioned midway on the Genettian scale.

In terms of levels of implication, Genette's own focus in *Palimpsestes* is on hypertextual relationships which are 'déclarée, d'une manière plus ou moins officielle' [more or less officially stated].[32] One of the critics to reject reader-based intertextuality (although the 'plus ou moins' here leaves considerable room for personal interpretation), he states that attendance to more implicit relationships both opens too wide a field of study and 'fait un credit, et accorde un rôle [...] peu supportable, à l'activité herméneutique du lecteur' [invests the hermeneutic activity of the reader [...] with an authority and a significance that I cannot sanction].[33] The number of works for young readers in which the relationships with one or more earlier versions of the katabasis is explicitly signalled is relatively small, and overt references, recognizable as such without reference to the surrounding context are few and far between. Direct quotation, without any form of transformation, is particularly rare. With the exception of Hayley's epigraph, the source of which is clearly signalled, the only example of such a reference is to be found in *Voyage* where Axel, recently embarked on his katabasis, declares it to be 'le *facilis descensus Averni* de Virgile' (140) [It was Virgil's *facilis descensus Averni*'] which quotes the Sibyl's words to Aeneas prior to his journey:

> [...] facilis descensus Averno:
> noctes atque dies patet atri ianua Ditis;
> sed revocare gradum superasque evadere ad auras,
> hoc opus, hic labor est. (VI, 126)

[[...]it is easy to go down to the underworld. The door of black Dis stands open
night and day. But to retrace your steps and escape to the upper air, that is the
task, that is the labour.]

In *Voyage*, attention is drawn to the intertextual status of the phrase through its
inclusion in Latin, through the use of italics, and through the presence of the
originating author (although not the specific text). Even in such a case of direct
quotation, it should be noted that transformational processes are nevertheless at
work since the positioning of the phrase and its enunciator are altered: imparted by
the guide prior to the hero's journey in *Aeneid* VI, it is transferred, in *Voyage*, to the
traveller once the journey is already underway.

Quotations from earlier katabatic narratives which undergo quite basic forms of
transformation are also apparent in the works for young readers. The heading to
chapter 18 of *King Solomon's Mines*, 'We Abandon Hope', part translates and renders
in the indicative the imperative of the famous injunction inscribed on the entrance
to the underworld in the third canto of Dante's *Inferno*: 'Lasciate ogne speranza,
voi ch'intrate' ['ABANDON ALL HOPE, YOU WHO ENTER HERE']. Hayley draws
more extensively (although also more freely) on the same lines from Dante in the
inscription of the gateway through which Serena passes:

> Thro' me ye pass to Spleen's terrific dome:
> Thro' me, to Discontent's eternal home:
> Thro' me, to those, who sadden'd human life,
> By sullen humour, or vexatious strife;
> And here, thro' scenes of endless vapours hurl'd,
> Are punish'd in the forms they plagued the world;
> Justly they feel no joy, who none bestow,
> All ye who enter, every hope forego! (III, 53)[34]

The repetition of 'Thro' me' at the beginning of the first three lines firmly
establishes the relationship, although (with the exception of the retention of
'eternal' in the second line) the second halves of each line depart from the pre-text
in terms of the site evoked. The following four lines, concerning the nature of the
inhabitants and overall system, also depart from the pre-text before returning to a
direct translation of the injunction against hope in the final line.

If direct quotation is relatively uncommon, a slightly more common practice is the
comparison of abstract elements of the katabasis (a character, the general landscape,
a particular aspect of the setting) with those of an earlier version or versions of the
narrative. That Télémaque explicitly invokes his predecessors (Theseus, Hercules,
Orpheus) in order to demonstrate the superiority of his motives in itself constitutes
an intertextual reference to the invocations of Dante the pilgrim and Aeneas prior
to their own travels. In *Triumphs*, Serena is directly compared to Dante; her overall
journey, as well as a micro-event within that journey (the threatened separation
from the guide), is also likened to the experiences of her predecessor:

Far stronger fears her resolution melt,
Than those, which erst the Bard of Florence felt,
When, by the honour'd shade of Virgil led
Through all the dreary circles of the dead,
Hell's fiercest Demons threaten'd to divide
The living Poet from his shadowy Guide,
And bade him, friendless, and alone, return
Through the dire horrors of the dark sojourn. (III, 180)

In *Alphonse et Dalinde*, the hero's familiarity with classical literature is established in the course of his initial descent where he compares the underground to the cave of Cyclops and expresses his intention to imitate the bravery of Odysseus (71). He later associates aspects of his descent into the silver mine with those of classical katabasis: the miner who accompanies him into the underground 'lui retrace l'image du farouche batelier des enfers' [seemed the very counterpart of the ferocious Ferryman of Hell], while the water flowing down the walls of the mine shaft 'rappellent à son imagination les redoutables fleuves du Tartare' (181) [recalled to his imagination the fearful and tumultuous streams of Tartarus]. Indeed, like the subterranean tourists of the nineteenth century, several characters have recourse to classical, literary underworlds in order to describe their experiences.[35] In *King Solomon's Mines*, Quatermain uses the traditional leaf metaphor to describe the deaths of Kukuanaland's warriors and refers to the 'dark mass of water' discovered in the underground as 'this African Styx' (296).[36] The narrator/protagonist of 'La Fée Poussière' compares in broad terms the underground environment in which she finds herself ('un lieu terrible où tout était feu et flamme' [a terrible place where all was fire and flame]) to the land of the dead: 'On m'avait parlé de l'enfer, je crus que c'était cela' (397) [I had heard tell of the infernal region; I thought that was it]. In *Sans Famille*, the same form of general comparison is rejected but nevertheless evoked: 'Si la lumière manquait souvent, le bruit disait toujours qu'on n'était pas au pays des morts' (49–50) [If light was sometimes scanty, the noise would tell you that you were not in a city of the dead]. As Pierre Citron writes with reference to *Voyage*, but clearly also applicable to *Sans Famille*: 'l'idée de l'enfer n'est évoquée que fugitivement, et pour être aussitôt repoussée: mais, pour cela, il lui fallait être présente' [the notion of hell is evoked but briefly and is immediately dismissed, but for this to happen it has to be present].[37] Only in *Triumphs* are the quotations and comparisons not generated by the traveller but located in the external system of communication between narrator and reader, and (as we will see) it is by no means coincidental that it is a female character who is excluded in this way.[38] In each of the other cases, the quotations or comparisons form part of the hero's own consciousnesses and thus contribute to their characterization by implicitly establishing a certain outlook, cultural awareness and level of education.

However, the majority of the characters, and indeed, narrators, of the texts for young readers demonstrate no sign of awareness of earlier versions of katabasis. The vast majority of intertextual relationships between the hypertexts for young readers and their classical and medieval hypotexts are not 'déclarée, d'une manière plus ou moins officielle', but, like Genette's architextual relations, 'tout à fait muette' [completely silent] and thus fall beyond the parameters of *Palimpsestes*.[39] But despite the lack of explicit references, the episodes overall, as well as the abstract elements of which they are composed, can nevertheless be said to be intertextually related to earlier versions of the narrative. Because of what they do and where they go, each of the protagonists of the texts for young readers can be seen as incarnations of Odysseus, Aeneas, and Dante the pilgrim. Auxiliary characters can also be intertextually related to earlier figures. The 'enormous', 'barking' puppy encountered by Alice during the course of her katabasis can be regarded as a latterday Cerberus, quietened by the brave heroine by means of a stick rather than with mud or a cake until 'at last it sat down a good way off, panting, with its tongue hanging out of its mouth, and its great eyes half shut' (65).[40] Butcher aligns the prehistoric shepherd of *Voyage*, who 'brandissait de la main une branche énorme, digne houlette de ce berger antédiluvien' (267) [swung in his hand an enormous bough, an appropriately primeval crook for this shepherd from before the Flood] with Orion, 'a giant pursuing wild animals with a club in his hand' encountered by Odysseus in the *nekyia*.[41] The various continuities and transformations apparent in the texts for young readers in terms of the character-based intertextual relationships will be further examined in subsequent chapters.

    Various aspects of setting, as well as a range of micro-events which take place in the course of the journey below ground, also form the basis of intertextual relationships with earlier versions of the narrative. The key characteristics and features of the underground locale, and the similarities and differences apparent between the hypo-texts and the hypertexts in this regard will be examined in further detail in the following chapter. A wide variety of micro-events — from knowledge-generating encounters and attempted but impossible embraces to metamorphosis, loss of consciousness and the traversal of waterways — similarly connect the works for young readers with the pre-texts. Several such events will be discussed in the course of subsequent chapters and a single example will suffice here. The emergence of Haggard's travellers from the underground to find that 'there above us were the blessed stars' (297), and Axel's contemplation of 'un point brillant [...] une étoile dépouillée de toute scintillation' (137) [a brilliant object [...] a star, but not twinkling at all] can be related to Dante the pilgrim's similarly star-spangled return to the surface:

> tanto ch'i' vidi de le cose belle
> che porta 'l ciel, per un pertugio tondo.
> E quindi uscimmo a riveder le stelle. (XXXIV, 138)

> [Through a round aperture I saw appear
> Some of the beautiful things that Heaven bears,
> Where we came forth, and once more saw the stars.]

In *Sans Famille*, the same event and image is present through its negation, just as the comparison of the mine with the land of the dead is rejected but nevertheless evoked:

> Je me retournai instinctivement en arrière; mais déjà nous avions pénétré assez avant dans la galerie, et le jour, au bout de ce long tube noir, n'était plus qu'un globe blanc comme la lune dans un ciel sombre et sans étoiles.' (56)

[I instinctively looked back, but already we had penetrated some distance into the gallery, and the daylight at the end of this long black tube was no more than a white globe, like the moon in a starless, sombre sky.]

Implicit rather than explicit, the vast majority of intertextual references which can be discerned between the hypotexts and hypertexts depend on a process of cotextualization. As Hebel points out, 'allusions may be cotextualized by their immediate lexical surroundings and/or by their relation(s) to structural elements such as character or setting'.[42] Taken in isolation, a given element's status as intertextual reference may be overlooked, but does become apparent when taken in combination with other elements and with the surrounding narrative. In *Wonderland*, for example, dry or dead leaves frame the journey. At the beginning, it is the heroine who lands — *falls* — 'upon a heap of sticks and dry leaves' (38), while at its close, it is the leaves which, conversely, fall upon her: she awakens to find her sister 'gently brushing away some dead leaves that had fluttered down from the trees upon her face' (159–60). This is clearly a different, less direct intertextual reference than that apparent in *King Solomon's Mines*: rather than a metaphor used to describe death, leaves here form part of the décor. In *The Golden Key*, both aspects come together when a realm which appears to constitute the land of the dead is described as being 'chiefly made up of the shadows of leaves innumerable' (38). The leaves in both *Wonderland* and *The Golden Key* can easily be overlooked when taken in isolation but emerge as intertextual references when taken in conjunction with other elements. Furthermore, those references outlined above which *can* be identified in isolation, are further bolstered by the surrounding context: for example, the intertextual status of the chapter heading, 'We Abandon Hope', is reinforced by the events described within that chapter (the descent as a whole as well as a micro-event such as sighting of stars) and by the presence of a particular character, namely, the remarkably Sibylesque Gagool (see Chapter 3). Similarly, when taken in combination with other hypertexts, the intertextual status of the various references to stars or leaves is bolstered. A process of cumulative and mutual reinforcement, both across the range of textual elements within an individual text, and for a given textual element across the corpus, is, then, at work.

Authorial Intention

So far, we have established that the form of intertextual relationship with which we are concerned does not, on the whole, conform to the hypertextual relations with which Genette is concerned in *Palimpsestes* since, in most cases, it is neither 'massive' nor 'declarée'. A further fundamental — though nowhere explicitly stated — characteristic of Genettian hypertextuality is that of authorial intention. All of the types of work with which Genette is concerned — parody, burlesque, pastiche — involve conscious, deliberate reworking of the various hypotexts. We shall now consider the extent to which katabatic intertextual relationships can be attributed to deliberate authorial intention. On the basis of textual and extra-textual evidence, were the authors familiar with earlier katabases and do they appear to have had one or more of these narratives in mind when writing the texts with which we are concerned?

In those texts (i.e. *Télémaque*, *Triumphs*, *Alphonse et Dalinde*, *King Solomon's Mines*, *Voyage*, 'La Fée Poussière') where explicit references are made to an earlier version or versions of katabasis, it is clear that the authors were familiar with one or more of the pre-texts, or at the very least with the general notion of the underworld and its characteristics. Only a writer familiar with Virgil could, for example, place the aforementioned *facilis descensus* line in the mouth of his narrator, and indeed, as Lesser demonstrates, 'Verne repeatedly alludes to Virgil' in *Voyage*, even in cases where the reference is far from indispensable.[43] In the cases of *Télémaque*, *Triumphs*, *Alphonse et Dalinde* and 'La Fée Poussière', textual evidence is further supported by extratextual information. We know, for example, that Fénelon had already provided the duc de Bourgogne with tales adapted from the classics or based on mythology ('où', according to François Caradec 'se mêlent le souvenir de Virgile et d'Homère' [where memories of Virgil and Homer are intermingled]) as well as a translation and *abrégé* of the *Odyssey* itself.[44] Similarly, Hayley had already published, as a note to his *Essay on Epic Poetry*, a translation of *Inferno* 1–3 prior to writing the *Triumphs*.

Similar evidence can be marshalled for the two women authors. Although classical literature did not form part of Genlis's own education (which was, indeed, frequently neglected) she was nevertheless a prodigious reader who filled the many gaps in her knowledge herself.[45] Like Fénelon (whom she admired), she was entrusted with the education of a future monarch, namely, the duc de Valois (future king Louis-Phillipe). She instructed her royal ward, as well as her several other pupils, in all subjects except Latin.[46] Despite this apparent lacuna, her knowledge of the classical world was nevertheless sufficient to produce an *Abrégé de mythologie grecque* (1810).[47]

George Sand, on the other hand, was exposed to the classical world from an early age. In her *Histoire de ma vie*, she refers on more than one occasion to an *Abrégé de mythologie grecque*, whose images enabled her to learn 'les principales données de la fabulation antique' [the main themes of classical storytelling] which interested her 'prodigieusement' [prodigiously].[48] When she later came to read the text itself 'j'y prenais un grand plaisir; car cela ressemble aux contes de fées par certains côtés' [I enjoyed it a great deal; since it resembles fairy tales in some ways].[49] Although the author of this work is not cited, it may well have been the *Abrégé* of Genlis; Sand certainly read works by the comtesse in her youth, and the *Veillées* was read to her by her mother.[50] In addition, and unusually for a girl at this time (see below), Sand learnt both Latin and Greek and read a range of literary and philosophical 'greats', including Dante.[51] In later life, when Sand took charge of the education of her granddaughters, for whom the *Contes* were initially designed, we know from Aurore Lauth-Sand's memoirs that her lessons included reading and discussion of the Homeric epics in translation by Leconte de Lisle: 'nous lisions pendant près d'une heure, en alternant l'une et l'autre, cette belle épopée ou j'apprenais la légende des Dieux et des Héros avec un vif plaisir' [for almost an hour, both taking turns, we would read this beautiful epic where I learnt the legends of the gods and heroes with immense pleasure].[52] The elderly writer certainly seems to have succeeded in transmitting to her granddaughter her own enthusiasm for the classical world since in a letter of 1872 she describes Aurore (then aged six) as being 'dans une rage de mythologie, elle coupe et colle des casques de papier, pour faire de sa poupée une Minerve, elle sait tous les dieux de l'Olympe sur le bout de son doigt et pourrait nous raconter l'*Iliade*' [obsessed with mythology, she cuts and pastes paper masks to make her doll into Minerva, she knows all the gods of Olympia off by heart and could tell us the story of the *Iliad*].[53] Furthermore, Sand also appears to have been familiar with at least one other katabasis produced specifically for young readers. Verne's *Voyage* was not only influenced by Sand's earlier novel, *Laura* (1864), but also seems to have itself helped shape 'La Fée Poussière'.[54]

In those texts where the relations with earlier versions of katabasis are implicit, it is possible to establish with some certainty that they were not, however, entirely coincidental given the authors' familiarity with some form of the narrative. MacDonald learnt both Greek and Latin throughout the course of his education and he would later read and expound the *Aeneid* with his children, Greville and Caroline Grace.[55] He also 'had a secure mastery of Dante', producing translations and, in later life, giving talks and lecture courses on the author of the *Commedia*.[56] Indeed, according to William Raeper, Dante was for MacDonald 'the poet of poets and unrivalled in his moral and spiritual vision'.[57] References to Dante are apparent throughout MacDonald's work but it was the fantasies which were most marked by this influence. Many of the 'complex theological ideas' of *At the Back of the North Wind* are 'drawn from Dante', and there is even mention of an earlier Italian traveller named Durante — meaning 'Lasting, for his books will last as long as there are enough men in the world worthy of having them'.[58]

Furthermore, from 1858 onwards, MacDonald was a close friend of Lewis Carroll and indeed the MacDonald family were amongst the very first readers of the *Alice* manuscript. Critics have established a number of connections and lines of influence running backwards and forwards between various works by the two writers.[59] Thus, because of the presence in both works of a tiny golden key which gives Alice access to the beautiful garden and enables Tangle and Mossy to reach the land of shadows, it has been argued that *Wonderland* may have been influenced by *The Golden Key* which, although not published until 1867, Carroll could have read in manuscript form by 1862.[60] However, with reference to *Wonderland* and its relationship with earlier canonical pre-texts, Brockway states that 'there is no suggestion of conscious derivation or adaptation of this descent theme on Carroll's part'.[61] Certainly, although Carroll did begin to learn Italian in his twenties, he states baldly in a letter of 1890 that he has never read a word of Dante.[62] Docherty consigns this to 'teasing equivocation' and points to the writer's friendship with the Dante enthusiast, George MacDonald.[63] Carroll may, then, have been indirectly familiar with Dante through MacDonald just as part of Sand and Genlis's exposure to the classical world occurred through their reading of Genlis and Fénelon respectively. In terms of the classical pre-texts, Cohen describes Carroll as being 'steeped in classical literature': having begun the study of Latin at home, he then pursued classical studies at Richmond and Rugby and then at Oxford.[64] Even after his appointment as Mathematical Lecturer, Carroll continued to read classical literature, as the 'system of readings' he devised for himself in 1855 attests.[65]

Even where specific extratextual details are unavailable, the familiarity of the writers with at least one of the katabatic pre-texts can nevertheless be assumed. Although canonical status took time, Dante was well known and widely admired in both England and France by the nineteenth century. Painters such as Ingres, Delacroix and Dante Gabriel Rossetti drew on his work for subject matter. By the middle of the century, the *Commedia* 'seems to have been a popular best-seller' in England, and in France it became so popular that it was translated into Old French in order to 'favoriser l'étude de la vieille langue' [promote the study of the ancient language].[66]

Familiarity with the katabases of Homer and Virgil on the part of the writers for young readers was even more likely. In both France and England, the realm of classical myth and literature was, particularly in the nineteenth century, 'an atmosphere to be breathed in without thinking'.[67] Writing in a work aimed at young readers at the end of the nineteenth century, Grace H. Kupfer observes that Greek and Roman mythology 'have become an inseparable part of art and literature'.[68] Classicism pervaded culture at large in both countries. Joseph A. Kestner refers to the presence of classical allusions in 'familiar letters, the popular press, parliamentary debates, social treatises, and scholarly texts', while Hugh Osborne points to the deployment of Latin tags in chapter headings in novels, as epigraphs to poetry, and as captions to cartoons.[69] Although both critics are concerned with England, the situation was clearly the same in France where, to give but one example, Victor Hugo quotes and reverses Virgil's 'formonsi pecoris custos, formonsior ipse' [Fair was my flock, but fairer I, their shepherd] (*Eclogue* V, 44) in the heading to chapter three of the fourth part of *Notre Dame de Paris*: 'Immanis pecoris custos, immanior ipse' — which is quoted in turn by Verne in *Voyage* (267).[70] The Victorians also 'knew their Virgil well. In educated circles he was read with interest and respect and frequently quoted, even in the House of Commons', and thus 'remained a public property, a cultural monument like the Albert memorial'.[71] This is confirmed by C. E. Bowen, who, in his *Virgil in English Verse* of 1887, wrote that: 'Hundreds of Virgil's lines are for most of us familiar patterns, which linger in our memory, and around which our literary associations cluster'.[72] Equally, Homer's 'words and phrases had sunk deep into the minds of educated men, so that a passing reference to them would be recognized and understood'.[73]

The katabatic pre-texts have so permeated Western culture that even those who have never read them can be said to be influenced by them. As Docherty, in his discussion of Dante and Carroll, points out, a given work can be known without actually having been read: 'Many people who have not read Dante nevertheless have a fair knowledge of his journey underground, just as many people who have never read Homer still have a fair knowledge of the journeyings of Odysseus.'[74]

Whether or not they were deliberately incorporated by the authors, the presence of the katabatic narrative in these texts serves to confer respectability and enhance their status via association with prestigious, consecrated literary works. As Evans observes with reference to the Vernien œuvre, but equally applicable to each of the katabatic works for young readers, literary allusions 'function so as to firmly anchor his narratives to a recognizable cultural tradition, and thereby broaden Verne's own literary authoritativeness by identifying his novels more closely with those of the canonical literature(s) of his time'.[75] This form of intertextual legitimization is, one might argue, particularly sought after and needful with respect to the marginalized realm of children's literature.

Such issues of function and effect are now frequently considered by critics to be of greater interest and importance than those of authorial familiarity and intention. Clayton and Rothstein, for example, state that '[a]t most, knowing something about the author adds coherence to already framed hypotheses about a text'.[76] Susan Suleiman adopts a similar stance in an article entitled 'Dialogue and Double Allegiance: Some Contemporary Women Artists and the Historical Avant-Garde', in which she brings together works by artists of different periods, nationalities and genders whose knowledge of each other she postulates but cannot firmly establish. In a note to this article she argues that although biographical information can strongly assist an argument, it is by no means essential.[77] For Jonathan Culler, a text's intertextual status (what he refers to as its presuppositions)

> is not essentially or even primarily a question of what the writer knows, certainly not a question of what he has in mind, for the relevant presuppositions may be deeply sedimented in his past or in the past of his discipline; and indeed it is a characteristic experience that one's presuppositions are best revealed by another.[78]

Function and effect are as much, if not more, to do with readers as authors, and many (though as we have seen by no means all) versions of intertextual theory do indeed participate in a general shift away from author-centred criticism towards greater attention to the reader.[79] When texts are targeted at a particular audience, it seems reasonable that readerly competence should receive at least as much consideration as authorial intention. In the final part of this chapter we will therefore consider the capacity of young readers specifically to recognize the intertextual relationships we have been discussing.

Readerly Competence

Several critics have drawn attention to the limited intertextual capacities of the young reader. Christine Wilkie, for example, argues that 'children's intersubjective knowledge cannot be assured', while Stephens states that 'there can be no presumption that the [child] audience has been previously exposed to specific pre-texts or conventions of narrative'.[80] For his part, Hunt argues that whereas adult readers 'are always reading variations on themes and structures they have absorbed before', this 'can't be true of the child reader.'[81]

If we assume for the time being that young readers were unfamiliar with the katabatic pre-texts and that all references, implicit or explicit, passed over their heads and were available only to the older ranks of the frequently multi-generational readerships, what are the implications of this non-recognition? What function, if any, do intertextual references perform? Most importantly, perhaps, to what extent does non-recognition compromise the young reader's overall understanding of the hypertexts of our corpus? Genette argues that although it does place limits on a reader's appreciation, non-recognition of intertextual relationships never fundamentally affects the comprehensibility of the hypertext: 'le recours à l'hypotexte n'est jamais indispensable à la simple intelligence de l'hypertexte' [a simple understanding of the hypertext never necessitates resorting to the hypotext].[82] Similarly, with reference to novels for young readers by Robert Cormier and Jill Paton Walsh, Wilkie argues that 'a perfectly coherent reading of the text is possible without the reader's knowledge of the intertextual poetic allusions' to works by Dylan Thomas and Gerard Manley Hopkins respectively.[83] Thus, a young reader's failure to establish connections between, for example, the katabasis of *King Solomon's Mines* and earlier versions of the narrative, does not impinge upon his or her comprehension of the text, and indeed each of the hypertexts can be read fruitfully in isolation, without 'recours à l'hypotexte'.

Even if the relationships are not established by the reader, their presence nevertheless serves important functions. Where direct, explicit references to earlier works are apparent, the reader may register the gesture towards some earlier unknown work, recognizing the existence of an intertextual reference without being able to identify its precise source. Although such references could be simply passed over, they may prompt the reader to fill the gaps in their knowledge, to seek out the unknown references: who is Virgil? Who is the Bard of Florence? What are 'les redoutables fleuves du Tartare'? and so on. Daniel Compère's claim that 'la reference littéraire ne tient jamais un rôle didactique' [literary allusion never has a didactic function] is, I would argue, unfounded.[84]

Furthermore, if the relationships are not recognized by the targeted young reader *during* the reading of the hypertext, the foundations have nevertheless been laid for recognition in any *subsequent* encounter with earlier versions of katabasis. C. S. Lewis describes a similar process when he underlines the decisive role of works read at an early age:

> Parrot critics say that *Sohrab* is a poem for classicists, to be enjoyed only by those who recognize the Homeric echoes. But I [...] knew nothing of Homer. For me the relation between Arnold and Homer worked the other way; when I came, years later, to read the *Iliad*, I liked it partly because it was reminiscent of *Sohrab*. Plainly, it does not matter at what point you first break into the system of European poetry. Only keep your ears open and your mouth shut and everything will lead you to everything else in the end — *ogni parte ad ogni parte splende*.[85]

An individual reader's trajectory does not necessarily correspond to the chronological order of production. Works produced at a later date may constitute, for a given reader, the hypotext for an earlier work. If a reader encounters *Voyage* and then *Aeneid* VI (and *if* the relationship is made), it is the chronologically later work of children's literature which serves as hypotext for the chronologically earlier work. Thus, to adopt Lewis's phrase, Aeneas is reminiscent of Axel rather than vice versa. Just as *Sohrab* enables Lewis to 'break into the system of European poetry', so too do each of the works of children's literature under consideration here serve as an entry point into a wider literary arena, exposing the young reader in a highly economical, efficient manner, to a narrative apparent in a range of foundational texts. They thus serve essentially the same function of initiating the young reader 'into the dominant literary codes of the culture' as the targeted adaptations of canonical works discussed above, although usually in a less deliberate and overt fashion.[86] In addition to this broadly didactic, initiatory role, the relationships between these texts can also contribute to the reader's enjoyment: part of the pleasure Lewis derives from his reading of the *Iliad* is due to the fact that it reminds him of *Sohrab*. In the same way, the hypertexts may also serve to increase the appeal of the works with which they are related.

It is, then, altogether possible that at the time of their initial encounter with the works of children's literature under consideration here, young readers would not be in a position to identify their relationships with earlier versions of katabasis. But as Piégay-Gros points out, intertextuality is by no means the preserve of erudite readers, and we should be extremely wary of underestimating the young reader's capacities.[87] As Barthes makes clear, the reader 'n'est pas un sujet innocent, antérieur au texte [...]. Ce 'moi' qui s'approche du texte est déjà lui-même une pluralité d'autres textes, de codes infinis ou plus exactement: perdus (dont l'origine se perd)' [is not an innocent subject, anterior to the text [...]. This 'I' which approaches the text is already itself a plurality of other texts, of codes which are infinite or, more precisely, lost (whose origin is lost)].[88] Despite the conception of the child as *tabula rasa*, originating in Romanticism but still very much in evidence today, there is no reason why Barthes's plural self should apply to adult readers alone. Even the least experienced reader has already entered language and started to become accustomed to its conventions. A survey carried out by Wolf and Hicks demonstrates that dialogism is 'not unique to adulthood'; children as young as three can *produce* dialogical discourse, which at the very least implies their potential to recognize it.[89] Indeed, as Lawrence R. Sipe points out, '[t]here is evidence that very young children spontaneously make [...] intertextual links' which, he shows, can be used by young readers to at times quite spectacular hermeneutic and aesthetic effect.[90]

Furthermore, awareness of cultural and historical conditions, attendance to what Hans Robert Jauss refers to as the prevailing 'horizons of expectation', means that it *is* sometimes possible to assume previous exposure to certain types of literature and conventions, and even to specific pre-texts. Thus, for example, Fénelon's previous works for his ward mean that we can assume that the duc de Bourgogne was able to recognize at least some of the many references within *Télémaque*.[91] Such specific assumptions are only possible in a limited number of cases, but it is nevertheless possible to postulate more broadly. The typical targeted reader of these texts received a considerable degree of exposure to the classical world both at school and at home. Familiarization with classical literature and mythology began young, and indeed if, as we have seen, classicism was so prevalent, this was in large part due to its importance in the early stages of life: 'la reference mythologique a baigné l'enfant, constituant pour lui un veritable *medium*' [a child was steeped in mythological references which served as a true *medium* for him].[92] In addition to the rewritings of specific works referred to in the foregoing discussion, a huge number of collections of retold myths and legends were also produced throughout the period spanned by this study. In addition to Genlis's *Abrégé,* other examples produced in France include: Nicolas-Jean Hugo de Bassville's *Élémens de mythologie avec l'analyse des poëmes d'Homère et de Virgile, suivie de l'explication allégorique à l'usage des jeunes personnes de l'un et l'autre sexe* (1784); Pierre Blanchard's *Mythologie de la jeunesse* (1801), which ran to at least eleven editions; Jules-Raymond Lamé Fleury's *Mythologie racontée aux enfants* (1833 and reprinted throughout the century); and Élisabeth Müller's *Mythologie pittoresque. La Fable racontée au jeune âge* (1867). English examples of such collections include: Rose Lawrence's *Cameos from the Antique; or the cabinet of Mythology* (1831); John Allen Giles's, *First Lessons in Classical Mythology, adapted to the use of little children* (1853); Charles Kingsley's *The Heroes* (1856) and Grace Kupfer's *Legends of Greece and Rome* (1897). The latter aimed to 'hold the reader's interest and to make him familiar with the chief characters in the mythical play, — characters that he will meet again and again in literature and art.'[93] Proserpina, Orpheus and Eurydice all feature in Kupfer's work, and this inclusion of underworldly figures and katabatic narratives is typical of other texts of this type consulted: Baudet features Pluton, Orpheus and Eurydice; Lamé Fleury includes Proserpine and Hercule ('aux enfers'); Müller devotes a whole section to Tartare and its inhabitants; and Bassville includes a 'Déscription des Enfers' as well as a summary of both the *nekyia* and *Aeneid* VI.

Moreover, 'les études classiques dominaient l'enseignement secondaire' [classical studies dominated secondary teaching] until the twentieth century in both England and France.[94] Even when new subjects such as modern languages and sciences were introduced, classics remained the largest single category of curriculum content, and Clarke refers to the nineteenth century as the 'golden age' of classical education.[95] Although perhaps hardly conducive to a 'genuine understanding' or engagement, pedagogical practices nevertheless ensured a high degree of familiarity with classical literature: as Theodore Zeldin points out, 'small children were made familiar with 'literature' [he later offers the *Aeneid* as an example] in a thorough way at an early age: even if they could not understand it, they could recite it.'[96] In the seventeenth century, the pupils of Port Royal competed in reciting Virgilian verse, and in the nineteenth century, copying out lines of Virgil and Homer was a punishment frequently meted out at Rugby, and a means of maintaining discipline at Oxford.[97]

This form of education was deliberately elitist, reserved largely for young middle-class males. As we have seen, Sand and Genlis were sufficiently proficient to 'ground' their own pupils — male and female — in aspects of classical literature, and several of the aforementioned collections of classical myth and legend were produced by women. At least one such collection was also clearly targeted at both girls and boys, and Aurore Lauth-Sand was unlikely to have been the only young female reader to find herself 'dans une rage de mythologie'. Yet such girls who were exposed directly to the classical world and classical literature were the exception rather than the rule. The education of middle-class girls throughout the period under consideration frequently did not extend beyond the acquisition of superficial 'accomplishments'.[98] Kingsley's comments in the preface to *The Heroes* simultaneously underline universal relevance and gender-specific practices:

> Some of you have heard already of the old Greeks; and all of you, as you grow
> up, will hear more and more of them. Those of you who are boys will, perhaps,

spend a great deal of time in reading Greek books; and the girls, though they may not learn Greek, will be sure to come across a great many stories taken from Greek history, and to see, I may say every day, things which we should not have had if it had not been for these old Greeks.[99]

Likewise, some members of the working classes did know the classics in the original or, more commonly, adapted form, and Homer, Virgil and Dante were often included in targeted libraries. Yet the very development of English Literature as a discipline was under the impetus of what might now be referred to as 'widening participation'. It was modern English and not ancient Greek or Latin which was felt to be most valuable for the working classes.[100]

Even if the classical world and its literature was not uniformly part of childhood culture in this period, its prominence within a particular, privileged and powerful part of society means that it was wholly possible that at least some young readers were capable of recognizing the relationships between the hypertexts and their hypotexts. The relationships between the different hypertexts may also have been recognized: so many schoolchildren read *Télémaque*, for example, that they may well have been in a position to relate, say, *Voyage*, to Fénelon's text instead of or as well as to the *Aeneid*.[101] Young readers may have established connections between the hypertexts and deliberately targeted versions of the earlier works rather than the original pre-texts. This being the case, the repetition of the general, abstract pattern is more important than the recurrence of specific signifiers which are likely to undergo change in the process of adaptation.

The identification of such relationships enables an enhanced, more enriched appreciation of the hypertext, as well as some insight into the general connectedness of texts. But as Flint points out, the recognition of quotation and indeed intertextual relationships more generally, not only involves the reader in the active construction of meaning, but also confirms 'one's confident membership of a cultural group'.[102] Chandler argues that 'identification of the appropriate code serves to identify the interpreter [...] as a member of an exclusive club, with each act of interpretation serving to renew one's membership'.[103] The club membership generated by these texts is particularly exclusive and high-profile. In France, possession of a classical education was 'seen as a means by which one could move into the liberal professions or the civil service', and in more general terms, 'one of the accepted badges of middle-class status'.[104] Likewise, in England, knowledge of the classics 'authenticated culture and class' and constituted 'the apanage of an economically privileged minority'.[105] Thus, whether these intertextual relationships are recognized during the reading of the hypertexts or at some later point, the texts for the young reader serve both to educate and to empower young readers by further familiarizing them with or by initiating them into foundational works, and thus enabling them to situate themselves within 'l'univers culturel de [leur] temps' [the cultural universe of their time].[106]

Usually formed on the basis of episodes rather than entire works, frequently implicit, and not always a manifestly deliberate aim of the author, katabatic intertextual relations clearly do not meet the requirements of Genettian hypertextuality. But whether or not their authors, or indeed their readers, were aware of it, each of the texts for young readers is nevertheless intertextually related to foundational works of classical and medieval literature. These relationships are particularly worthy of our attention given their ability to empower the young reader by introducing them to, or further familiarizing them with, a prestigious, highly enabling, cultural arena.

If the corpus of texts examined by Genette in *Palimpsestes* is, then, different from our own, the various categories of transformation which he outlines and for which he supplies a highly precise nomenclature nevertheless provides the framework for a detailed exploration of the various similarities and differences between the katabases for young readers and their classical and medieval hypotexts. Such will be our concern in the subsequent chapters of this study.

Notes to Chapter 1

1. Michael Worton and Judith Still, 'Introduction', in *Intertextuality: Theories and Practices*, ed. by Michael Worton and Judith Still (Manchester/New York: Manchester University Press, 1990), pp. 1–44 (p. 1).
2. Michel Butor, 'Suggestion', *L'Arc*, 39 (1969), 99–101 (p.100).
3. Julia Kristeva, Σημειωτική: *Recherches pour une semanalyse* (Paris: Seuil, 1969), p. 85; *Desire in Language: A Semiotic Approach to Literature and Art*, trans. by Thomas Gora, Alice Jardine and Leon S. Roudiez (Oxford: Blackwell, 1980), p. 66.
4. Michael Riffaterre attempts to mark off 'true' intertextuality from aleatory intertextuality, i.e. 'des rapprochements accidentels dûs à des similitudes de lexique, de situation, à des ressemblances sur le plan de la référence apparente ou réelle au monde verbal' [accidental connections due to similarities in lexicon, in situation, or to resemblances on the level of apparent or real reference to the non-verbal (sic) world] (Michael Riffaterre quoted and translated in Thaïs E. Morgan, 'Is there an intertext in this text?: Literary and Interdisciplinary Approaches to Intertextuality', *American Journal of Linguistics*, 3 (1985), 1–40 (p. 27)). Riffaterre is by no means alone in making this move: Laurent Jenny also differentiates intertextuality from 'une simple allusion ou réminiscence' ('La Stratégie de la forme', *Poétique*, 27 (1976), 257–81 (p. 262); while Daniel Compère objects to all but the most concrete form of allusion on the grounds that anything lacking typographic, stylistic or narrative marks cannot be regarded as intertextual but merely 'le simple rapprochement établi entre deux textes par le caprice du lecteur' [the simple connection of two texts made according to the whim of the reader] (Daniel Compère, *Jules Verne: Écrivain* (Geneva: Droz, 1991), p. 163).
5. Morgan, p. 26.
6. Andrew D. Weiner, 'Sidney/Spenser/Shakespeare: Influence/Intertext/Intention', in *Influence and Intertextuality in Literary History*, ed. by Jay Clayton and Eric Rothstein (Madison: University of Wisconsin Press, 1991), pp. 245–70 (p. 246). Piégay-Gros also recognizes the existence of scales of intertextuality: 'si toute œuvre est intertextuelle, des différences de degré ou d'infléchissement peuvent cependant être distinguées' [if all texts are intertextual, differences of degree and of emphasis can nevertheless be distinguished] (Natalie Piégay-Gros, *Introduction à l'Intertextualité* (Paris: DUNOD, 1996), p. 8).
7. This strategy is also advocated by Heinrich F. Plett, 'Intertextualities', in *Intertextuality*, ed. by Heinrich F. Plett (Berlin/New York: Walter de Gruyter, 1991), pp. 3–29 (p. 6).
8. Genette, pp. 8–14.
9. Genette, p. 321.
10. Genette, p. 9.
11. Owen Miller, 'Intertextual Identity', in *Identity of the Literary Text*, ed. by Mario J. Vallès and Owen Miller (Toronto/Buffalo/London: University of Toronto Press, 1985), pp. 19–40 (p. 40).
12. Genette, p. 9.
13. Genette, p. 13.

14. Genette, p. 19.

15. John Stephens, *Language and Ideology in Children's Fiction* (London/New York: Longman, 1992), p. 86; John Stephens and Robyn McCallum, *Retelling Stories, Framing Culture: Traditional Story and Metanarratives in Children's Literature* (London/New York: Garland, 1998), p. 3.

16. Marc Soriano, *Guide de littérature pour la jeunesse*, 2nd edn (Paris: Delagrave, 2002), p. 30.

17. Soriano, p. 30.

18. Stephens and McCallum, p. 3.

19. Stephens and McCallum, p. 6.

20. An identically titled text, produced by H. L. Havell, appeared two years later in the *Told Through the Ages* series.

21. Alfred John Church, *L'Odyssée contée aux enfants. Le récit d'Homère simplifié par A. J. Church*, trans. by J.-R. Lugné Philipon (Paris: Vuibert, 1923).

22. Général L. M., *L'Énéide racontée à mes petits enfants* (Limoges: Droquet and Ardent, 1935), p. 4.

23. William Raeper, *George MacDonald* (Tring: Lion Publishing, 1987), p. 322.

24. Rose Emily Selfe, *How Dante climbed the mountain. Sunday readings with the children from the 'Purgatorio'* (London: Cassell, 1887), p. 26, iv. Selfe also published *Selections from the first nine books of the 'Croniche Fiorentine'. Translated for the use of students of Dante and others* (London: Constable, 1896).

25. Mary MacGregor, *Stories from Dante told to the children* (London/New York: Jack/Dutton, 1909), p. 13. At least one adaptation of Dante was also produced in the United States: Elisabeth Harrison, *The Vision of Dante. A story for little children and a talk to their mothers* (Chicago: Chicago Kindergarten College, 1894).

26. Genette, p. 242.

27. J. L. Goré, 'Le Télémaque, périple odysséen ou voyage initiatique?', *Cahiers de l'Association Internationale des Études françaises*, 15 (1963), 59–78 (p. 60).

28. Plett, 'Intertextualities', p. 7.

29. Plett, 'Intertextualities', p. 20.

30. Shlomith Rimmon-Kenan, *Narrative Fiction: Contemporary Poetics* (London/New York: Routledge, 1999), p. 13.

31. Rimmon-Kenan, p. 15.

32. Genette, p. 19.

33. Genette, p. 19.

34.

> 'Per me si va ne la città dolente,
> per me si va ne l'etterno dolore,
> per me si va tra la perduta gente.
>   Giustizia mosse il mio alto fattore;
> fecemi la divina podestate,
> la soma sapïenza e 'l primo amore.
>   Dinanzi a me non fuor cose create
> se non etterne, e io etterna duro.
> Lasciate ogne speranza, voi ch'intrate.' (III, 1)

[THROUGH ME YOU ENTER INTO THE CITY OF WOES,
THROUGH ME YOU ENTER INTO ETERNAL PAIN,
THROUGH ME YOU ENTER THE POPULATION OF LOSS.
JUSTICE MOVED MY HIGH MAKER, IN POWER DIVINE,
WISDOM SUPREME, LOVE PRIMAL. NO THINGS WERE
BEFORE ME NOT ETERNAL; ETERNAL I REMAIN.
ABANDON ALL HOPE, YOU WHO ENTER HERE.]

35. John F. Sears, *Sacred Places: American Tourist Attractions in the Nineteenth Century* (Amherst: University of Massachusetts Press, 1998), pp. 35, 39.

36. The shades of *Aeneid* VI rush to the bank 'quam multa in silvis autumni frigore primo / lapsa cadunt folia' (VI, 309) [as many as are the leaves that fall in the forest at the first chill of autumn];

and the underworld inhabitants of canto III respond to Charon: 'Come d'autunno si levan le foglie / l'una appresso de l'altra, fin che 'l ramo / vede a la terra tutte le sue spoglie' (III, 112) [As leaves in quick succession sail down in autumn / Until the bough beholds its entire store / Fallen to the earth]. Quatermain uses the same metaphor to describe the infliction of death rather than its condition: 'the mass of struggling warriors, men falling thick as leaves in the autumn wind' (206).

37. Pierre Citron, 'Sur quelques voyages au centre de la terre', in *Nouvelles recherches sur Jules Verne et le voyage I* (Paris: Librairie Minard, 1978), p. 74.

38. See Udo J. Hebel, 'Towards a Descriptive Poetics of Allusion', in *Intertextuality*, ed. by Heinrich F. Plett (Berlin/New York: Walter de Gruyter, 1991), pp. 135–64 (p. 146).

39. Genette, p. 12.

40. Docherty aligns the puppy encountered *during* the course of Alice's with the leopard that Dante the pilgrim faces *prior to* his journey. No mention is made of Cerberus, who, because both canine and a subterranean inhabitant, is in many ways closer to Alice's adversary. That other katabatic travellers including Aeneas and Psyche also encounter the monstrous dog highlights the limitations of Docherty's focus on a single earlier version of the narrative (Docherty, 'Dantean Allusions in Wonderland', p. 13).

41. Jules Verne, *Journey to the Centre of the Earth*, trans. by William Butcher, 3rd edn (Oxford/New York: OUP, 2008), p. 230.

42. Hebel, p. 154.

43. Lesser, p. 40.

44. François Caradec, *Histoire de la littérature enfantine en France* (Paris: Albin Michel, 1977), p. 63.

45. Gabriel de Broglie, *Madame de Genlis* (Paris: Librairie Académique Perrin, 1985), p. 23.

46. Broglie, pp. 28, 136.

47. Stéphanie de Genlis, *Abrégé de mythologie grecque. Arabesques Mythologiques, ou les Attributs de toutes les Divinités de la Fable* (Paris: Barrois, 1810).

48. George Sand, *Histoire de ma vie*, ed. by Damien Zanone, 2 vols (Paris: Flammarion, 2001), I, 154.

49. Sand, *Histoire de ma vie*, I, 238.

50. Sand, *Histoire de ma vie*, I, 247–50.

51. Hortense Dufour, *George Sand: La Somnambule* (Monaco: Éditions du Rocher, 2002), p. 108.

52. Quoted in Sand, *Contes d'une grand-mère*, p. 481.

53. George Sand, *Correspondance*, ed. by Georges Lubin, 24 vols (Paris: Garnier, 1964–90), XXIII, 337.

54. Piero Gondolo della Riva, 'George Sand inspiratrice de Jules Verne', in *George Sand et son temps III: Hommage à Annarosa Poli*, ed. by Elio Mosele (Geneva: Slatkine, 1994), pp. 1109–16 (p. 1113); Kiera Vaclavik, 'George Sand & Jules Verne: A Missing Link', *French Studies Bulletin*, 90 (2004), 8–10.

55. Raeper, pp. 30, 40, 41, 43, 65; Spina, p. 16

56. Spina, pp. 27–28.

57. Raeper, p. 322.

58. Raeper, p. 322; George MacDonald, *At the Back of the North Wind* (New York: Routledge, 1871; repr. New York/London: Garland, 1976), p. 114.

59. See, for example, John Docherty, *The Literary Products of the Lewis Carroll–George MacDonald Friendship* (Lewiston, NY/Queenston, Ont./Lampeter: Edwin Mellen, 1995); Raphael B. Shaberman, *George MacDonald: A Bibliographical Study* (Winchester: St Paul's Bibliographies, 1990), pp. 115–28.

60. Lewis Carroll, *Alice's Adventures in Wonderland and Through the Looking Glass*, ed. by Roger Lancelyn Green (London: OUP, 1971), p. 254.

61. Brockway, p. 36.

62. Morton N. Cohen, *Lewis Carroll: A Biography* (London: Macmillan, 1995), p. 52; Docherty, 'Dantean Allusions in Wonderland', p. 13.

63. Docherty, 'Dantean Allusions in Wonderland', p. 13.

64. Brockway, p. 36; Cohen, p. 224.

65. Cohen, p. 60.

66. Nick Havely, 'Introduction: Dante's Afterlife, 1321–1998', in *Dante's Modern Afterlife: Reception and Responses from Blake to Heaney*, ed. by Nick Havely (London: Macmillan, 1998), pp. 1–16 (p. 2); Albert Counson, 'Dante en France', *La Revue moderne*, 48 (1904), 232–52 (p. 252).

67. Christopher Stray, *Classics Transformed: Schools, Universities and Society in England, 1830–1960* (Oxford: Clarendon Press, 1998), p. 47.

68. Grace H. Kupfer, *Legends of Greece and Rome* (London: Heath, 1922) [1st edn 1897], p. 5.

69. Joseph A. Kestner, *Mythology and Misogyny: The Social Discourse of Nineteenth-Century British Classical Subject Painting* (Madison/London: University of Wisconsin Press, 1989), p. 14; Hugh Osborne, 'Hooked on Classics: Discourses of Allusion in the Mid-Victorian Novel', in *Translation and Nation: Towards a Cultural Politics of Englishness*, ed. by Roger Ellis and Liz Oakley-Brown (Cleveden: Multilingual Matters, 2001), pp. 120–66 (p. 140).

70. Victor Hugo, *Notre-Dame de Paris* (Paris: Livre de Poche, 1972), p. 188.

71. Norman Vance, 'Virgil and the Nineteenth Century', in *Virgil and his Influence: Bimillenial Studies*, ed. by Charles Martindale (Exeter: Bristol Classical Press, 1984), pp. 169–92 (p. 169).

72. Quoted in Stray, p. 65.

73. Richard Jenkyns, *The Victorians and Ancient Greece* (Cambridge, MA: Harvard University Press, 1980), p. 204.

74. Docherty, 'Dantean Allusions in Wonderland', p. 13.

75. Arthur B. Evans, 'Literary Intertexts in Jules Verne's *Voyages Extraordinaires*', *Science-Fiction Studies*, 23 (1996), 171–87 (p. 171).

76. Jay Clayton and Eric Rothstein, 'Figures in the Corpus: Theories of Influence and Intertextuality', in *Influence and Intertextuality in Literary History*, ed. by Jay Clayton and Eric Rothstein (Madison: University of Wisconsin Press, 1991), pp. 3–36 (p. 15).

77. Susan Rubin Suleiman, 'Dialogue and Double Allegiance: Some Contemporary Women Artists and the Historical Avant-Garde', in *Mirror Images: Women, Surrealism and Self-Representation*, ed. by Whitney Chadwick (Cambridge, MA/London: MIT Press, 1998), pp. 128–54 (p. 152).

78. Jonathan Culler, *The Pursuit of Signs: Semiotics, Literature, Deconstruction* (London/Henley: Routledge and Kegan Paul, 1981), p.102.

79. Logically, any theory which denies that the author is the ultimate source or guarantor of intertextuality must locate it in the reader. But this is not always the case, thus Riffaterre — who appears to move towards this position — ultimately locates intertextuality in neither the author nor the reader but in the text itself. The assignation of consciousness to the text rather than the author is discussed by Will McMorran in, 'From Quixote to Caractacus: Influence, Intertextuality, and *Chitty Chitty Bang Bang*', *The Journal of Popular Culture*, 39: 5 (2006), 756–79 (pp. 757–58).

80. Christine Wilkie, 'Relating Texts: Intertextuality', in *Understanding Children's Literature*, ed. by Peter Hunt (London/New York: Routledge, 1999), pp. 130–37 (p. 131); Stephens, *Language and Ideology in Children's Fiction*, p. 85.

81. Peter Hunt, 'What do we lose when we lose allusion? Experience and Understanding Stories', *Signal*, 57 (1988), 212–22 (p. 222).

82. Genette, p. 554.

83. Wilkie, p. 134.

84. Compère, *Jules Verne: Écrivain*, p. 89.

85. C. S. Lewis, *Surprised By Joy: The Shape of My Early Life* (London: G. Bles, 1955), p. 56. Lewis quotes *Inferno* VII, 75 [each part shines on all the others].

86. Wilkie, p. 135.

87. Piégay-Gros, p. 3.

88. Roland Barthes, *S/Z* (Paris: Seuil, 1970), p. 16; *S/Z*, trans. by Richard Millar (London: Cape, 1975), p. 10.

89. Dennie Wolf and Deborah Hicks, 'The Voices within Narratives: The Development of Intertextuality in Young Children's Stories', *Discourse Processes*, 12, (1989), 329–51.

90. Lawrence R. Sipe, '"Those two gingerbread boys could be brothers": How Children Use Intertextual Connections During Storybook Readalouds', *Children's Literature in Education*, 31 (2000), 73–90 (p. 73).

91. Caradec, p. 63.

92. André Blanc, 'Fonction de la référence mythologique dans le *Télémaque*', *Dix-Septième Siècle*, 125 (1979), 373–88 (p. 377).

93. Kupfer, p. 6.

94. William den Boer, 'Préface', *Les Études classiques aux XIXe et XXe siècles: Leur place dans l'histoire des idées*, ed. by William den Boer (Geneva: Fondation Hardt, 1980), no page numbers.

95. R. D. Anderson, *Education in France, 1848–1870* (Oxford: Clarendon Press, 1975), pp. 24, 89; Stray, p. 185; M. L. Clarke, *Classical Education in Britain, 1500–1900* (London/New York: Cambridge University Press, 1959), p. 84.

96. Stray, p. 66, cf. also pp. 46, 187; Theodore Zeldin, *France, 1848–1945*, 2 vols (Oxford: Clarendon Press, 1977), I, 173.

97. Pierre Thomas Du Fossé, *Mémoires pour servir à l'histoire de Port-Royal*, 2 vols (Geneva: Slatkine, 1976), I, 170: 'Comme notre classe éstoit composée de ceux qui étoient les plus avancez dans les études, nous faisions des défis d'émulation les uns contre les autres, à qui réciteroit un plus grand nombre de vers de Virgile, sans faire de fautes' [As our class was made up of those most advanced in their studies, we challenged each other to recite the most lines of Virgil without making a mistake]; Cohen, pp. 19, 57.

98. Jenkyns, p. 64; R. L. Archer, *Secondary Education in the Nineteenth Century* (London: Cass, 1966), pp. 231, 245.

99. Charles Kingsley, *The Heroes, or Greek Fairy Tales For My Children* (London: Macmillan, 1865) [1st edn 1856], p. vii.

100. Martyn Lyons, 'New Readers in the Nineteenth Century: Women, Children, Workers', in *A History of Reading in the West*, ed. by Guglielmo Cavallo and Roger Chartier (Cambridge: Polity, 2003), pp. 313–44.

101. 150 editions and 80 translations of *Télémaque* were produced by 1830 alone, and the text has been described by François Caradec as 'le roman le plus lu et le plus traduit de notre littérature' [the most read and translated novel of our literature] (Caradec, p. 65). In the first half of the eighteenth century, *Télémaque* was one of the most published and advertised books on this side of the Channel. (Ronald Paulson, 'Models and Paradigms: *Joseph Andrews*, Hogarth's *Good Samaritan*, and Fénelon's *Télémaque*', *Modern Language Notes*, 91 (1976), 1186–1207 (p. 1201)).

102. Kate Flint, *The Women Reader, 1837–1914* (Oxford: Clarendon Press, 1993), p. 259.

103. Daniel Chandler, *Semiotics: The Basics* (London: Routledge, 2002), p. 200.

104. Zeldin, p. 297; Anderson, p. 8; Robert R. Bolgar, 'Latin Literature: A Century of Interpretation', in *Les Études classiques aux XIXe et XXe siècles*, ed. by den Boer, pp. 91–126 (p. 107).

105. Jenkyns, p. 63; Bolgar, p. 107.

106. Blanc, p. 373.

CHAPTER 2

The Underground Landscape
and its Inhabitants

In *Palimpsestes*, Genette outlines a series of 'transpositions thématiques' [thematic transpositions] which are of two basic forms: 'la transposition diégétique' [diegetic transposition] concerning setting and character and 'la transposition pragmatique' [pragmatic transposition] involving actions or events.[1] The more common of the two forms, and that with which we are principally concerned in this study, are 'transpositions diégétiques' in which one encounters 'la même action (ou presque) dans un autre univers' [the same (or almost the same) action in another world].[2] A given action 'peut être transposée d'une diégèse à une autre, par exemple d'une époque à une autre, ou d'un lieu à un autre, ou les deux à la fois' [can be transposed from one period to another, or from one location to another, or both] as well as from one 'milieu social' [social setting] to another.[3] As a result of changes to the setting in which an event takes place, the character who acts can also undergo alterations in terms of their age, sex and nationality.[4] All such changes, Genette argues, tend to bring character and setting closer to the targeted readership: 'le mouvement habituel de la transposition diégétique est un movement de translation (temporelle, géographique, sociale) *proximisante*: l'hypertexte transpose la diégèse de son hypotexte pour la rapprocher et l'actualiser aux yeux de son propre public' [the habitual movement of diegetic transposition is a movement of proximization: the hypertext transposes the diegesis of its hypotext to bring it up to date and closer to its own audience (in temporal, geographic, or social terms)].[5]

In this chapter, our focus shall be on the 'transpositions diégétiques' discernible in katabases targeted at young readers in terms of the underground landscape and its inhabitants (the transpositions concerning the other key players in the katabasis, i.e. the travellers who venture into the underground realm and their accompanying guides, will be examined in the following chapter). Because of the nature of their setting and their targeted audience, these texts offer an interesting opportunity to explore the extent to which textual components can be brought closer without loss of identity and essential characteristics. How much 'proximisation' can a setting undergo before it becomes something else altogether? To what extent can hell be 'brought closer' and *remain hell*, especially given that by the nineteenth century in particular, physical underground locales had become a part of everyday life as places of work, scientific endeavour, tourism, and transportation?[6] Moreover, the audience targeted by these texts is one for which specific types of material are, it is widely thought, deliberately avoided or suppressed. Genette argues that in rewritings:

On n'y supprime pas seulement ce qui pourrait ennuyer le jeune lecteur ou excéder ses facultés intellectuelles, mais aussi et surtout ce qui pourrait 'choquer', 'toucher' ou 'inquiéter' son innocence, c'est-à-dire bien souvent lui livrer des informations qu'on préfère lui soustraire encore pour quelque temps: sur la vie sexuelle, il va de soi, mais aussi sur bien d'autres réalités ('faiblesses' humaines) dont il n'est pas urgent de l'avertir et de lui donner l'idée.[7]

[What is suppressed in this case is not only anything that might bore young readers or exceed their intellectual ability but also and especially anything that might 'shock,' 'trouble,' or 'upset' their innocence — i.e., anything that might provide them with information we prefer to withhold from them for some time still: information on sexual matters, of course, but also on many other realities (human 'foibles') which it is not urgent to bring to their awareness or attention.]

Although not specified, key elements of the katabasis — death, sin, evil — almost certainly fall within the category of 'realités' Genette has in mind here. Many people are of the opinion that children should be shielded from dark, difficult material, and Marian Pyles has observed that in contrast with the books of more experienced readers, those for young audiences 'frequently celebrate the joys and infinite possibilities of life. They likewise traditionally have happier endings and produce more resolved conflicts.'[8] Yet mortality is by no means absent from books for young readers; Pyles goes on to discuss the 'abundance of material that deals [...] with the subject of death'.[9] It can be portrayed in children's literature as the outcome of, and appropriate punishment for, bad behaviour and disobedience.[10] Moreover, certain texts in the pre-Romantic period in particular had no qualms about threatening their young readers with punishments in the next world in order to regulate their behaviour in this.[11] But what of katabatic narratives specifically? When compared with katabases targeting a general audience, do those produced for young readers incorporate and emphasize these elements to the same extent, or are they instead reduced and played down in order to protect?

Classical and Medieval Katabases

In each of the pretexts, the underground is a sacred space, special and unique. This is underlined by its difficulty of access, and its geographical and/or temporal distance. The classical katabases are embedded within narratives set in what was already, to their initial audiences, a distant, mythical past. The descent of Odysseus takes place in the faraway, fantastic land of the Cimmerians 'shrouded in mist and cloud' (XI, 17), and its precise start point is difficult to establish. In the *Aeneid*, on the other hand, the physical entity of the cave marks the entry to the underground which, situated in 'Euboicis Cumarum' (VI, 2) [the Euboean colony of Cumae] of 'Hesperium' (VI, 6) [the land of Hesperia] (i.e. Italy), is both much more concrete than that of Homer and brought closer to a Roman audience. But if the locale is more easily pinpointed, access to the underground involves a series of rites, including most notably the location and appropriation of the Golden Bough, even more complex and testing than those faced by Odysseus. In the *Inferno*, Dante, like Virgil, gives the underworld a very clear entrance point and also effects a form of *translation proximisante*. In this case, however, the descent is brought closer temporally rather than geographically; it is transferred from the remote past to the almost contemporary world of the initial reader, and more specifically, the evening of Good Friday in the year 1300. On the other hand, Dante's underground is the least clearly situated in physical terms. The environs are wooded but no further details are provided.

The underworlds are presided over by a ruler or rulers who are referred to repeatedly. Whereas they are never encountered in either the *nekyia* or *Aeneid* VI, Dante the pilgrim not only meets with Satan but clambers over his immense body in order to return to the surface. Many other figures inhabiting the undergrounds are encountered in each of the narratives, including some (such as the judge Minos and the boatman Charon) who are recurrent presences. The underworld of *Aeneid* VI houses figures such as these, with clearly designated roles, as well as a diverse range of allegorical figures such as 'consanguineus Leti Sopor' (VI, 278) [Sleep, Death's sister], and fearsome creatures including Centaurs, Scyllas, Gorgons and Harpies (138–39). Dante's underworld also incorporates a rich cast of monsters such as Cerberus, Geryon, the Minotaur, and the Harpies, and of menacing workers and tormentors including Minos, Plutus, Phlegyas, and, perhaps most memorably, the Malebranche: 'demon cornuti con gran ferze' (XVIII, 35) [demons — horned // And carrying large scourges].

Such figures are present only because of the peculiar function of the underground which is to receive, house and punish the more or less diverse ranks of the dead. One of the principal characteristics of the latter is their physical intangibility: the underground of the *nekyia* is home to 'the senseless, burnt-out wraiths of mortals' (XI, 475–76), while that of *Aeneid* VI is occupied by 'exsanguis [...] umbras' (VI, 401) [bloodless shades], by 'sine corpore vitas / admoneat volitare cava sub imagine formae' (VI, 292) [disembodied spirits, a mere semblance of living substance]. In both cases, they prove frustratingly impossible to grasp. In the *Inferno*, the weightlessness of the dead is emphasized by Phlegyas's boat which dips down only when the pilgrim boards (VIII, 28). But despite the stress on insubstantiality, death is very much like life, a continuation of it. The underworld constitutes an abode of the dead, a place in which the dead are housed and, as the domestic terminology suggests, the inhabitants of the underground preserve a strong sense of animation. If the travellers repeatedly seek to embrace their loved-ones it is in part because of their misleadingly life-like appearance. Dante the pilgrim refers to the shades at one point as 'vanità che par persona' (VI, 36) [emptinesses, which seem / Like real bodies], and in both the *Inferno* and the classical katabases, the dead are, in Robert Pinsky's words, 'full of a vigorous other-life'.[12] Although they cannot embrace or be embraced by the living, the shades are nevertheless able to remember, to feel sorrow, and to converse in a largely unlimited way. Likewise, the bodies of the dead preserve the marks and scars inflicted in life.

Whereas the underground at first houses the dead in their entirety, it later becomes accessible only to the dead of a particular sort. In the *nekyia*, the inhabitants are largely undifferentiated, although there is a broad separation between the mythological sinners who undergo specific torment and the rest of the dead whose general condition is itself highly unpleasant, far worse than the lowest form of life: Achilles tells Odysseus that he would 'rather slave on earth for another man — / some dirt-poor tenant farmer who scrapes to keep alive — / than rule down here' (XI, 489–91). In *Aeneid* VI there is a much more marked separation between the damned inhabitants of Tartarus (and within this group those who are and are not tortured) and the blessed residents of the Elysian Fields (who for their part are divided between those who stay and those who return to the surface). The Virgilian underground is unique in that it offers, in the Elysian Fields, a death vastly superior to the life which preceded it, as well as the opportunity to be a temporary visitor rather than a permanent resident. Yet despite the various divisions and segregations apparent here, all categories of the dead are still present in the underworld. However, with the advent of Christianity and the displacement of the blessed to Heaven, the underground becomes reserved exclusively for sinners, who are, in the *Inferno*, themselves subject to a highly complex system of classification. Over time, then, the underground's role becomes exclusively rather than partially one of punishment for sin, leading to an evacuation of virtually all characteristics of a positive nature.

Indeed as Brunel observes, it is perhaps in order to undergo physical punishment that the dead remain embodied in the manner outlined above.[13] The torments of the dead are frequently horrific and presented in graphic detail. In the course of his travels, Odysseus views three figures being punished for their crimes: Tityus, who is stretched out over nine acres, unable to chase away the vultures who pluck at his liver; Tantalus, who can never reach the water and fruits which surround him; and Sisyphus who must continue to labour at his never quite successful rock-rolling task. Within the walls of Tartarus in *Aeneid* VI, Tisiphone lashes the shades and, as in the *nekyia*, Tityus is once more prey to a vulture who feeds endlessly:

> [...] rostroque immanis vulture obunco
> immortale iecur tondens fecundaque poenis
> viscera, rimaturque epulis habitatque sub alto
> pectore, nec fibris requies datur ulla renatis. (VI, 597)

> [a huge vulture with hooked beak cropped his immortal liver and the flesh that was such a rich supplier of punishment. Deep in his breast it roosts and forages for its dinners, while the filaments of his liver know no rest but are restored as soon as they are consumed.]

Above the heads of the Lapiths, Ixion and Pirithous, 'atra silex iam iam lapsura cadentique / imminet adsimilis' (VI, 602) [the boulder of black flint is always slipping, always seeming to be falling] and a feast is laid out for all to see but for none to enjoy. In the *Inferno*, the punishment famously fits the crime: according to the system of *contrepasso*, the torture undergone by the shades is suited to each kind of sin 'often by extending or distilling or reenacting the sin itself'.[14] Thus, the lustful are buffeted about in the wind (V), gluttons are chewed by Cerberus (VI), murderers are boiled in blood (XII) and fomenters of schism are cut apart (XXVIII). Likewise, the thieves of the eighth circle who, as Robert Pinsky states, 'ignored the boundary of *thine* and *mine* in life now merge as shades, their shells of personal identity made horribly permeable'.[15]

The physical surroundings within which these punishments take place themselves receive an ever-increasing level of attention. In the *Odyssey*, the landscape is never described directly; its features and overall nature are instead inferred from dialogue. It is, for example, in Anticleia's address to her son that we learn that the underground is 'the world / of death and darkness' (XI, 155). As a result, the underground traversed by Odysseus remains somewhat mysterious, vague and intangible, especially when compared to descriptions of the palace of Ithaca, in books XX–XXII in particular.

It is Virgil who, according to Alice Turner, provides 'the first thoroughly graphic description of Hell'.[16] Even before the descent begins, we learn from the Sibyl's instructions to Aeneas that: 'tenent media omnia silvae, / Cocytusque sinu labens circumvenit atro' (VI, 131) [[t]he middle of that world is filled with woods and the river Cocytus glides round them, holding them in its dark embrace]. Aeneas enters the underworld via 'spelunca alta fuit vastoque immanis hiatu, / scrupea, tata lacu nigro nemorumque tenebris' (VI, 237) [a huge, deep cave with jagged pebbles underfoot and a gaping mouth guarded by dark woods and the black waters of a lake]. Although the silence of the underworld is frequently alluded to, aural details are included throughout the narrative: near the walls of Dis, Aeneas and his guide 'hinc exaudiri gemitus, et saeva sonare / verbera, tum stridor ferri tractaeque catenae' (VI, 557) [could hear the groans from the city, the cruel crack of the lash, the dragging and clanking of iron chains], whereas in Elysium, with its 'virgulta sonantia silvae' (VI, 704) [copses of rustling trees], they listen instead to the singing of the blessed. Details concerning the sounds of the underworld are further supplemented by visual and olfactory elements, such as the 'glaucaque' [grey-green] hue of the reeds (VI, 416), or the 'fauces grave olentis Averni' (VI, 201) [evil-smelling throat of Avernus].

But as Turner points out, it was in the Middle Ages that the most elaborate landscaping of the underworld took place involving the development of a complex iconography apparent in numerous visual as well as textual representations.[17] Unsurprisingly, therefore, it is in Dante's *Inferno*, which, as illustrator Michael Mazur notes, 'even includes measurements', that by far the most concrete, tangible underworld topography emerges.[18] Dante the pilgrim frequently asserts the ineffability of the underground locale, as, for example, with reference to the schismatics encountered in the eighth circle:

> Chi poria mai pur con parole sciolte
> dicer sel sangue e de le piaghe a peino
> ch'i' ora vidi, per narrur più volte?
>   Ogne lingua per certo verria meno
> per lo nostro sermon e per la mente
> c'hanno a tanto comprender poco seno. (XXVIII, 1)

> [Who could find words, even in free-running prose,
> For the blood and wounds I saw, in all their horror —
> Telling it over as often as you choose,
> It's certain no human tongue could take the measure
> Of those enormities. Our speech and mind,
> Straining to comprehend them, flail, and falter.]

Such assertions are, of course, highly ingenuous since they are made in the very process of describing the scene. The very first things which Dante the pilgrim remarks are the 'sospiri, pianti e alti guai' (III, 22) [sighs, groans and laments] issuing from the underground and, as in *Aeneid* VI, sounds, sights and smells are all recorded. The textures of the landscape, the materials from which its different features are built, are also described: the walls of the city of Dis 'mi parean che fero fosse' (VIII, 78) [seemed cast / Of solid iron'], and the 'alta ripa' [deep-cut bank] on which the travellers stand is 'facevan gran pietre rotte in cerchio' (XI, 1) [[f]ormed by a circle of massive, fissured rock]. As these quotations suggest, a high level of precision is achieved through the extensive employment of metaphors, adjectives and adverbs.

The landscapes which emerge directly or indirectly are, for the most part, highly unpleasant. While in the *Odyssey* the underground is equally dismal throughout, in both the *Aeneid* and the *Inferno* there is a close correlation between the nature of the landscape and the nature of its inhabitants. The most meritorious enjoy pleasant, indeed idyllic, surroundings in the Elysian Fields:

> [...] locos laetos et amoena virecta
> Fortunatorum Nemorum sedesque beatas.
> largior hic campos aether et lumine vestit
> purpureo, solemque suum, sua sidera norunt. (VI, 638)

> [the land of joy, the lovely glades of the fortunate woods and the home of the blest. Here, a broader sky clothes the plains in glowing light, and the spirits have their own sun and their own stars.]

Existence in this realm is infinitely superior to that on the surface. In the *Inferno*, the Limbo of the first circle includes a pleasant, well-lit place complete with 'nobile castello' [noble castle], 'bel fiumicello' [handsome stream] and 'fresca verdura' [fresh green meadow] (IV, 90–96) inhabited by the unbaptized but otherwise honourable poets of Antiquity. Yet Limbo is a mere pocket within the first circle and the Elysian Fields are preceded, of course, by the highly unpleasant realm of Tartarus. Taken together, the undergrounds are predominantly negative places in which existence is infinitely worse than on the surface, as is clear in the widespread use of adjectives such as 'joyless' (*Odyssey* XI, 94), 'horrendas' [fearful] (*Aeneid* VI, 327), 'trista' [dismal], 'buia' [grim], 'sconsolata' [bleak] (*Inferno* III, 78; III, 130; VIII, 77) etc. As opposed to the glowing light of the Elysian Fields, darkness is one of the principal negative characteristics of these underworlds for visitors and inhabitants alike: Aeneas refers to his passage 'per umbras / per loca senta situ cogunt noctemque profundum' (VI, 461) [through the shades of this dark night in this dark and mouldering place] while Deiphobus speaks of 'tristis sine sole domos, loca turbida' (VI, 534) [our sad and sunless homes in this troubled place]. The prevailing gloom of the underworld is also alluded to in the *nekyia* (XI, 155, 157).

If the underground is infinitely worse or — more occasionally — better than the surface, it is also strongly reminiscent of it. In his description of the various aspects of the underground, Dante frequently has recourse to those of the surface, as in the following description of the route taken from an 'alp-like place' into the seventh circle:

Qual è quella ruina che nel fianco
di qua da Trento l'Adice percosse,
o per tremeto o per sostegno manco,
che da cima del monte, onde si mossa,
al piano è sì la roccia discoscesa,
ch'alcuna via darebbe a chi sù fosse:
cotal di quel burrato era la scesa ; (XII, 3)

[[...] This side of Trent,
There is a place a landslide fell and struck
The Adige's flank: because of unstable ground
Or earthquake, rocks once tumbled from the peak
And formed a passage where people can descend.
Such was the footing we had down that ravine.]

But it is not only in Dante's comparisons of surface and underground that a certain 'contamination' of the two realms is apparent.[19] As Pierre Brunel observes: 'L'autre monde a, comme le nôtre, un relief, des fleuves et un climat que les peuples semblent avoir souvent conçu d'après le leur' [the other world has, like ours, relief, rivers and a climate that peoples seem to have conceived in accordance with their own].[20] The underground locales of *Aeneid* VI and the *Inferno* include several architectural structures of varying degrees of size and grandeur such as entryways, walls, cities and towers. The undergrounds also encompass a range of natural features such as trees, reeds and lawns, as well as various weather conditions including, rain, fog, snow and hail. One of the most prevalent natural physical features of the underworld is water, described by Brunel as 'un élément constant du paysage infernal' [a constant element in the landscape of hell].[21] Odysseus must first cross a vast expanse of water before he can enter the realm of the dead, which, given the torments of Tantalus, must itself contain some form of water. There are several waterways in the underworlds of both the *Aeneid* and the *Inferno* — perhaps most memorably those which are crossed by the travellers in the boats of Charon (*Aeneid*) and Phlegyas (*Inferno*). That the underworld landscape of these narratives 'reproduisent volontiers notre séjour' [readily reproduce our own realm] is perhaps, Brunel suggests, because 'le regard du vivant reste prisonnier des categories' [the vision of the living is locked within categories].[22] Just as the dead are strikingly lifelike, so too the underground environment, for all its sacredness and separation, is strongly recognizable and closely related to the surface.

Katabases for Young Readers

As we saw in Chapter 1, *Télémaque* and *Triumphs* are closely modelled on *Aeneid* VI and the *Inferno* respectively and their underground landscapes are, naturally, analogous to them in terms of their physical features, population and function. In each text physical entities mark both the entrance to the underworld and the intertextual relationship with the pre-text. Thus, Télémaque enters a poisonous cavern amidst tremors and howls, while Serena is escorted through an inscribed gateway. Within the underground itself, key physical features of the pre-texts such as waterways and architectural structures are also retained. Similar, too, are the overall conditions of the underground and the way in which they are described. Thus, Serena passes '[t]hro' long, long tracts of darkness' (III, 47) in order to enter a realm of 'shadowy horrors' (III, 203), the 'gloomy', 'drear'/'dreary' features of which are constantly emphasized (e.g. III, 190, 42, 536). In the palace of Spleen, the occasional flash of light serves only to emphasize the prevailing gloom:

> A sudden light soon struck her dazzled view;
> But 'twas a light of such infernal hue,
> As double horror to the darkness gave,
> With dread reflection from a dusky wave. (III, 99)

Like Dante, Hayley refers to surface conditions in order to describe this chiaroscuro:

> Such, as on earth, to Superstition's eye,
> Denounces ruin from the northern sky,
> While she discerns, amid the nightly glare,
> Armies embattled in the blazing air. (III, 208)

In *Télémaque*, although the final reference to the underground realm overall is to 'ces sombres lieux' [my trans: this gloomy place] (410–11), the conditions are, as in *Aeneid* VI, somewhat more varied in this respect. Tartarus is characterized by its darkness (385, 388, 393). But as in the Virgilian pre-text, the Champs Elysées are as bright and diffused with light as Tartarus is dark and gloomy (397). Fénelon too has recourse to the surface in order to convey this luminosity, but here the emphasis is on difference rather than similarity since the light of the Champs Elysées 'n'est point semblable à la lumière sombre qui éclaire les yeux des misérables mortels' (397) [not like that gloomy gleam which enlightens the eyes of wretched mortals].

As in their pre-texts, both realms house allegorical figures, workers and rulers with whom the travellers communicate. Minos makes another appearance in *Télémaque* and Charon is present in both works for young readers. In *Télémaque*, Pluton and Proserpine are attended by a whole host of 'images funestes' [horrid images] including 'la Mort [...] les noirs Soucis, les cruelles Défiances, les Vengeances' (389) [Death [...] black Care, cruel Jealousy; Revenge]. Similarly in *Triumphs*, Spleen's own abode is surrounded by the offspring of Pride, Fear and Disorder'd Wit, and the ruler is attended by Disease, Detraction, Disappointment and Discontent as well as her Prime Minister, Ennui. The final realm is ruled over by Misanthropy with his followers Satire, Sarcasm, Irony, Derision and Malice.

But, as before, the principal population of the undergrounds is the dead who are punished or (in *Télémaque*) rewarded for their behaviour on earth. In *Triumphs* the inhabitants are exclusively negative and of a specific type deliberately attuned to the condition of the protagonist and targeted reader, namely, 'those, who sadden'd human life / By sullen humour, or vexatious strife' (III, 55). Serena thus encounters infants born in loveless unions, beggars, and alcoholics, as well as three principal groups of 'fiends' (III, 20): the Fierce (made up of Scolds and Termagents); the Fretful; and finally the Sullen or Envious. The inhabitants of the underground in *Triumphs* are 'punish'd in the forms they plagued the world' (III, 58), i.e. according to a Dantesque system of *contrepasso*. Thus, having emptied a vase onto the head of her husband, Socrates, the scolder Xantippe is now tortured by drops of liquid fire falling from a suspended vase (III, 371–75).

Fénelon's underground is inhabited by shades of all classes, but Télémaque encounters monarchs alone, i.e. a form of the dead directly relevant to both the hero and the targeted reader, heirs to the thrones of Ithaca and France respectively. In Tartarus, Télémaque encounters numerous kings who had committed a range of crimes including those who had 'cherché les richesses par des frauds, des trahisons et des cruautés' [endeavoured to acquire wealth by fraud, treachery, and cruelty] as well as 'les ingrats, menteurs, flatteurs' (390) [the ungrateful, liars, flatterers]. A group of kings are at the mercy of their own former slaves: the slaves of Naborphasan taunt their erstwhile master as they hold him in chains (387). Another shade who had been virtuous in life for his own sake rather than for the gods undergoes no physical torment from the Furies 'parce qu'il leur suffit de l'avoir livré à lui-même et que son propre cœur venge assez les dieux méprisés' [because they thought it enough to have delivered him over to himself, and to let his own heart take vengeance on him for his contempt of the gods]. He is pursued everywhere by 'les rayons perçants de la vérité' (392) [the piercing rays of truth]. The simple truth also punishes several other inhabitants, the sight of which 'les perce, les déchire, les arrache à eux-mêmes' (394) [enrages, distracts and confounds them]. The punishment meted out for these crimes is thus largely psychological in the manner of the boulder poised to fall within the walls of Tartarus in *Aeneid* VI. Such eschewal of the graphically presented physical torment which prevails in the earlier narratives can be read as an attempt to shield the young reader in the manner outlined by Genette.

Clearly then, both Hayley and Fénelon effect *translations proximisantes* in terms of the inhabitants of their underworlds. Indeed, they are 'proximisante' to such an extent that, despite their possession of many key features, they can no longer be said to constitute *the* underground — Hell — at all. In each case, the texts clearly present *an* underworld not *the* underworld; a particular form of 'hell', based on others, and with a particular purpose. Although they constitute the sole underworlds of their texts, they still do not possess the singular quality of earlier locales. This is partly because of the very tangible presence of the pre-text within the narrative: this underground cannot be singular given that there is (at least) *an* other. The same could of course be said for the Virgilian and Dantesque underworlds, but in the two reworkings for young readers the intertextual non-singularity is combined with, and reinforced by, other factors. In the case of *Triumphs*, the underground is simply too worldly to be otherworldy. Although traditional forms of sin (such as Pride and Envy) are present, they are brought down to the level of mere bad (indecorous, insufficiently feminine) behaviour. Artifice and parody abound and in this sense Hayley's underworld is in many ways closer in spirit to that of Aristophanes' *Frogs* than to Dante's *Inferno*. In *Télémaque*, an alternative afterlife system always hovers nearby and is gestured towards throughout. Thus, the reversals of fortune which evoke the parable of Dives and Lazarus, the piercing light of truth, and the references to eternal youth, all evoke a Christian afterlife with which the Abbé and his ward (as well as subsequent young readers) were of course all too familiar.

The non-singular status of the underground landscapes — the fact that they are *not hell* — is even more readily apparent in the other texts for young readers. None of the undergrounds constitutes the final destination of all living beings or of all sinners in the afterlife. The caves into which Alphonse initially descends and the underground of *King Solomon's Mines* retain a sacred quality in that they constitute burial chambers for members of the Guanche sect and for the Kukuan kings respectively. Alphonse finds himself 'au milieu de plus de deux cents cadavres rangés debout contre les murs' [in the midst of two hundred dead bodies, arranged, standing, against the wall], none of which 'paroissoit tomber en corruption, et n'exhaloit la plus légère odeur [...] tous avoient conservé leur peau et leurs traits' (72) [seemed to suffer putrefaction, or sent forth the least smell [...] they had all preserved their features]. The petrified remains of the twenty-seven Kukuan kings in *King Solomon's Mines* 'wrapped in a shroud of ice-like spar' are equally well preserved (268). Furthermore, at the head of the table around which these forms are placed, 'holding in his skeleton fingers a great white spear, sat *Death* himself, shaped in the form of a colossal human skeleton, fifteen feet or more in height' (266). But like any cemetery or burial ground, these undergrounds merely store inanimate remains rather than housing walking, talking shades as in the pre-texts.

All the other undergrounds are occupied in some way, but the presence of living beings only increases their dissemblance from the earlier sacred locales. The mines of *Alphonse et Dalinde, Princess* and *Sans Famille* are places of industry and labour. Despite their very tangible dangers, they are places in which to make a living rather than places of the dead. In the narration which precedes Rémi's initial descent, the traditional underworld is evoked only in order to be rejected: 'on n'était pas dans le pays des morts' (50) [you were not in a city of the dead]. Although a particular set of procedures must be followed, it is not particularly difficult to get access to the underground: Rémi simply replaces his injured friend, whilst Alphonse merely obeys his mentor who organizes the excursion into the mine. As opposed to both the workers and the shades of traditional katabases, the miners are not permanent but temporary residents of the underground who, unless prevented by some form of accident, return to the surface on a regular basis. The boundary between surface and underground is, thus, much less absolute than in earlier narratives. Even for the targeted middle-class reader with little or no direct experience of mining communities, the undergrounds are recognizably places of *this* world rather than the next. This is particularly true of *Sans Famille* where — since the descents occur in nineteenth-century Varses — both temporal and geographical *translations proximisantes* are effected.

In addition, the reader has a much greater exposure to, and familiarity with, the underground environment than in earlier texts. In *Princess*, a description of the underground locale is included on the very first page of the text and by the time Irene undertakes her descent in chapter 20, no less than six chapters have already taken place below ground. Alexis's account of the mine in *Sans Famille* serves to establish the nature of the subterranean setting prior to the actual descents. In *Paradis*, details concerning the proportions and features of the underground locale accumulate with every story preceding the katabasis proper which itself refers only to the nature of the door leading to the Sibyl's realm. In this way, the exceptional and extraordinary quality of the landscape is reduced.

In *Paradis* and *Princess*, monstrous beings do occupy the underground locale, but however malevolent (and this is not unambiguously the case) they are not dead. In *Paradis*, the German knight's realization that the inhabitants of the underground 'étaient vraiment des démons' [were really demons] is confirmed when he witnesses 'la reine et les autres dames [...] se transformaient toutes ensemble en couleuvres et en serpents' (35) [the queen and other ladies [...] all turn into snakes and serpents], a form of metamorphosis with clear connotations of Eden and evil. But whatever their powers of transformation, there is no indication that the Queen and her courtiers are dead, nor are their numbers sufficient to constitute *the* (all-encompassing) underworld. In *Princess* the underground is not only workplace to the miners but also home to the goblins referred to at one point by Curdie's wise mother as 'those demons' (182). This 'strange race of beings' (2), has developed high levels of cunning, mischief and strength, and is physically repulsive: 'not ordinarily ugly, but either absolutely hideous, or ludicrously grotesque both in face and form' (4). The underground population has its rulers, as well as a government and a population of 'animal companions' (4) who emerge onto the surface from time to time and are even more monstrous than the goblins themselves (97–100). Yet as opposed to the demons and fearsome creatures of earlier texts, the nature of the goblins is *caused by* rather than simply reflected in the landscape. In an age of Darwinism and Taine's identification of 'race, moment, milieu' as historical determiners, it is precisely the underground environment which has brought about the degeneration of both the goblins and their companions. In the closing lines of the text MacDonald nonetheless pulls back from such absolute determinism: existence below ground is not inherently or immutably detrimental since most of the goblins who remain underground 'grew milder in character, and indeed became very much like the Scotch Brownies. Their skulls became softer as well as their hearts [...] and by degrees they became friendly with the inhabitants of the mountain and even with the miners' (241).

The inhabitants of other undergrounds may be rather peculiar or behave somewhat bizarrely, but they are by no means out and out representatives of evil. On the contrary, the venerable, wise old men of *The Golden Key* are strongly spiritual and, with their majestic beauty and direct, simple manner, clearly associated with goodness rather than evil. Wonderland houses a rich and diverse population made up for the most part of talking animals, but also fantastical creatures (the Mock Turtle, Gryphon and March Hare), and (pseudo-)human figures (the Mad Hatter, as well as the rulers — the King and Queen of Hearts — and their walking, talking playing-card court). In most cases, their moral status goes unremarked, and even the violent, hard-talking Queen of Hearts and the Duchess are impotent and ridiculous rather than truly evil or dangerous (see chapter 3). In *Voyage*, the underground cavern is populated, like a textual Jurassic Park, by various amoral creatures including eyeless fish, a plesiosaurus and ichthyosaurus, as well as, in the 1867 version of the text, a prehistoric shepherd and his mastodon herd.[23] In 'La Fée Poussière', the underground is also populated by a diverse range of 'habitants' (403) [inhabitants] which, although the narrator/protagonist of 'La Fée Poussière' finds it rather hard to believe, are equally amoral and impulse-led.

The destinations of these journeys are, then, of a fundamentally different order to those traversed in the classical and medieval pre-texts. With the exception of *Télémaque*, the sacred qualities of the underground are entirely eliminated. Given this fundamental shift in identity, what is striking is the sheer number of aspects of the traditional underground locales which do nevertheless remain in place in the texts for young readers. Firstly, despite temporal 'translations proximisantes' which are frequently effected, some sense of otherworldliness is retained by the fact that the journeys frequently take place in locations distant (and different) from that of the travellers and their targeted readers: La Sale's German knight undertakes his journey in Italy; the Portuguese Alphonse embarks on his first descent in Tenerife and his second in Denmark (the supplementary journey of later editions occurs on the Scottish isle of Staffa); the descent of the German Axel and Lidenbrock in *Voyage* occurs in Iceland, while that of the English travellers of *King Solomon's Mines* takes place in the fictional country of Kukuanaland in South Africa. Moreover, difficulty of access, the need to perform specific tasks, overcome obstacles and complete extensive journeys, remains an important part of several texts, and usually far exceeds the realist requirements of the difficult act of journeying below the earth's surface. Axel and his uncle must crack a code, and travel through Germany, Denmark and Iceland using several modes of transport before arriving at the Sneffels peak which they are able to enter only due to a precise alignment of earth and sun. The travellers of *King Solomon's Mines* must also undertake a long and arduous journey through lands known and unknown, and participate in civil war, before gaining access to the underground by coopting the diabolical Gagool. In *Paradis*, the German knight and his squire face a range of obstacles including a vertiginous bridge and forceful winds before finally reaching the Sibyl Queen's domain. Just as Aeneas is instructed by the Sibyl to find the golden bough, so too do both the narrator/protagonist of 'La Fée Poussière' and Irene in *Princess* gain access to the underground by obeying the orders of their female mentors and accomplishing specific tasks (slipping on a ring; calling out three times).

In addition, key physical features of the classical and medieval undergrounds remain very much in place and, as discussed in the previous chapter, serve as intertextual markers. In each of the katabases for young readers, gloomy darkness continues to prevail. For example, when Alphonse reaches the bottom of the staircase during his first descent, 'il lève la tête et ne voit plus le jour' [he looked upwards, but could no longer see the light of day], then passes through 'un long corridor obscur' [my trans: long dark corridor] within 'ce lugubre souterrain' (71) [this dreary vault]. Likewise, as Alice falls down the well 'it was too dark to see anything' below her, and when she reaches the bottom, 'she looked up, but it was all dark overhead' (29). In *King Solomon's Mines*, Quatermain refers repeatedly (if rather unvaryingly) to the obscurity of various parts of the underground locale including 'the dark doorway' (265), 'a gloomy apartment' (265), 'that dark place' (272), 'a dark hole' (272), 'the dark passage' (273), the 'darkness of the chamber' (295) and the 'darkness of the tunnels' (295). The same insistence is equally apparent in *Princess*, where the underground is a place of 'universal and constant darkness' (142), and the 'lower regions of darkness' are frequently contrasted with the 'upper regions of light' (100). That the passage of time has no effect within the underground since the light of day never enters — 'the morning made no difference here. It was all dark, and always dark' (131) — is stated no less than three times at different points in the text.

Demonstrating a clear concern for plausibility and verisimilitude, each of the writers incorporates some form of light source which enables the travellers to navigate these predominantly dark spaces. These can take the form of candles, lamps and torches brought from the surface by the travellers themselves or already *in situ* in the underground locale: torches burn in the undergrounds of *Alphonse et Dalinde*; small overhead apertures provide light in *Paradis* and *King Solomon's Mines*; a 'feeble light' shines on the gateway in *Triumphs*; and the 'long, low hall' of Wonderland is 'lit up by a row of lamps hanging from the roof' (29). In 'La Fée Poussière', it is the fairy herself who, like Hayley's sprites, helpfully becomes 'toute lumineuse et rayonnait comme un flambeau' (398) [wholly luminous and radiant as a torch]. These light sources do not only have a practical function of plausibility but can also give rise to spectacular effects of illumination.[24] As in the Virgilian underground, the gloom is thus dispelled by areas of gorgeous brightness. On arriving in the silver mine, Alphonse is 'frappé de la lumière d'une vive clarté' [surprised by the sudden appearance of light], the silver chamber being 'éclairé par une infinité de lampes et de flambeaux. Tout brille et tout éblouit dans ces régions souterraines. Les lumières se réfléchissait et se répètent sur l'argent des murs et des voûtes, et sur le cristal des eaux limpides qui traversent le salon' (182) [lighted by an infinity of lamps and flambeaux. All is shining, all dazzles in these subterranean regions; the lights are reflected and multiplied by the silver walls and vaults, and the crystal waters, which wind along the hall]. The undergrounds of the two MacDonald texts contain comparable locales: in *The Golden Key*, the home of the Old Man of the Earth is a 'glimmering cave' (55), while in *Princess*, the walls of the goblin hall 'were, in many parts, of gloriously shining substances, some of them gorgeously coloured besides, which powerfully contrasted with the shadows' (65). The labyrinthine passages of the underground in *Voyage* are frequently illuminated in the same way: when the light of the surface still penetrates, '[l]es mille facettes de la lave des parois le recueillaient à son passage et l'éparpillaient comme une pluie d'etincelles' (137) [[t]he thousand facets of the lava on the walls picked it up on the way down and scattered it everywhere like a rain of sparks], and when daylight disappears, the Ruhmkorff lamps with which the travellers are equipped produce similar effects. Moreover, in *Voyage*, as in *Télémaque* and *Aeneid* VI, spaces characterized principally by their gloom and darkness are juxtaposed with an area of striking, supernatural light; the vast underground cavern is lit by 'une lumière 'spéciale' [qui] en éclairait les moindres détails' (202) [a special light which revealed the smallest details].

Further elements from classical and medieval undergrounds which are by no means as intrinsic to the landscape from the point of view of verisimilitude as the darkness discussed above are also retained. Water remains 'un élément constant' in the katabases for young readers, a 'motif that seems to run through all underground children's books', as Wendy Lesser observes.[25] Indeed, in a number of texts, as in the *Aeneid* and *Inferno*, several different forms of water are present. The mine of *Sans Famille* initially incorporates 'un petit ruisseau' [little rivulet] running between the tracks (56), but this will soon be replaced by no less than a 'cascade', an 'avalanche' of water (67). Wonderland's lovely garden has 'cool fountains' (30) and the many-doored hall soon, thanks to Alice's tears, includes its own pool. During much of her descent, Irene follows the course of a 'little stream' (403), and in *Voyage*, the lifesaving stream named the Hans Bach leads the travellers to the underground cavern with its 'vaste nappe d'eau, le commencement d'un lac ou d'un océan' [vast expanse of water, the beginning of a lake or ocean] which 's'étendait au-delà des limites de la vue' (200) [stretched away out of view]. The immensity of the waterways encountered is also emphasized in *Paradis* where the travellers must cross 'une très grosse rivière' (29) [a very wide river] in order to enter the realm of the Reine Sibylle. As this suggests, waterways are more than mere elements of the backdrop: as in *Télémaque* and *Triumphs*, they are crossed in some form of vessel (*Voyage*) or via a bridge (*Paradis*), passed through (*Princess, The Golden Key*), or inadvertently entered into by the travellers (*Wonderland, The Golden Key, King Solomon's Mines, Sans Famille*). They thus serve as obstacles to the journey, can vary the landscape, and (where vessel and crossing is concerned) constitute a further form of intertextual reference.

In terms of their overall nature, the underground locales of several texts may possess certain positive features, but the overwhelming impression is nevertheless one of negativity. In *Princess*, the underground may contain the 'magnificent cavern' (64) of the goblin hall, but overall the surface is infinitely superior to the depths. Similarly, in *King Solomon's Mines*, Quatermain describes the stalactite chamber as 'the most wonderful place that the eyes of living man ever lit on', eulogizing 'the overpowering beauty and grandeur' (262) of the stalactites within 'this beautiful place' (264). The 'overpowering' character of this beauty hints at a response, typical of the sublime, combining admiration and fear, and this is even more pronounced in the next 'awe-inspiring' chamber which presents 'a ghastly sight' and 'grisly wonders' (266, 270). Naturally enough, once immured within its walls, Quatermain's descriptions become unequivocally negative: the treasure-chamber is 'accursed', the underground as a whole in which 'the horrors of the night' are spent, is 'a ghastly hole', and, in hindsight, an 'awful dungeon that was so near to becoming our grave' (298). Other undergrounds are wholly devoid of redeeming features. In *Alphonse et Dalinde*, for example, this is emphasized in the case of the first underground into which the hero descends via the repetition of the adjectives 'funeste' and 'affreux' [dreary, dismal] by both protagonist and narrator (71–74). Although clearly not the case, the underground of 'La Fée Poussière' is so horrific that the narrator/protagonist assumes it to be hell.

Not only do the undergrounds for young readers retain key features and the overall qualities of classical and medieval undergrounds, but the way in which they are presented also recalls earlier strategies and methods. Like Dante the pilgrim, Quatermain and Axel both stress the ineffable nature of the underground in the very process of its description: '[i]t is', claims Haggard's hero, 'impossible for me to convey any idea of the overpowering beauty and grandeur of these pillars of white spar' (262). Similarly, in the underground cavern, Axel states: 'Toutes ces merveilles, je les contemplais en silence. Les paroles me manquaient pour rendre mes sensations [...] A des sensations nouvelles, il fallait des mots nouveaux, et mon imagination ne me les fournissait pas' (204) [I reflected upon all these marvels in silence. Words to describe my feelings failed me entirely [...] New words were needed for new sensations, and my imagination could not provide them].

Another very common technique is the presentation of the unknown via the known; the comparison of elements of the underground to those of the surface. In *Sans Famille*, attention is drawn to the similarities between the two realms in terms of their layout: 'Ces galeries se croisaient, et çà et là, comme à Paris, il y avait des places et des carrefours; il y en avait de belles et de larges commes les boulevards, d'étroites et de basses comme des rues du quartier Saint-Marcel' [These galleries crossed each other, and here and there, as in Paris, there were squares and cross-roads. Some of these open spaces were wide and handsome, like boulevards; some of them narrow and mean, like the streets in the Quartier St Marcel]. But what differentiates surface and underground is the way in which these passages are lit: 'toute cette ville souterraine était beaucoup moins éclairée que les villes durant la nuit, car il n'y avait point de lanternes ou de becs de gaz, mais simplement les lampes que les mineurs portent avec eux' (49) [this subterranean town was much worse lighted than other towns are during the night, for there are neither lanterns nor gas: only the lamps which the miners carried with them]. Indeed, most comparisons between surface and underground establish differences rather than similarities. In *Voyage*, Axel contrasts the absolute darkness of the underground tunnels which 'faisait de moi un aveugle dans toute l'acception du mot' [made me a blind man in the full sense of the word], with the conditions on the surface where, even 'au milieu des plus profondes nuits, la lumière n'abandonne jamais ses droits! Elle est diffuse, elle est subtile, mais, si peu qu'il en reste, la rétine de l'œil finit par la percevoir!' (187–88) [in the middle of the darkest nights, light never entirely gives up its rights. It is diffuse, it is subtle, but however little remains, the retina ends up receiving it]. A similar technique is employed in *King Solomon's Mines* when Quatermain states that: 'On the surface of the earth there is always some sound or motion, and though it may in itself be imperceptible, yet does it deaden the sharp edge of absolute silence.' (286) Familiar conditions and objects are thus used to stress the alterity of the underground which may not be hell but is nevertheless very different to the surface.

In addition to analogies or contrasts concerning light and darkness, sound and silence, comparisons with the surface are also frequently employed in order to convey the size and scale of the underground locale. In order to reach his workplace, Alexis is obliged to 'faire trois fois plus de chemin que n'en font ceux qui montent aux tours de Notre-Dame de Paris' (48) [three times the distance necessary to be accomplished by those who ascend the towers of Notre Dame in Paris]. The same comparison with the ecclesiastical architecture of the surface in order to aid comprehension of the sheer scale of the underground locale is also apparent, in a more extended form, in *King Solomon's Mines*:

> Let the reader picture to himself the hall of the vastest cathedral he ever stood in, windowless indeed, but dimly lighted from above [...] and he will get some

idea of the size of the enormous cave in which we stood, with the difference that this cathedral was loftier and wider than any built by man. (262)

The conceit is pursued in the description of the stalactites ('in the form of a pulpit') and the smaller caves adjoined to the main cavern ('as chapels open out of great cathedrals') (264). Similarly, in the labyrinthine passages of the underground in *Voyage*, 'une succession d'arceaux se déroulait devant nos pas comme les contrenefs d'une cathédrale gothique' [a succession of arches unfolded in front of us like the counter-naves of a Gothic cathedral], shortly after which 'notre tête se courbait sous les cintres surbaissés du style roman' (144) [we had to bow our heads under low semicircular arches in the Roman style]. But if these features are analogous to the architecture of the surface, the underground cavern leaves it, in Lidenbrock's view at least, very much in the shade: 'Que sont les arches des ponts et les arceaux des cathédrales' [What are bridge arches and cathedral vaults], he exclaims, 'auprès de cette nef d'un rayon de trois lieues, sous laquelle un océan et ses tempêtes peuvent se développer à leur aise?' (213) [next to this nave forty miles in diameter, beneath which an ocean and its storms can behave as they wish?] The sacred thus does have a place in these essentially secular spaces, even if only to demonstrate the way in which the natural dwarves and triumphs over the man-made.

If the comparison of surface and underground utilized by Dante is frequently apparent in the katabases for young readers, the attention to detail and precise description of the *Inferno* is, however, extremely rare. Only in *Voyage* is a high degree of attention paid to the underground landscape throughout the narrative. Both the claustrophobic, labyrinthine passages initially traversed and the vast underground cavern subsequently entered are described with considerable precision. However, the majority of the katabatic narratives for young readers err on the side of less is more in this regard, adopting what we might refer to as a Homeric approach. In *Paradis*, *Sans Famille* and *Princess*, detailed description of the subterranean setting during the narration of the journey can be dispensed with since the nature of the landscape has, as we have seen, been more or less fully established prior to the actual descent. Such an explanation does not account for the absence of description in other texts, however. In *Wonderland*, for example, little attention is paid to the physical landscape at any point. In a text in which the heroine changes size so frequently and in such an extreme manner (see Chapter 3), the specific objects of the setting are evoked almost exclusively in terms of their dimensions: whereas the home of the March Hare and its tea-table and the rose tree whose flowers are in the process of being painted are all 'large' (91, 93, 105), the White Rabbit lives in a 'neat little house' in which there is a 'tidy little room' (55, 56), the Duchess inhabits 'a little house [...] about four feet high' (77), and the Mock Turtle sits on 'a little ledge of rock' (125).

Illustration offers a further opportunity for concretizing the underground land-scape and the 1522 manuscript of *La Salade* and four of the nineteenth-century texts were illustrated when they first appeared in volume form. Just as Verne's text provides the most detailed textual account of the underground, so too do the accompanying illustrations of Edouard Riou supply the greatest visual precision — text and image together thus providing the most concrete of all the subterranean

FIG. 2.1. Gigantic mushrooms in *Voyage au Centre de la Terre*. Édouard Riou, 1867
Source: http://www.renepaul.net/collection_verne1

spaces of these texts. In the largely landscape-based images the high degree of detail is combined with an expansiveness and pronounced panoramic quality. Of the thirty-one images corresponding to the subterranean scenes, the majority represent small — indeed minuscule — figures within a massive landscape. The presence of the characters provides the viewer with a point — however minimal — of identification. It serves, more importantly, to emphasize the scale of the setting, frequently commented upon by Axel in the narrative (Fig. 2.1).[26]

Close correspondences between text and image are equally apparent in the other texts, which is to say that very little attention is paid to the underground landscape. *Paradis* is accompanied by a highly detailed image which presents only the exterior rather than the interior of the mountain (Fig. 2.2). In a further image, in which a knight is greeted by two women, the figures of the foreground dominate (Fig. 2.3).

John Tenniel's celebrated illustrations closely follow the textual precedent set by Carroll in this regard, the near total absence of detail concerning the landscape within the narrative being reproduced in the essentially character-focused images (23 out of a total of 46 of which feature Alice herself) where the inclusion of the very immediate surroundings serves simply to anchor or ground the protagonist presented (Fig. 2.4).[27]

FIG. 2.2 (above). The mountain leading to the subterranean abode
of the Reine Sibylle. Artist unknown, *c*.1440
FIG. 2.3 (below). Underground greetings in *Paradis*
Artist unknown, *c*.1440

FIG. 2.4. Character focus in one of Tenniel's illustrations for *Wonderland*
John Tenniel, 1865

Arthur Hughes' illustrations for *Princess* as a whole pay more attention to the setting of the text (e.g. the opening image is of the castle and surrounding scenery), but the three illustrations which accompany the specifically katabatic episode of the text are, like those of Tenniel, strongly character-based (Figs. 2.5 and 2.6; see also the cover image of the present work). The same is also true of Emile Bayard's illustrations to the Hetzel edition of *Sans Famille*, seven of which depict events taking place in the mine (see Fig 2.7). In the illustrations of both Hughes and Bayard, the protagonists seem squeezed into the available space, successfully conveying the darkness and claustrophobia generated by the underground locale even if there are no precise details concerning the nature of the surroundings. Overall, the lower level of attention paid to the subterranean setting is typical of children's literature which frequently concentrates on incident rather than lengthy description and can be seen as a deliberate effort to spare the young reader from 'ce qui pourrait [l']ennuyer'.[28]

However, Genette's other remarks concerning the tendency to shield and protect children from harsh realities are not borne out by the katabatic narratives. Although the undergrounds cannot, as we have seen, be classed as hells, it is by no

FIGS. 2.5 (left), 2.6 (right): Two of Hughes's three illustrations for the katabasis of *Princess*
Arthur Hughes, 1872; by courtesy of Senate House Library, University of London

FIG. 2.7. Cramped, dark conditions in
the mine of *Sans Famille*.
Émile Bayard, 1880

FIG. 2.8. Ancient remains
en masse in *Voyage*.
Édouard Riou, 1867
Source: http://www.renepaul.net/
collection_verne1

means the case that a whitewashing of 'difficult' elements occurs. Death remains
almost omnipresent in these narratives. As we have already seen, undergrounds
can be deliberately designated to store the remains of the dead. Although without
a commemorative purpose and indeed unbeknownst to mankind as a whole, the
underground of *Voyage* has the same function. The cavern contains a sprawling
expanse of animal remains (255), the account of which is accompanied by an
illustration by Riou (Fig. 2.8). Axel and Lidenbrock later discover 'un corps
humain absolument reconnaissable' [a perfectly recognizable human body], as well
preserved as those of the more conventional burial grounds of *Alphonse et Dalinde*
and *King Solomon's Mines*:

> ce cadavre, la peau tendue et parcheminée, les membres encore moelleux — à
> la vue du moins — , les dents intactes, la chevelure abondante, les ongles des
> mains et des orteils d'une grandeur effrayante, se montrait à nos yeux tel qu'il
> avait vécu. (259)

> [this body was before our eyes exactly as it had lived — complete with
> stretched, parchment-like skin, limbs still fleshy and soft, apparently at least,
> teeth still preserved, a considerable head of hair, and finger- and toe-nails of a
> frightening length.]

Moreover, the extraordinary *living* forms which Verne's travellers go on to encounter further extend the chthonic dimension of the underground since, as in 'La Fée

Poussière', these are creatures which, on the surface, are not only dead but long and emphatically extinct. Thus, just as the dead enjoy a certain degree of animation in the classical and medieval underworld, so too can the undergrounds of Verne and Sand be regarded as places sheltering 'des morts qui vivent encore' [the still living dead].[29]

Although in texts such as *Paradis* and 'La Fée Poussière' there is no significant sense of physical danger, the vast majority of the texts bear out Lesser's view that death constitutes 'the ever-present threat inherent in the subterranean adventure' for young readers.[30] As Thélismar tells Alphonse following the explosion in the silver mine, '[l]a mort [...] a passé sur nos têtes' (183) [death has passed over our heads], and one miner who turns out to be none other than the hero's father is initially thought dead. In *Sans Famille* death is constantly hovering in the wings: the very first figure encountered is 'une folle' [a mad-woman] whose husband has been killed in a mining accident (42), and Rémi will later visit the home of a widow whose bereavement had also been caused by the mine. Furthermore, Rémi himself, like the heroes of *King Solomon's Mines*, and *Voyage*, must confront his own mortality. In all three texts, a number of possible sources of death, including hunger, thirst and asphyxiation, stack up ominously against the heroes: 'Si nous ne sommes pas noyés ou brisés' [If we aren't drowned or torn to pieces], Axel observes during the perilous return to the surface, 'si nous ne mourons pas de faim, il nous reste toujours la chance d'être brûlés vifs' (287) [if we don't starve to death, there's still the chance we might be burned alive]. The heroes undergo periods of incarceration which range in duration from twenty-eight hours (Axel's separation from his uncle and Hans) to two weeks (*Sans Famille*), during which the death of the travellers becomes increasingly imminent, as is reflected in the terminology employed: 'tombeau' (*Voyage* 164, *Sans Famille* 81), 'living tomb' (*King Solomon's Mines* 287), 'sépulcre' (*Sans Famille* 87), 'grave' (*King Solomon's Mines* 283). Both Rémi and Axel refer to the underground as a 'prison' (*Voyage* 155, 168; *Sans Famille* 81), while Quatermain describes it as a 'prison-house' (284) and 'awful dungeon' (298). Axel refers to the whole of the first part of his katabatic travels as 'un emprisonnement' (204) [my trans: an imprisonment], and, separated from Lidenbrock and Hans, he feels he has been 'enterré vif' (184) [buried alive]. This is also how Rémi describes the situation of himself and the other miners trapped underground (81).[31] In *Princess*, Irene rescues Curdie from imprisonment in the mine, and the threat of her own abduction is present throughout the text. Clearly, then, the punishment of incarceration, formerly meted out to the evil inhabitants of the underworld, is here displaced onto the travellers themselves. Mining accidents which left workers imprisoned underground were an all too common occurrence in nineteenth-century England and France, and also featured in mining narratives for both adult and young readers of the period.[32] The inclusion of imprisonment in *Sans Famille* can thus be attributed to realist and generic convention, whereas its inclusion in the other texts of our corpus can instead be read as symptomatic of a period which, as a result of archaeological enterprises revealing the ruins of past civilizations, was 'haunted by [the] prospect of future burial'.[33]

Although there is no such incarceration in the *Alice* books, death is constantly threatened in *Wonderland*, and not only in the Queen of Hearts's repeated calls for decapitation. During the initial fall, Alice decides against dropping the marmalade jar 'for fear of killing somebody' (27), and during her first transformation in the hall, she begins to worry that the process, 'might end [...] in my going out altogether, like a candle' (32). Death lurks even in the most apparently carefree, innocent situations: when playing with the puppy Alice 'was terribly frightened all the time at the thought that it might be hungry, in which case it would be very likely to eat her up in spite of all her coaxing' (64), or during the conversation at the tea-table where, she realizes, the changing of places cannot go on indefinitely (99). As Carpenter notes: 'The state of Nothingness or Not Being, which at the very least is death and at its worst is something more frightening, lies just around every corner'.[34]

But death is not only threatened in the texts for young readers. Almost without exception the underground is also, to adopt the *King Solomon's Mines* chapter title, 'The Place of Death' in a way that is not apparent in traditional katabases. The first underground into which Alphonse descends is not only a place in which remains are housed but also, for the very first time, a place in which death actually *occurs*. The hero, it is made clear, acts only out of self-defence, but when attacked by the twelve Guanches, his response is unhesitating and fierce:

> tirant de longs poignards attachés à leur ceinture, ils fondent tous ensemble sur Alphonse, qui, mettant l'épée à la main, les reçoit avec intrépidité. Le combat fut sanglant et opiniâtre. L'adresse et la valeur d'Alphonse triomphèrent de la force; et quoique seul contre douze hommes furieux, il fut vainqueur. Il reçut deux blessures légères; mais il en coûta la vie à la plus grande partie de ses adversaires, et le reste épouvanté prit la fuite.' (73)

> [They drew the long daggers which they carried at their girdles, and fell instantly altogether on Alphonso, who, brandishing his sword, received them with intrepidity. The combat was obstinate and bloody; the address and valour of Alphonso triumphed over numbers, and though alone against twelve enraged foes, he was the conqueror. He received two slight wounds, but his sword was mortal to most of his adversaries, and the rest fled, terrified and howling.]

With the exception of *Wonderland*, where, as we have seen, death is nevertheless a very tangible presence, the undergrounds of each of the nineteenth-century texts similarly serve as the backdrop for death. In *Voyage*, the travellers look on from the raft as the plesiosaurus, vanquished in its epic battle with the ichthyosaurus, enters its death throes and then expires in a watery grave (232). In 'La Fée Poussière', although referred to only indirectly in dialogue, it is clear that Sand's narrator/protagonist witnesses a vast number of deaths during her journey: she deplores 'tous ces massacres' [all these massacres] which occur in this landscape 'qui appartient à ces dévorants qui vivent les uns des autres' (401) [belonging to these devouring creatures who live upon one another]. In both *Voyage* and 'La Fée Poussière', the deaths are essentially amoral, a question of the survival of the fittest rather than a battle between good and evil.

The underground of *The Golden Key* is unique in that it is the place in which, in the course of her journey, the traveller herself dies. Tangle initially visits the Old Man of the Sea, who is — fairly unmistakably — no less than Death himself: as this 'grand man, with a majestic and beautiful face' tells Tangle, '[s]ome people call me the Old Man of the Sea. Others have another name for me, and are terribly frightened when they meet me taking a walk by the shore. Therefore I avoid being seen by them, for they are so afraid, that they never see what I really am' (54). Tangle's own death in the course of this sojourn is confirmed as she later travels down the scorching descent towards the cave of the Old Man of the Fire: 'Her head was under water, but that did not signify, for, when she thought about it, she could not remember that she had breathed once since her bath in the cave of the Old Man of the Sea' (58). Such a fate would usually denote a failed katabasis, but death does not here prevent the continuation of the journey. Rather than a punishment for sin, it is instead an extension of life, bringing regeneration and repose: during her bath, Tangle 'grew happier and more hopeful than she had been since she lost Mossy' (53). Afterwards, '[a]ll the fatigue and aching of her long journey had vanished' (53), and she is able to see despite the darkness: 'For after being in that bath, people's eyes always give out a light they can see by' (55). Like the inhabitants of earlier undergrounds, Tangle is clearly now a member of the animate dead.

On the other hand, the deaths which occur in *Princess*, *Sans Famille* and *King Solomon's Mines* do constitute acts of retribution, fully in line with the traditional underworld in which the evil are punished for their crimes. In *King Solomon's Mines*, the underground serves as the backdrop to the deaths of both the diabolical Gagool and the angelic Foulata. The demise of the latter is accidental and tragic, justifiable, as will become clear in Chapter 3, on the grounds of race and gender rather than morality. But Gagool's death is very clearly retributive in nature. Her crimes include the earlier carnage of the witch-hunt, the death of Foulata as well as her attempts (albeit foiled) to incarcerate the English travellers and probably da Silvestra before them. Her graphically described punishment is brought about by a massive slab of stone no longer merely poised to fall as in the walls of Tartarus but which crushes her to pieces, leaving the travellers 'standing in a bloody ooze' (283).

The retributional function of the underground is also preserved at the end of *Princess* in the watery deaths of many of the goblins. As in *King Solomon's Mines*, the deaths are the direct result of the malevolent scheming of the villains: it is in attempting to destroy the mine that the goblins inadvertently flood their own domain instead. The lesson of this just reward is spelt out unequivocally: 'They had been caught in their own snare; instead of the mine they had flooded their own country, whence they were now swept up and drowned' (237). The description of the 'dead goblins' 'tossing about in the current through the house' (237) is again fairly graphic.

Similarly, in *Sans Famille*, only Rémi and five others from a total of 150 miners eventually escape from the underground following the accident. While the majority of the deaths occur 'off-stage', that of a single miner, Compayrou, is described in detail. The miners come to interpret their imprisonment in the underground as a punishment sent by God and so repent their sins in acts of public confession. Compayrou eventually admits to having stolen a watch and allowing another man to serve a five-year prison sentence for his crime. The *magister* prevents the outright killing of the self-avowed criminal, but fully approves his total ostracism from the group. When Compayrou becomes feverish, the miners refuse to provide him with the water he requests, and, reaching for it himself, falls and drowns:

A peine se fut-il mis sur le dos que le charbon s'effondra sous lui, et sans qu'il pût se retenir de ses jambes écartées et de ses bras qui battaient le vide, il glissa dans le trou noir. L'eau jaillit jusqu'à nous, puis elle se referma et ne se rouvrit plus. (103–04)

[Scarcely had he placed himself upon his back, when the coal gave away under him, and without being able to hold himself back, with his legs widely stretched out, and his arms beating the empty space, he slipped into the black hole. The water spurted up until it reached us, then closed again, and never opened more.]

The precise manner of Compayrou's death — grasping for water — recalls the traditional torments of Tantalus who had, of course, committed crimes far in excess of poor Compayrou. The connection between water and retributive death already seen in *Voyage* and *Princess* is further extended (thus undermining Lesser's assertion, which holds true only for *The Golden Key*, that water is associated with rebirth in children's stories involving undergrounds).[35] Compayrou's death demonstrates the inescapable and fatal nature of all forms of sin and is warmly welcomed by the other miners as an expiation of the crime: 'Maintenant, tout va bien marcher, dit Pagès...'(104) ['Now, all will go well,' said Pagès...]. This response is by no means condemned but in fact reinforced by the text, since the punishment of imprisonment does indeed soon come to an end. Traditional features of the underworld thus remain central, even in one of the most resolutely secular subterranean settings.

The subterranean destinations of the katabatic journeys in the texts for young readers are in many ways very different to those of the classical and medieval pre-texts. They cannot be referred to as 'hell' in that their singularity and sacred quality are substantially reduced if not eliminated altogether, and their essential functions are radically different. Yet if the nature of the readership appears to have shaped certain shifts (such as the psychological punishment in *Télémaque* and the lower level of description), it did not, however, entail the evacuation of many of the essential features of the earlier narratives. Several of the physical features of the underground landscapes remain firmly in place. Moreover, if the inhabitants of the underworld are rarely both dead and evil, death and sin nevertheless remain present in these narratives, transferred from *diégèse* to *histoire*, from characters (the inhabitants) to events (deaths). Despite the obvious shifts, then, the chthonic and moral dimension of traditional katabasis constitute integral elements in the narratives for young readers; the sanitization process outlined by Genette simply does not occur in this respect.

Notes to Chapter 2

1. Genette, pp. 293, 418.
2. The distinction between the two forms is not absolute however: 'transpositions diégétiques' always involve some degree of 'transposition pragmatique' since the place in which a character does something, and who that character is, necessarily affects what he does and why he does it (Genette, pp. 419, 421).
3. Genette, p. 420.
4. Genette, p. 422.
5. Genette, p. 431.

6. See R. Williams, chapters 2–4, and Lesser, p. 5.

7. Genette, p. 331.

8. Marian S. Pyles, *Death and Dying in Children's and Young People's Literature: A Survey and Bibliography* (Jefferson, NC/London: McFarland, 1988), p. 9.

9. Pyles, p.11. See also, for example, Geneviève Arfeux-Vaucher, *La Vieillesse et la mort dans la littérature enfantine de 1880 à nos jours* (Paris: Éditions Imago, 1994); Kiera Vaclavik, 'Death for Beginners: Nineteenth-Century Katabatic Narratives for Young Readers', in *Birth and Death in Nineteenth-Century French Culture*, ed. by Nigel Harkness, Lisa Downing, Sonya Stephens and Timothy Unwin (Amsterdam/New York: Rodopi, 2007), pp. 127–38; Colin McGeorge, 'Death and Violence in Some Victorian School Reading Books', *Children's Literature in Education*, 29: 2 (1998), 109–17.

10. Gillian Avery, *Nineteenth Century Children: Heroes and Heroines in English Children's Stories, 1780–1900* (London: Hodder and Stoughton, 1965), pp. 212–14.

11. Children were long seen as being tainted with original sin, and, partly because it was felt that they were not too young to die and go to hell, a form of literature was produced, peaking in 1671, which was later dubbed the 'brand of hell' school. See Sheila Egoff, 'Precepts, Pleasures and Portents: Changing Emphases in Children's Literature', in *Only Connect: Readings in Children's Literature*, ed. by Sheila Egoff, G. T. Stubbs and L. F. Ashley (Toronto/New York: OUP, 1980), pp. 404–33 (pp. 405–06).

12. Robert Pinsky, notes to canto XXV, p. 412.

13. Brunel, p. 128.

14. Nicole Pinsky, notes to canto XXVIII, p. 419.

15. Robert Pinsky, notes to canto XXV, p. 412.

16. Alice Turner, *The History of Hell* (London: Robert Hale, 1995), p. 37.

17. Turner, p. 89.

18. Note to canto XI, p. 393.

19. Brunel, p.81.

20. Brunel, p. 93.

21. Brunel, p. 86.

22. Brunel, p. 81.

23. Felicia Miller Frank, 'Chateaubriand, Verne, and Méliès: L'Effet d'irréel — Liminal Landscapes and Magic Shows', *Nineteenth Century French Studies*, 23 (1995), 307–15 also draws the comparison between Verne's text and Spielberg's 1993 film (p. 310). Roughly three and a half thousand words were inserted at the end of chapter 37 in the 1867 version of the text.

24. Sears (pp. 40, 47) and R. Williams (pp. 106–07) refer to the spectacular light effects produced in nineteenth-century tourist sights such as the limestone caverns of Dudley or the Mammoth Cave of Kentucky. A recent trip to the Grotte de Marzal in the Ardeche, during which the lights were extinguished and lightning simulated, confirms that such practices continue to this day.

25. Lesser, p. 162.

26. See, in this context, Verne's letter to Hetzel concerning *Vingt mille lieues sous les mers*: 'I have received the drawings from Riou. I have several suggestions to make which I'll mention to him by return mail. I think he needs to make the people much smaller and the rooms much larger. And he needs to add much more detail[...]', trans. by and quoted in Arthur B. Evans, 'The Illustrators of Jules Verne's *Voyages Extraordinaires*', *Science-Fiction Studies*, 25 (1998), 241–47 (p. 244).

27. Richard Kelly, '"If you don't know what a Gryphon is': Text and Illustration in *Alice's Adventures in Wonderland*', in *Lewis Carroll, a Celebration: Essays on the Occasion of the 150th Anniversary of the Birth of Charles Lutwidge Dodgson*, ed. by Edward Guiliano (New York: Potter, 1982), pp. 62–74 (p. 63). The illustrations were coloured and slightly modified by Gertrude Thomson in the subsequent *Nursery Alice* of 1890.

28. Myles McDowell, 'Fiction for Children and Adults: Some Essential Differences', in *Writers, Critics, and Children: Articles from 'Children's Literature in Education'*, ed. by Geoff Fox et al. (New York/London: Agathon/Heinemann, 1976), pp. 140–57 (p. 141, pp. 147–49).

29. Daniel Compère, *Un voyage imaginaire de Jules Verne: 'Voyage au centre de la terre'* (Paris: Minard, 1977), p. 56. The same is true of *Wonderland* in a much more limited way with respect to the

Dodo — perhaps the most famous of all extinct species — who makes one brief appearance in the text but who does figure prominently in Tenniel's illustration of the episode.

30. Lesser, p. 163.

31. In the English translation, the chapter heading 'Dans la remontée' [literally, 'In the Upwelling'] becomes 'A Living Tomb'.

32. Most famously, in Zola's *Germinal* (1885), also G. A. Henty, *Facing Death; or, the Hero of the Vaughan Pit. A Tale of the Coal Mines* (1882); George E. Sargent, *Down in a Mine; or, Buried Alive* (1878); A. de Gériolles, *Sous Terre* (1910). R. Williams discusses a series of nineteenth-century mining disasters (pp. 89–90).

33. Williams, p. 43.

34. Humphrey Carpenter, *Secret Gardens: A Study of the Golden Age of Children's Literature* (London: Allen & Unwin, 1985), p. 60.

35. Lesser, p. 162.

CHAPTER 3

Gender Roles and Relations

In *Deconstructing the Hero: Literary Theory and Children's Literature*, Margery Houri-han draws on an extensive corpus, ranging from the *Epic of Gilgamesh* and the *Odyssey* to *Where the Wild Things Are*, in order to conduct a forthright critique of what she refers to as 'the hero story'. '[D]eeply entrenched' and 'ubiquitous' in Western culture, this powerful and influential narrative 'inscribes the set of related concepts, the fundamental dualisms, which have shaped Western thought and values'.[1] Foremost amongst these is that which sets male against and above female, presenting the former as 'the norm, as what it means to be human' and the latter as 'other — deviant, different, dangerous'.[2] The hero who dominates the text is a brave, frequently violent man of action who confronts and overcomes a series of adversaries, suppresses emotion in order to attain his goals, and is most comfortable in the company of other men.[3] Whilst demonstrating male supremacy and the importance of male endeavours, the hero story simultaneously 'defines good and bad femininity and inscribes the subordinate place of women'.[4] Female figures are few, and most remain in the domestic sphere; those encountered in the external realm of the adventure are powerful but often malevolent.[5]

Although very little has been made by critics of the gender dimension of katabasis, katabatic narratives are frequently embedded within hero stories of this type, and the extent to which the configurations outlined by Hourihan are apparent in the underworld constitutes the main focus of this chapter. We will first ask whether, on the basis of role allocation, and the portrayal of key protagonists and their interaction, alternatives are envisaged for the afterlife in traditional katabasis; or whether dominant modes are instead prolonged and replicated, just as key features of the surface are retained in the underground landscape. We will then consider what happens to these patterns when the katabasis is targeted at young readers specifically. It was in the course of the nineteenth century that, due to ever-sharper differentiation of male and female roles, authors and publishers began targeting gender specific readerships in a sustained manner.[6] We will explore the extent to which such developments have a discernible impact on katabases for young readers in terms of role allocation and the key traits attributed to central prota-gonists. Although, as we saw in the last chapter, Genette's observations concerning suppressions in children's literature do not hold for issues of mortality, to what extent are they borne out with regards to sexuality and to relations between the sexes? Is *this* the kind of 'adult' material which is suppressed, toned down or elided so as to protect the child reader?

Classical and Medieval Katabases

As in the hero story more generally, the katabases of the *Odyssey*, *Aeneid* and *Inferno* are very much '*his* story', in that '[t]he reader perceives the world of the text and the events which occur in it from the hero's point of view, or the point of view of a narrator who admires him and places him in the foreground, so that the story imposes his perspective and his evaluations'.[7] In each of the katabases, events are focalized principally through the hero, and in two of the three cases the journey to the underworld is narrated by the hero/traveller himself. Although the majority of the *Odyssey* is recounted by an extra-diegetic narrator, in books IX–XII it is Odysseus who narrates his travels, including the katabasis, to the Phaeacian king and his court. The intermezzo which returns us briefly to Phaecia (XI, 333–76) foregrounds the fact that the hero is narrator as well as actor. In the *Inferno*, Dante the poet also frequently asserts his presence via the self-reflexive, meta-literary comments which punctuate the poem (e.g. XXXII, 1–10).

The heroes who focalize and/or narrate the katabases are all — literally or meta-phorically — seasoned travellers of mature age. Prior to their descents, both Odysseus and Aeneas have already undertaken various heroic feats and engaged in extensive travels in order to return to, or to found, their homeland. For his part, Dante the pilgrim is, famously, '[n]el mezzo del cammin di nostra vita' (I, 1) [[m]idway on our life's journey] when he embarks upon his katabasis. Although they may benefit from the assistance of guides, these are essentially solitary undertakings; Odysseus and Aeneas leave the men they lead behind on entering the underworld. However, it is when prompted by others rather than by their own initiative that the travellers decide to set out on this particular journey. Circe tells Odysseus that he must journey to the land of the dead in order to find out how to return to Ithaca (X, 488–540), while in book V of the *Aeneid*, Anchises instructs his son to visit him in the underworld (V, 731). In the *Inferno*, Virgil advises Dante the pilgrim to undertake the descent (I, 88).

Neither Odysseus nor Dante the pilgrim relishes the prospect of this journey. The former meets Circe's instructions with gloom and despondency:

> So she said and crushed the heart inside me.
> I knelt in her bed and wept. I'd no desire
> to go on living and see the rising light of day. (X, 496–98)

Lost in the dark wood with his initial route blocked, Dante the pilgrim initially accepts Virgil's advice. But the pilgrim is soon wavering, questioning his capacity to undertake such a journey:

> E qual è quei che disvuol ciò che volle
> e per novi pensier cangia proposta,
> sì che dal cominciar tutto si tolle,
>   tal mi fec' ïo 'n quella oscura costa,
> perché, pensando, consumai la 'mpresa
> che fu nel cominciar cotanto tosta. (II, 37)

> [And then, like one who unchooses his own choice
> And thinking again undoes what he has started,

> So I became: a nullifying unease
> Overcame my soul on that dark slope and voided
> The undertaking I had so quickly embraced.]

It is only by revealing the intervention of the three blessed ladies in Heaven that Virgil is able to restore the pilgrim's courage.

If both Dante the pilgrim and Odysseus have considerable forebodings prior to the katabasis, all three travellers are extremely frightened by their experiences in the course of the journey. Odysseus states how, at the beginning and end of his visit, 'blanching terror gripped me' (XI, 43, 633). And although Aeneas strides fearlessly into the cave (VI, 263), he is soon drawing his sword in terror against the monstrous forms he encounters (VI, 290), and is bewildered and terrified by the commotion on the banks of the Styx and the sounds emanating from Dis (VI, 317, 559). In the *Inferno*, the terror experienced during the journey continues into its narration: 'e con pauro il metto in metro' (XXXIV, 10) [putting it in verse I find // Fear in myself still].

Indeed, katabatic travellers demonstrate none of the emotional detachment which Hourihan associates with the hero. Although they themselves do not undergo physical torture, they nevertheless witness the sufferings of others, including friends and loved-ones. Odysseus is particularly prey to emotion, as is clear from the tears he sheds during his encounters with Elpenor, Anticleia and Agamemnon. He is 'filled with pity' and 'throbbing with grief' (XI, 87) when he first sees his mother, and stands with Agamemnon 'trading heartsick stories, / deep in grief, as the tears streamed down our faces' (XI, 465–66). Aeneas also weeps as he reaches out to grasp the shade of Anchises (VI, 686). Although Dante the pilgrim increasingly responds to the sinners housed in the underworld with anger, indignation or contempt, in the early stages of the journey he too is strongly moved by their fate:

> Gran duol mi prese al cor quando lo 'ntesi,
> però che gente di molto valore
> conobbi che 'n quel limbo eran sospesi. (IV, 43)
>
> [[...] I heard
> These words with heartfelt grief that seized on me
> Knowing how many worthy souls endured
> Suspension in that Limbo.]

Having seen and heard about those 'enno dannati i peccator carnali' [who sinned in carnal things], 'pietà mi giunse' [[p]ity overwhelmed me] (V, 38, 72). Francesca's torment arouses the pilgrim's tears and her story causes him to collapse, overcome with pity (V, 103, 125).

But this susceptibility to emotion is the only way in which the katabatic travellers depart from Hourihan's characterization of the hero. Very much a man of action, who 'uses his club, or sword or gun to telling effect', the traveller's response to events and experiences can at times be combative and violent.[8] When the promise of fame on the surface fails to elicit the information which Dante the pilgrim seeks, he resorts to physical violence:

> Allor lo presi per la cuticagna
> e dissi: «El converrà che tu ti nomi,
> o che capel qui sù non ti rimagna». (XXXII, 96)

[Then I reached out and seized him by the hair
And shook his scruff. 'Now name yourself forthwith —
Or not a hair will remain,' I threatened him.]

Similarly, both Odysseus and Aeneas wield their weapons in the underground: it is in this way that Odysseus controls the approach of the shades to the speech-enabling blood, while Aeneas instinctively reaches for his sword on encountering the monstrous beasts which gather near the dark elm (VI, 285). The usual heroic behaviour is not, however, always effective in the underground; the hero's weapons cannot always be used 'to telling effect'. Aeneas's sword is of no use when confronted with the shades which, as the Sibyl points out, are 'sine copore vitas' (VI, 292) [disembodied spirits]. Similarly, Dante's threats go unheeded by Bocca degli Abati whose identity is finally disclosed only when another shade addresses him.

Nevertheless, the heroes are active participants who demonstrate considerable initiative in the course of the katabasis. Odysseus works out for himself a strategy with which to converse most effectively with the massed ranks of approaching shades; Aeneas approaches and engages in conversation with the underworld inhabitants unprompted; and Dante the pilgrim not only observes and speaks with the shades presented to him by Virgil, but also selects interlocutors for himself. Both Aeneas and Dante the pilgrim actively pose questions as well as listening attentively to their guides. Overall, the successful accomplishment of the emotionally difficult and at times physically challenging journey serves to showcase the hero's bravery and assiduity. It therefore either establishes or, in the cases of the classical heroes, further enhances their superior status, as is clear in Circe's words to Odysseus following the journey: 'You who ventured down to the House of Death alive, / doomed to die twice over — others die just once' (XII, 21–22). The fear and emotion demonstrated by the heroes emphasizes the difficulty of the enterprise and renders their achievement all the more remarkable.

Katabasis is, therefore, clearly a male prerogative, and this is the case not only in these texts but almost everywhere in pre-modern literature. Certain female figures do undertake descents, but for one reason or another do not qualify as katabatic travellers. Both the Sumerian Inanna and her later Mesopotamian incarnation, Ishtar, visit the depths — but both are goddesses rather than mortals. Persephone's initial journey when abducted by Hades is enforced rather than willingly undertaken, and she is immortal by the time she embarks upon her twice yearly travels between the surface and the depths. Indeed, the only female figure to unambiguously undertake a katabasis in classical literature is Psyche, whose story is embedded within Apuleius's *Golden Ass*.[9] Even here the descent is not entirely successful: although Psyche achieves the fourth and final task set by Venus, her curiosity impels her to open the successfully retrieved box, and this induces a state of deep sleep from which she in turn must be rescued by Cupid.

Although it is merely intimated and easily overlooked, Virgil's Sibyl also has claims to the title of female katabatic traveller. She has been granted extremely long life, but is not actually immortal, and appears to have already travelled through the underground with her own guide before setting out with Aeneas. She tells him that: 'sed me cum lucis Hecate praefecit Avernis, / ipsa deum poenas docuit perque omnia duxit' (VI, 564) [when Hecate put me in charge of the groves of Avernus, she herself explained the punishments the gods had imposed and showed me them all]. To an even greater extent than that of Psyche, the Sibyl's *katabasis* is submerged within the journey of a male figure. We are in fact encouraged to think of the Sibyl much less as a traveller in her own right than as Aeneas's guide. In this capacity, she is the custodian of knowledge and is referred to by Aeneas as his 'docta comes' (VI, 292) [wise companion]. She offers her frequently bewildered ward often detailed explanations and provides otherwise inaccessible information concerning aspects, such as the inhabitants of Tartarus, which cannot be directly observed by the traveller (VI, 147). She also gives directions and practical advice, and hurries Aeneas on where necessary. Interrupting the conversations which the hero has initiated with both Palinurus and Deiphobus, she reminds the hero in the latter case that: 'Nox ruit [...]; nos flendo ducimas horas' (VI, 539) [Night is running quickly by, [...] and we waste the hours in weeping]. It is the Sibyl who negotiates passage through the underworld with at times obstructive inhabitants and workers. She is the one who speaks with Charon and thus attains their traversal of the Styx, and she again who neutralizes Cerberus: only after the monster is asleep does Aeneas take command of the entrance (VI, 424). As in their entry into the underworld, the active Sibyl leads, with a deferential, obedient Aeneas following in her wake.

Yet this is a temporary rather than permanent state of affairs. The Sibyl's moral status is implicitly questioned: although described by Anchises in book V as 'casta' (V, 735) [chaste], she seems to have already ventured into a realm where she herself says that the chaste cannot enter (VI, 563) and when higher realms are reached she is replaced. In the second half of the journey, the male patriarch, Anchises, takes up the mantle of guide, providing information and leading both Aeneas and the Sibyl back out of the underground through the Gate of Ivory. Her secondary status is confirmed when, at the end of book VI, she disappears unmentioned.[10] The Sibyl's replacement by a superior male guide and her erasure at the close of the narrative thus serves to redress the balance of male–female power established in the first part of the journey.

Dante would also later replace the Sibyl by casting Virgil as the traveller's companion in the *Inferno*, although his guide is imbued with many of her attributes. He too informs, chides, hurries and provides practical assistance — carrying his ward when crossing difficult terrain or when pursued by the Malebranche (XIX, 31–45; XXIII, 37–51).) To a much greater extent than the relationship between Aeneas and the Sibyl, that of Dante the pilgrim and Virgil is one of tangible mutual respect and affection. At the end of canto XXIII, the pilgrim describes himself 'dietro a le poste de le care piante' (XXIII, 148) [[f]ollowing in the tracks of his dear feet] and earlier in the same canto, Virgil's tenderness and attentiveness is emphasized:

> Lo duca mio di sùbito mi prese,
> come la madre ch'al romore è desta
> e vede presso a sé le fiamme accese,

> che prende il figlio e fugge e non s'arresta,
> avendo più di lui che di sé cura,
> tanto che solo una camiscia vesta; (XXIII, 37)

> [My leader took me up at once, and did
> As would a mother awakened by a noise
> Who sees the flames around her, and takes her child,
> Concerned for him more than herself, and flies
> Not staying even to put on a shift:]

The guide's maternal affection is stressed again almost immediately afterwards: Virgil carries the pilgrim 'come suo figlio, non come compagno' [[n]ot like his mere companion, but like his child] (XXIII, 51).

Despite this proximity and complicity, Virgil too will later be replaced by a superior guide. Neither hell nor purgatory is an appropriate place for the chaste Beatrice who takes over when Dante the pilgrim reaches the highest realm. Virtuous women are thus distanced from the medieval underworld but not all female figures are excluded from it. Indeed, each of the travellers encounters female shades and residents of the underworld. Odysseus meets his mother and then a long line of other women, each of whom is remarkable for, and defined by, her relationships with men: 'all were wives and daughters once of princes', 'the daughters and wives of great men' (XI, 227, 329). The only female shades encountered by Aeneas are the victims of unhappy love (VI, 442), but mention is also made of various female monsters and guardians (Tisiphone, the Scyllas, the Gorgons, and the Furies). In addition to the 'fierce' female Erinyes who guard the city of Dis, Dante the pilgrim encounters female residents in three of the nine circles of the underworld: Virgil points out Camilla, Penthesilea and Lavinia in the first circle of Limbo as well as various female figures in the pouches of the eighth circle reserved for the fraudulent. In the first pouch, housing seducers and panderers, he indicates a character from Terence's play, *Eunuchus*:

> Appresso ciò lo duca «Fa che pinghe»,
> mi disse, «il viso un poco più avante,
> sì che la faccia ben con l'occhio attinghe
>   di quella sozza e scapigliata fante
> che là si graffia con l'unghie merdose,
> e or s'accoscia e ora è in piedi stante.
>   Taïde è, la puttana [...] (XVIII, 127)

> [[...]Then my leader gave me advice:
> 'Extend your gaze a little farther ahead,
> So that your eyes may fully observe the face
> Of that disheveled strumpet who in the mire
> Scratches her body, as she stands or squats,
> With shit-rimmed fingers — she is Thaïs, the whore]

In the tenth pouch inhabited by falsifiers, the shade of Master Adam points out Potiphar's wife ('la falsa ch'accusò Gioseppo' (XXX, 97) [this false one [who] made / Her accusation defaming Joseph]) while the shade of Capocchio directs attention to the incestuous 'Mirra scellerata' (XXX, 38) [Myrrha the infamous]. In the second circle, both male and female shades who had committed carnal sins are buffeted by the winds of Hell. Virgil does make cursory reference to male sinners, but — with ten as opposed to two lines devoted to them — he pays a great deal more attention to female figures:

> «La prima di color di cui novelle
> tu vuo' saper», mi disse quelli allotta,
> «fu imperadrice di molte favelle.
>   A vizio di lussuria fu sì rotta,
> che libito fé licito in sua legge,
> per tòrre il biasmo in che era condotta.
>   Ell' è Semiramìs, di cui si legge
> che succedette a Nino e fu sua sposa:
> tenne la terra che 'l Soldan corregge.
>   L'altra è colei che s'ancise amorosa,
> e ruppe fede al cener di Sicheo;
> poi è Cleopatràs lussurïosa.
>   Elena vedi, per cui tanto reo
> tempo si voles, e vedi 'l grande Achille,
> che con amore al fine combatteo.
>   Vedi Parìs, Tristano»; (V, 52)

['First amongst these you wish to know,' he said,
'Was empress of many tongues — she so embraced
Lechery that she decreed it justified
Legally, to evade the scandal of her lust:
She is that Semiramis of whom we read,
Successor and wife of Ninus, she possessed
The lands the Sultan rules. Next, she who died
By her own hand for love, and broke her vow
To Sychaeus's ashes. After her comes lewd
And wanton Cleopatra. See Helen too,
Who caused a cycle of many evil years;
And great Achilles, the hero whom love slew
In his last battle. Paris and Tristan are here — ']

Male travellers not only observe but sometimes make efforts to converse with female inhabitants. While the speech of certain women (such as Anticleia in the *Odyssey* and Francesa in the *Inferno*) is presented directly, the vast majority speak at one remove, if they speak at all. In the *Odyssey*, the speech of the female residents is closely controlled by the hero: he will not let his mother approach the blood and speak with him until he has first conversed with Tiresias, and he uses his sword to maintain an orderly approach of the illustrious women. While the speech of the first of these is reported indirectly ('Tyro, born of kings, / who said her father was that great lord Salmoneus, / said that she was the wife of Creusa...' (XI, 235–37)), in the other cases the 'who said...' is replaced simply by 'who...', with Odysseus offering his own resumé of the key experiences and relationships of the various figures — usually either their sexual trysts with a god or the children they had borne. In the *Aeneid*, female figures are again associated with voicelessness, though here it is used as a weapon against the male traveller. Aeneas approaches and calls out to Dido, but his spurned lover maintains a stony silence and will not meet his gaze (VI, 469).

Refusing to comply with his commands, she leaves an impotent Aeneas to look on as she returns to her husband (VI, 472). Whether or not the female figure in question relates her own experiences, the encounters tend to underline the fractious nature of male–female relations. Dido leaves Aeneas in the underground just as he had abandoned her on the surface; their relationship in the land of the living and of the dead is marked by pain, disjunction, and rupture. That she finds solace in the arms of her betrayed husband does little to alleviate the conflictual vision of male–female relations. In the *Inferno*, the pilgrim sympathizes with the plight of Francesca and Paolo who, unlike Dido and Aeneas, are united in the underground. Yet their story is nevertheless one of prohibited union and betrayal which again clearly demonstrates the disastrous and fatal effects of romantic relationships between the sexes.

This portrayal is pursued in the various conversations between male traveller and male inhabitant, many of which are concerned with women and with sexual relations. In the course of these interactions, explicit and virulent expressions of hostility towards individual women and womankind more generally take place. Throughout the *Odyssey*, Agamemnon's murder by his wife and her lover serves as a threatening possible outcome for the hero's own homecoming, and in Book XI, Agamemnon is able to tell his former comrade first-hand of the terrible fate that befell him. He places the blame squarely not with his actual murderer, Aegisthus, but with Clytaemnestra, who he refers to variously as 'my own accursed wife', '[m]y treacherous queen', 'that whore', and 'the queen hell-bent on outrage' (XI, 410, 422, 424, 432). In *Aeneid* VI, Virgil also incorporates the denunciation of an infamous woman, even though its justification as counter-example no longer pertains since Aeneas is aiming to found a new nation rather than return home to wife and family. Helen's betrayal is graphically and forcefully presented in Deiphobus's horrifically disfigured form:

> Atque hic Priamiden laniatum corpore toto
> Deiphobum videt et lacerum crudeliter ora,
> ora manusque ambas, populataque tempora raptis
> auribus et truncas inhonesto vulnere naris. (VI, 494)

[Here too he saw Deiphobus, son of Priam, his whole body mutilated and his face cruelly torn. The face and both hands were in shreds. The ears had been ripped from the head. He was noseless and hideous.]

Whereas Deiphobus restricts his censure to Helen, whose name he cannot bring himself to utter (VI, 511), Agamemnon casts the net of his condemnation wide enough to include *all* women: 'she [...] bathes in shame not only herself but the whole breed of womankind, even the honest ones to come, forever down the years' (XI, 433–34). Shocked by these revelations, Odysseus seems to agree and adds, with reference to the men who had die for Helen's sake, that Zeus's most reliable weapon is 'women's twisted wiles' (XI, 437). Agamemnon warns Odysseus never to fully confide in his own wife and even if he then reassures the hero of Penelope's integrity, he is soon counselling Odysseus to approach Ithaca under cover, since 'the time for trusting women's gone forever!' (XI, 456).

Clearly, then, the hero story pattern outlined by Hourihan is also fully evident when the travellers descend below the surface. In the underworld, male figures occupy the key roles and female figures, who tend not to talk but to be talked about, are marginalized. Various encounters underline the sexual infidelity of women as well as the fatal consequences of female behaviour. Women are thus associated with sexuality, physicality and death. The classical and medieval underground is a place dominated by active male figures in which the failure of male–female relations is frequently evoked and where hostility towards women is often palpable.

Adventure Stories for Young Readers

In many works for young readers, katabasis remains a decidedly male prerogative. In *Paradis*, *Télémaque*, *Alphonse et Dalinde*, *Voyage*, *King Solomon's Mines* and *Sans Famille*, male travellers journey into the underground in what is, in virtually all cases, very much '*his* story'. As in earlier katabases the modes of narration employed in these texts concentrate attention on the male traveller and his experience. In the three nineteenth-century texts, events are related by the travellers themselves. In *Télémaque* and *Alphonse et Dalinde*, the katabases are presented by an omniscient, extra-diegetic narrator, but focalized through the heroes. Although there is a degree of fragmentation in *Paradis*, the male first-person narrator relates his own descent as well as those of other male travellers.

These narratives take place within adventure stories — a genre which not only 'depicted a world in which all significant events were dominated by male characters' but which was produced for the most part by male writers and 'written almost exclusively for boys'.[11] In the katabatic narratives, not only is there proximity between character and targeted reader according to gender but also via age. Although several travellers (such as those in *King Solomon's Mines*) are mature adults, others are at the beginning rather than 'midway through' their lives. Télémaque, Alphonse, and Axel are all young adults, positioned between adulthood and child-hood. Calypso addresses Télémaque in book I as 'jeune étranger' [young stranger] and notes the contrast between Mentor's age and the hero's youth (66). Alphonse is seventeen when his story begins. In *Voyage*, the illustrations of Axel, like those of Hans, clearly present a grown man (Fig. 3.1) but rather than the child that critics sometimes see, he is — as his name implies — a bachelor on the cusp of adulthood and adolescence, significantly younger than his fellow travellers.[12]

Rémi, on the other hand, is just eight years old when his adventures begin and still a child (only ten or eleven) by the time he journeys into the underground. Given the widespread and often controversial employment of children in the mines of both England and France in the nineteenth century, this *translation proximisante* in no way flouts realism so as to pander to a young readership.[13]

In addition to modifications to the age of the protagonist, another important shift in the nineteenth-century texts is that the descent is no longer confined to a single individual or a guide–traveller pair but is instead a collective affair, a team event. In *Voyage*, the journey is undertaken by both Lidenbrock and Axel as well as their Icelandic guide, Hans. In the company of Gagool and Foulata, all three English travellers enter the underground in *King Solomon's Mines*. In *Sans Famille*, Rémi is

FIG. 3.1. Axel on the cusp in *Voyage*
Édouard Riou, 1867; source: http://www.renepaul.net/collection_verne1

never alone in the underground: he initially descends into the mine with Gaspard, visits the *magister*'s cave with its occupant, and is trapped underground with a total of five other miners.

Whatever the size of the group, the journeys of these texts are, as opposed to the earlier narratives, almost always self-determined. The travellers may have heard of similar enterprises which prompt them to action, but it is they who decide to embark upon the descent rather than in accordance with specific instructions received from others. Like Aeneas, Télémaque descends in search of his father, but he resolves to undertake the journey himself rather than being summoned to him in a dream.

These (relatively minor) differences aside, the travellers otherwise conform closely to their katabatic predecessors. With the exception of La Sale's knight and Alphonse, they are all extremely frightened by their subterranean experiences. In the cavern leading to the underworld, Télémaque's 'corps était couvert d'une sueur glacée' (385) [body was covered all over with a cold sweat] and the sights of Tartarus 'faisaient dresser les cheveux de Télémaque sur sa tête' (395) [made his hair stand on end]. In *Sans Famille*, Rémi's extreme fear is reiterated in the course of both descents into the mine (56, 65, 70, 108), and at one point, key elements of the traditional underworld constitute the source of his fears: 'J'avais peur de l'eau, peur de l'ombre, peur de la mort' (85) [I was afraid of the water, afraid of the darkness, afraid of death]. The heroes of *King Solomon's Mines* enter the underground 'in some fear and trembling' (262), and the burial chamber, from which Quatermain attempts to flee, makes Curtis sweat and Good swear (266). Axel is terrified by the prospect of the journey which he undertakes only in order to avoid being outdone by others and continues to be gripped by fear at various points in the course of the descent. Nor are his fellow travellers immune from such sentiments: Axel, Lidenbrock and the ever-sanguine Hans are all 'glacés d'effroi' (245) [frozen with terror] as they cross the underground sea during the storm.

Like their classical and medieval predecessors, the heroes are also frequently subject to their emotions. Towards the end of his séjour in the underground, La Sale's knight 'commença à se sentir le cœur gros' (35) [began to have a heavy heart], while Alphonse is strangely unsettled during his descent into the silver mine: 'un pressentiment secret l'émeut et le trouble... Il se sent attendri; il a peine à démêler lui-même ce qui se passe au fond de son cœur' (181) [my trans: a secret premonition disturbs and perturbs him... He felt moved and found it difficult to understand himself what he was experiencing]. Having identified the miner injured in the explosion as his long-lost father, the hero collapses like Dante the pilgrim:

> [...] il jette un œil mouillé de pleurs sur ce triste objet... il frémit... récule... s'élance vers lui... le regard encore d'un air égaré; son sang se glace dans ses veines; ses cheveux se hérissent sur sa tête, et comme s'il eût été frappé de la foudre, sans pouvoir prononcer une seule parole, il tombe évanoui à côté de l'infortuné dont la vue vient de produire en lui une aussi terrible révolution [...] (184)

> [his eyes, dim by tears, were cast towards the mournful Object — he shuddered! — started back! — sprang again towards him! — beheld him with distraction in his countenance! — his blood froze in his veins! — his hair stood an [*sic*] end; and, as if a thunderbolt had struck him, he fell speechless and lifeless to the earth!]

Télémaque sympathizes with the unhappy Nabopharsan persecuted by his own former slaves (386), and is even more moved by the words of his great-grandfather (402–03). The physical resemblance which Télémaque discerns between Arcésius and his father 'attendrit son cœur: des larmes douces et mêlées de joie coulèrent de ses yeux' (403) [melted his heart, and tears of joy trickled down his cheeks].

In the nineteenth-century texts, considerable stress is also placed on the physical challenges of the journey. Following the indescribable 'horrors of the night' spent in the treasure chamber (286), the groping passage through the labyrinthine passages of the underground leaves the travellers of *King Solomon's Mines* 'thoroughly worn out with fatigue' (294). In the mine, Rémi is afflicted not only by 'tourments de l'esprit' [mental torment] increased by the absence of light, but also 'les tourments du corps' [bodily pain], including headache, physical constriction and hunger (94,

108). In *Voyage*, during the convulsive return to the surface, 'une faim violente' (286) [a violent hunger] is only one of the adversities faced by the travellers: 'Pendant les instants de halte, on étouffait; pendant les moments de projection, l'air brûlant me coupait la respiration' (296) [During the pauses, we suffocated; when we were moving, the burning air took my breath away]. In these texts, it is the travellers themselves rather than the inhabitants of the underworld who not only undergo the punishment of incarceration, as we saw in the previous chapter, but who also experience extreme physical and psychological torments.

Moreover, the actions of the heroes are at times severely circumscribed. Trapped in the *remontée*, Rémi and the miners depend entirely on the efforts of others for their rescue, as the following exchange makes clear:

> — Eh bien! et nous, dit Bergounhoux après un moment de silence, qu'est-ce que nous allons faire?
> — Que veux-tu faire ?
> — Il n'y a qu'à attendre, dit le magister.
> — Attendre quoi ?
> — Attendre; veux-tu percer les quarante ou cinquante mètres qui nous séparent du jour avec ton crochet de lampe? (74)

> ['Well, and ourselves,' said Bergounhoux, after a moment's silence, 'what are we going to do?'
> 'What do you want to do?'
> 'There is nothing for it but to wait,' said the magister.
> 'Wait for what?'
> 'Wait. Are you going to cut through the forty or fifty mètres that separate us from daylight with your lamp-hook?']

In *Voyage*, following the detonation of the dynamite intended to remove the rock impeding their descent, the travellers are reduced to a passive, impotent state: 'À partir de ce moment, notre raison, notre jugement, notre ingéniosité n'ont plus voix au chapitre, et nous allons devenir le jouet des phénomènes de la terre' (278) [From that moment on, our reason, our judgement, our ingenuity were to have no influence at all on events: we were to become the mere playthings of the Earth]. They are later carried upwards towards the surface by 'un movement que nulle puissance humaine ne pouvait enrayer' (282) [a motion that no human force could influence]. In *King Solomon's Mines*, the travellers are utterly immobilized by the realization that they are immured in the underground: 'For a few minutes we stood horrified there over the corpse of Foulata. All the manhood seemed to have gone out of us. The first shock of this idea of the slow and miserable end which awaited us was overpowering' (282). Quatermain later refers to 'that dreadful inaction, which was one of the hardest circumstances of our fate' (288).

Yet all of this only serves to underline the heroism, skill and bravery of the travellers. Despite their fears and the apparently hopeless situations in which they find themselves, the travellers all nevertheless successfully return to the surface. The essential qualities of the classical and medieval travellers are apparent and at times even extended in the heroes of these texts. Despite his tender age, Rémi demonstrates considerable initiative and courage. Rather than waiting to be rescued, he goes to impressive lengths to save himself. He has already heroically saved the *magister's* life when, much later in the imprisonment and in a state of considerable physical debilitation, he goes on an aquatic reconnaissance mission to find an alternative means of escape. If all are men (or boys) of action, some of the young male travellers are even more violent and combative than their predecessors. Thus, Télémaque not only bears his sword into the underworld, but, unlike Aeneas, is able to brandish his weapon to good effect, successfully separating the shades as he passes: 'il remarque les ombres légères qui voltigent autour de lui, et il les écarte avec son épée' (385) [he observes a multitude of flitting ghosts hovering about him, which he drives away with his sword]. Genlis's swashbuckling hero is by far the most combative of the katabatic travellers; thanks to '[l]'adresse et la valeur d'Alphonse' (73) [the address and valour of Alphonso], he inflicts death and injury on his adversaries, as we saw in the last chapter.

In addition to bravery, determination and endurance, a further key to the success of these journeys is team work and group solidarity. In *King Solomon's Mines* a combination of practical know-how and physical prowess finally enables the travellers to pursue their journey: when Quatermain realizes that fresh air is circulating in the treasure chamber they renew their efforts to find an alternative means of egress, which, once discovered, can be passed through due to the sheer might of Curtis. But it is not just for his physical prowess that Curtis is relied upon. When Quatermain and Good give way to despair, they have his 'broad shoulder' upon which to — literally — cry (288). The man who has proved himself a skilled, brave and ferocious warrior, is equally capable of offering selfless nurture:

> Ah, how good and brave that great man was! Had we been two frightened children, and he our nurse, he could not have treated us more tenderly. Forgetting his own share of miseries, he did all he could to soothe our broken nerves [...] (288)

Similar scenes are equally apparent in the other nineteenth-century texts. On two occasions in *Voyage*, a usually brusque Lidenbrock holds a debilitated Axel in his arms, caring for and speaking to his 'enfant' (195) [boy] with unaccustomed tenderness. Axel is grateful and moved by his uncle's words and attentions: 'Je fus touché de ces paroles, n'étant pas habitué aux tendresses du farouche professeur. Je saisis ses mains frémissantes dans les miennes. Il se laissa faire en me regardant. Ses yeux étaient humides' (156) [I was touched by these words, not being used to such tenderness from the tough professor. I seized hold of his trembling hands in mine. He allowed me to do this, while looking at me. His eyes were damp]. Following the imprisonment in the mine in *Sans Famille*, Rémi states that: 'De pareilles angoisses supportées en commun unissent les cœurs; on souffre, on espère ensemble, on ne fait qu'un' (124) [Sufferings like ours, borne in common, unite hearts; people who have suffered and hoped together become attached]. In addition to this spiritual union, the *magister* at one point holds a sleeping Rémi in his arms to prevent the hero falling into the water below. Just as Dante the pilgrim evokes his guide's maternal affection, so too does Rémi describe himself as 'un enfant sur les genoux de sa mère' [a child upon its mother's knee], and expresses his admiration for the elderly miner who is 'non seulement un homme à la tête, mais encore un bon cœur' (98) [not only a clear-headed man, but a good-hearted one too]. The groups of travellers are, thus, self-sufficient and autonomous, including protagonists who are men enough to adopt the conventionally feminine roles of care and nurture where necessary.

The guide figures that feature in almost all the descents at some point are, accordingly, almost always male. Arcésius and Thélismar alone offer guidance to Télémaque and Alphonse respectively, but in other texts, multiple guide figures are apparent. In *Sans Famille*, Rémi, like Aeneas, has different guides for different functions: Alexis serves an initiatory function comparable to that of the Sibyl since his highly informative narrative prepares Rémi for his descent. The hero's first true guide, Alexis's uncle Gaspard, accompanies the hero in the course of his initial descent into the mine, providing concrete, practical advice. But since Gaspard proves unable to satisfy Rémi's more theoretical questions, a second superior guide is introduced just as guidance passes from the Sibyl to Anchises. The *magister* is an elderly miner and, as his name suggests, an autodidact who has acquired his learning by reading and by conversing with mining engineers. His role is further extended during the principal descent and imprisonment when he is no longer solely Rémi's guide, but also leader of the group as a whole. In *Voyage*, various guides are in operation simultaneously rather than consecutively. The overarching guide is Arne Saknussemm who has left a series of clues which the travellers follow. Two of the three travellers who enter the underground also, in different ways, perform the role of guide. The taciturn Hans is initially engaged in order to guide the travellers on the surface, but he continues to prove extremely useful below ground, as, for example, when he procures the desperately needed drinking water and thus ensures the continuation of the journey. However, he cannot, strictly speaking, be said to guide the other two characters in a terrain as unknown to him as it is to them. It is Lidenbrock who (at times erroneously) decides on the route to follow, thus merging the roles of guide and leader like the *magister* in *Sans Famille*. Samivel refers to Lidenbrock performing 'le rôle de l'initiateur indispensable aussi bien à Enée, qu'à [...] Dante' [the role of initiator as indispensable to Aeneas as to Dante].[14]

Only in *King Solomon's Mines* does a female figure guide the male travellers into the underground. Gagool's monstrousness and lack of femininity is established from the outset (9). In her first appearance in the narrative she is barely human, let alone female, and strongly associated with death:

> [...] I observed the wizened monkey-like figure creeping up from the shadow of the hut. It crept on all fours, but when it reached the place where the king sat, it rose upon its feet, and throwing the furry covering off its face, revealed a most extraordinary and weird countenance. It was (apparently) that of a woman of great age, so shrunken that in size it was no larger than that of a year-old child, and was made up of a collection of deep yellow wrinkles. Set in the wrinkles was a sunken slit, that represented the mouth, beneath which the chin curved outwards to a point. There was no nose to speak of; indeed, the whole countenance might have been taken for that of a sun-dried corpse had it not been for a pair of large black eyes, still full of fire and intelligence, which gleamed and played under the snow-white eyebrows, and the projecting parchment-coloured skull, like jewels in a charnel house. As for the skull itself, it was perfectly bare, and yellow in hue, while its wrinkled scalp moved and contracted like the hood of a cobra. (147)

Gagool's physical appearance clearly presents her as the 'nadir of degeneration'.[15] Furthermore, her regression appears to be of a particular, sexually induced, form, given the striking resemblance she bears to a syphilitic child who, in the nineteenth century, was '[o]ften described as a "small, wizened, atrophied, weakly, sickly creature," resembling a "monkey or little old man," suffering, apish, shriveled, and prematurely aged'.[16] Her stature and shrunken features align her with various portrayals of the Sibyl in classical literature.[17] Moreover, the suggestion that she has undertaken an earlier journey (253), as well as her age and 'preternatural knowledge', all align her with the Virgilian Sibyl: Gagool's knowledge of the underground 'places the men entirely in her power', with Quatermain himself being obliged to beg for her life since '[s]he, and she only, knows the secret' (245).[18] But if the Virgilian Sibyl's moral status is implicitly undermined, Gagool is unambiguously evil. Whereas the Sibyl voluntarily assists Aeneas in the underground, Gagool, compelled to do so on pain of death, leads the travellers into the underground but aims to permanently inter them in the depths. And while the morally ambiguous Sibyl is replaced, Gagool, the out and out representative of female threat and danger, is violently killed off, crushed to death beneath a slab of stone (280). Male dependency on a treacherous female figure is, thus, thoroughly avenged, the underground the place in which female threat is most fully demonstrated, but also that in which it is punished.

By contrast, the heroines of these texts tend not to enter the underground but are kept pristine and protected on the surface. The self-sacrificing, nurturing Foulata may have all the credentials of the Victorian Angel in the House, but the fact that she ventures below at all itself suggests that she is compromised in some way. The taint on her character is of course her skin tone, as she herself recognizes just prior to her death in a statement which, via reference to the physical world, naturalizes the whole process: 'I know that he cannot cumber his life with such as me, for the sun cannot mate with the darkness, nor the white with the black' (281). The true angels of these texts, Lise in *Sans Famille* and Graüben in *Voyage*, serve as Beatrice-like beacons in that they constitute the fixed point to which the hero's thoughts periodically turn during his journey. The characterization of both heroines conforms to the ideals of womanhood widely promulgated in the nineteenth century. This is particularly striking in the case of Lise whose perfection is only enhanced by the fact that, for the majority of the text, she is mute. (It is only in the penultimate chapter that, like one of the *nekyia*'s illustrious women, she gains her voice, thanks to the hero who had earlier initiated her into the written word as well.) Lise is very clearly portrayed as an Angel in miniature: as she cares for the hero during a period of illness, he comes to think of her as his 'ange gardien' [guardian angel], and henceforth as 'un être idéal, entouré d'une sorte d'auréole' [an ideal being, surrounded by a sort of halo] whom he expects at all times to 's'envoler avec de grandes ailes blanches' (I, 282) [[fly] away upon great white wings]. Lise is, then, simply too angelic, too heavenly, to be permitted to enter the underworld realm where her presence, like that of Graüben, is spiritual rather than physical. The physical and emotional intimacy achieved between the male travellers thus contrasts with the distance maintained between the heroes and their female objects of affection.

Female figures in any capacity are, indeed, few and far between in the under-grounds of these texts. The vast majority of the undergrounds are inhabited by male or non-gender-specific figures. Whereas in *Germinal* women work in close proximity to men in the underground, in *Sans Famille* all of the miners are male. Where female figures are present or merely referred to in these narratives, the connotations are, however, the same as those of the classical and medieval pre-texts. In *Paradis*, the Sibyl's court is made up of women *and* men: 'des groupes de dames et de demoiselles, de chevaliers et d'écuyers' (32) [groups of ladies and their ladies in waiting, knights and squires]. As in the descent of Guerino, upon which La Sale drew in *Paradis*, the demonic nature of the entire population is confirmed by physical metamorphosis which occurs every Saturday. But if in the earlier Italian narrative, *all* the underground inhabitants — 'les hommes comme les femmes' [men and women][19] — are transformed, in *Paradis* it is the female residents and ruler alone who take on the form of the traditional Christian symbol of evil: 'elles se transformaient toutes ensemble en couleuvres et en serpents' (35) [they all turned into snakes and serpents]. The dangers posed by the deceitful sexually active woman discussed by male figures in earlier narratives are here foregrounded, graphically embodied in the shape-shifting, unstable female body. La Sale's portrayal of the Sibyl emphasizes the only implicit moral ambiguity of her classical namesake. This Sibyl Queen who, like Dante's Semiramis, is 'imperadrice di molte favelle', is a subterranean siren, a femme-fatalesque Devil incarnate.

Female figures have a much lower profile in Fénelon's katabasis. In the course of his journey, Télémaque meets only one female figure — an entirely mute and inert Persephone. The insignificance of women has, moreover, already been established when Télémaque seeks to legitimize his actions and bolster his confidence via comparison with earlier katabatic questers. If Orpheus can win over the underworld deities with the loss of a mere women, his own chances, he thinks, are good: 'Je suis plus digne de compassion qu'Orphée; car ma perte est plus grande: qui pourrait comparer une jeune fille, semblable à cent autres, avec le sage Ulysse, admiré de toute la Grèce?' (383) [I am more worthy of compassion than Orpheus, as my loss is greater; for, who can compare a young woman, equaled by so many others, with the sage Ulysses, admired by all Greece?] Yet references to fractious male–female relations and to treacherous women nevertheless punctuate the narrative. Nabopharsan tells the young hero that: 'une femme que j'aimais et qui ne m'aimait pas m'a bien fait sentir que je n'étais pas un dieu: elle m'a empoisonné; je ne suis plus rien' (386) [a woman whom I loved and who did not love me soon made me sensible that I was not a god; she poisoned me, and I am now no more]. Arcésius later points out Thésée 'qui a le visage triste: il a ressenti le malheur d'être trop crédule pour une femme artificieuse' (403) [in whose countenance there appears a little melancholy: he has felt the ill effects of his credulity to an artful woman]. He also indicates Agamemnon who, in a fusion of the Homeric and Virgilian narratives, 'porte encore sur lui les marques de la perfidie de Clytemnestre' (404) [who yet bears the marks of Clytemnestra's perfidy].

In certain texts the portrayal of women and of male–female relations is not limited to the roles protagonists perform, the ways they behave and the things they

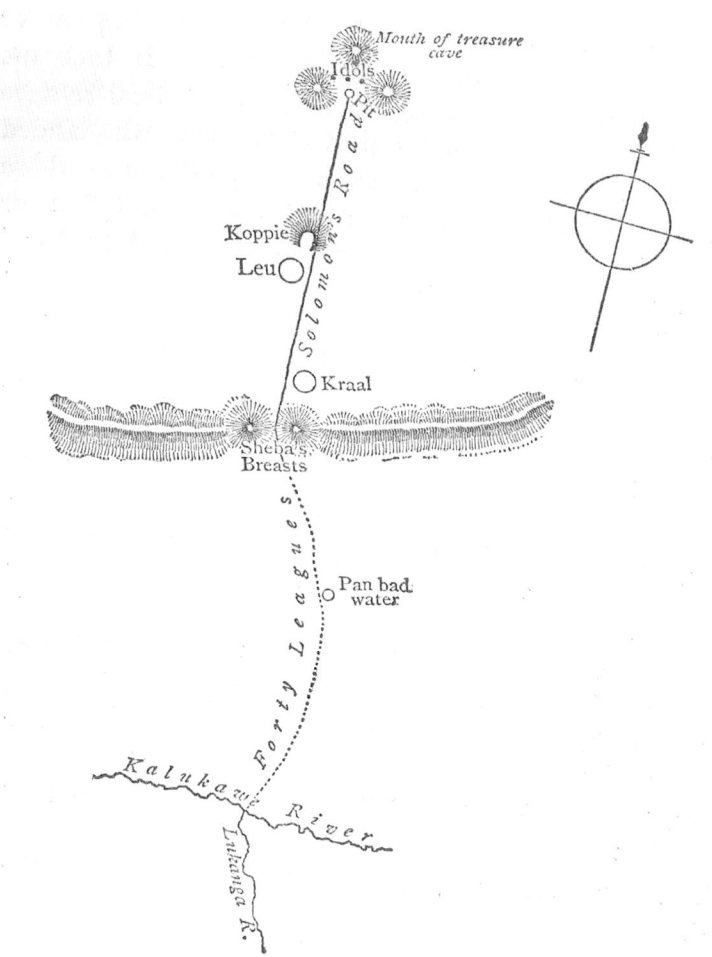

FIG. 3.2. The renowned treasure map of *King Solomon's Mines*
Artist unknown, 1885

say. In *King Solomon's Mines* and *Voyage* the landscape itself is not only 'anthro-pomorphized' but, as in much nineteenth-century discourse, feminized and eroti-cized.[20] The most overt and widely discussed case is that of both text and image in *King Solomon's Mines*. Anne McClintock opens *Imperial Leather* with an analysis of the treasure map of chapter 2 (Fig. 3.2) which, she makes clear, takes the form of an inverted female body 'spread-eagled and truncated', in which 'the only parts drawn are those that denote female sexuality'.[21] At the heart of the map are two peaks, named 'Sheba's Breasts' by da Silvestra and frequently referred to as such by the English travellers, from which mountain ranges extend horizontally in the form of armless hands. At the top of the map, above the navel-like 'Koppie', are situated the three peaks which enclose the 'mouth of the treasure cave' into which the travellers eventually descend having already successfully scaled 'Sheba's Breasts' (27). The pictorial representation is reinforced textually by a general feminization of the

FIG. 3.3. The treasure map featured in the *Magasin d'Éducation et de Récreation*
Artist unknown, 1888. By courtesy of the University of Liverpool Library.

landscape: the sky blushes 'like the cheek of a girl' (76), the moon (always referred to with a female pronoun) is described as appearing 'in all her chastened glory' (72) and as 'beautiful and serene' (77). Most striking and explicit is the following description of the mountain peaks which:

> are shaped exactly like a woman's breasts [and at times the mists and shadows beneath them take the form of a recumbent woman, veiled mysteriously in sleep]. Their bases swelled gently up from the plain, looking, at that distance, perfectly round and smooth; and on top of each was a vast round hillock covered with snow, exactly corresponding to the nipple on the female breast. (85)[22]

In the French translation of the text which appeared in Hetzel's *Magasin d'Édu-cation et de Récreation* this aspect of the text underwent major modification.[23] If some feminization of the landscape is retained and two references to the 'mamelons' [nipples] of the peaks are included, there is only one (typographically inaccurate) reference to the mountains themselves as 'les Seins de Phéba' [Phéba's Breasts].[24] The previously cited description of the mountains is entirely cut. While it is true that the text as a whole was reduced, it seems unlikely that it was merely spatial constraints which dictated these particular excisions. The map is transformed into a much more authentic-looking colour document in which only the faintest outline of the original map can be traced (Fig. 3.3). However, the manuscript itself (rather than what is inscribed upon it) here takes the form of a female torso seen from behind with Da Silvestra's writing clothing in part the flesh-coloured form. Hips, waist and even a breast are visible, with the crease emphasizing the spine and buttocks. In the *Magasin*'s version of the map, the eroticization is, then, transferred rather than entirely eliminated.[25]

In *Voyage*, the feminization of the underground is by no means as overt as that of *King Solomon's Mines* or even other works by Verne such as *Les Indes Noires* in which the mine — 'le véritable personnage féminin' [the true female protagonist] of the text — is a kind of Sleeping Beauty resuscitated by the princely miners.[26] Yet the feminization of the landscape is nevertheless discernible by the end of the text and especially when read in conjunction with *King Solomon's Mines*. Verne's travellers access the underground only after clambering up one of a pair of volcanic peaks, from which Axel enjoys the same kind of perspective view across Iceland as Quatermain et al. experience with regard to Africa. But it is the account of the travellers' mode of departure from the underground which most clearly evokes a feminized landscape. Although the travellers are described as being 'vomis, expectorés dans les airs' (293) [regurgitated, spat out], their journey clearly evokes the contractions of labour: in a series of violent movements, they leave an immense, fertile cavern via a narrow passage before emerging onto the surface 'à demi nus' (299) [half-naked].[27]

The more or less overt feminization of the underground of these texts further contributes to the presentation of the nature of women specifically and of male–female relations more generally. Although at times wonderful and praised, the feminized landscape, and by extension woman in general, is, in *Voyage* and *King Solomon's Mines*, frequently hostile, threatening, and dangerous. The feminized underground is far from passive, no mere 'walkover': the immense and immersing, overwhelming and engulfing female landscape is a place of death and fear, a place which immobilizes, imprisons and explicitly unmans (see Quatermain's response to the fallen door cited above). As we have seen, the travellers frequently undergo setbacks, imprisonment and physical torments, but it is excessive, and indeed inaccurate, to claim that the travellers are either 'devoured' or 'consumed' by the feminized underground.[28] The travellers survive the journey, emerging — however ingloriously — from the underground. The very fact that the feminized underground must be actively engaged with and battled against — the travellers obliged to engage in what Andrew Martin has referred to as 'geographical grappling with the earth mother' — actually serves the interest of the construction of a dynamic, proactive masculine identity.[29] The feminized 'landscape of difficulty' serves to highlight the determination, physical strength, endurance and prowess of the male travellers.[30] Furthermore, if the underground of *King Solomon's Mines* is a female space, the deaths of Gagool and Foulata can be read as a punishment not only for their evil deeds and/or their race, but also for their arrogation of male pursuits and prerogatives.[31] Drawing on one of the standard formulae used with reference to hero stories, Scheik observes that in *King Solomon's Mines* the 'female landscape has been penetrated and escaped, and in the process the adventurers do not "do and die"; rather, the men *do*, and the women *die*'.[32]

In these adventure stories, the age of the travellers, their increased initiative, and the undertaking of the journey in groups rather than alone, all constitute departures from earlier katabatic narratives. Several of the key elements of the traditional katabasis are nevertheless retained here: like their predecessors, the travellers are emotional and fearful but also dynamic, courageous and resourceful. In some cases, the successful accomplishment of the journey constitutes male victory over, and dominance of, a sexualized female, and a generally hostile attitude towards women is frequently apparent in these texts. Virtually no female figures enter or are present in the underground, and, as in earlier narratives, those who do so are associated with danger, sin and/or sex. In the one case of male reliance on a female figure (in the relationship between Gagool and the English travellers), that dependency is wholly avenged. The intense and close relationships between male protagonists contrast strongly with male–female relations which are only successful if distant. Idealized femininity is, in these texts, associated with immobility, stasis, and the surface.

Fantasy and Fairy Tale for Young Readers

In the works of fantasy or fairy tale which make up the remainder of our corpus, something quite different occurs. In five of the eleven works for young readers overall and in more than half (four of the seven) nineteenth-century texts, what Genette refers to as *transexuation* takes place: the central role of traveller is allocated to a female rather than male figure.[33] As opposed to the katabases undertaken by the Sibyl or Psyche, as well as the abortive journeys of Gagool and Foulata, those of Serena, Alice, Tangle, Mossy and the narrator/protagonist of 'La Fée Poussière' are not submerged within the travels of male heroes. The surrounding narrative is devoted either entirely (*Triumphs*, 'La Fée Poussière', *Wonderland*) or in large part (*The Golden Key*, *Princess*) to the female protagonists who undertake the journey. When the female katabatic travellers of these texts do not take centre stage they at least share it: both MacDonald texts feature what Zipes refers to as 'a composite hero', a girl–boy pairing made up of Mossy and Tangle on the one hand and Irene and Curdie on the other.[34] Given that at least three of the texts were initially targeted at a specifically female readership (*Triumphs*, 'La Fée Poussière', *Wonderland*), the shift in gender clearly constitutes a *translation proximisante*.

The journeys undertaken by the female travellers are as much of a trial and feat of endurance as those undertaken by male travellers. They are always emotionally harrowing and in some cases also physically demanding. The katabasis is particularly gruelling in the MacDonald texts: having flung herself down the passage to the Old Man of the Fire, Tangle endures terrible heat and feels 'scorched to the bone' (58).

For her part, Irene follows the thread through a range of rough terrains which 'tried her dreadfully' (154), before coming to the pile of rocks, the removal of which makes her back ache and her hands and fingers bleed (158). Serena's passage through the Abode of Spleen is also physically exhausting: 'her weary feet she drags / Thro' winding caverns, and o'er icy crags' (III, 519). All of the female travellers except Tangle are extremely frightened in the course of the katabasis, although not usually to any greater extent than their male counterparts. The darkness of the underground and its goblin rulers both scare Irene, but her distress is most acute on coming to the pile of rocks which seems to block her route (404). In *Triumphs*, the 'trembling' (III, 48, 148), 'shuddering' (III, 360, 402) Serena is in a perpetual state of distress: 'terrors shake her tender soul' (III, 176), she obeys her guide '[i]n silent tremor' (III, 518), and finally faints like Dante the pilgrim in a 'fearful trance' (III, 644). The narrator/protagonist of 'La Fée Poussière' is stunned and amazed by her experience, the creatures she encounters triggering 'une véritable térreur' (400) [great terror]. Hourihan argues that Alice 'is not especially distressed' and 'is not afraid' during her journey.[35] But Hourihan's desire to present *Wonderland* as a subversion of the male hero story in which the unfazed traveller feels no need to dominate those she encounters means that she overlooks explicit statements to the contrary. We are clearly told that Alice is extremely frightened by her encounters with the angry White Rabbit and the potentially hungry puppy (56, 64) as well as her rapid shift in size having eaten the mushroom (73). She prevails upon the occupants of the Duchess's kitchen to take care with the baby, 'jumping up and down in an agony of terror' (84). Furthermore, in the course of her travels through Wonderland, Alice is increasingly driven to despair, and experiences anger, frustration, confusion, and loneliness. She is bullied and berated repeatedly by the other characters and referred to throughout as 'poor Alice' (e.g. 128). Overall, then, the katabases require, and the female travellers prove themselves capable of, as much fortitude, courage and perseverance as their male counterparts.

But there are many significant ways in which female katabatic travellers and their narratives differ from those of male protagonists. Only in 'La Fée Poussière', where the female traveller both narrates and focalizes, is attention fixed on female experience to the same extent as it is focused on male experience in the adventure stories. In Sand's story, everything seen or said is presented from a specifically female perspective. In the other texts, a third-person omniscient narrator presents the journeys of the female traveller to the reader. This can facilitate access to the heroine's thoughts and feelings and, in both *Wonderland* and *The Golden Key*, Alice and Tangle are the principal focalizers of events. Elsewhere, however, the focus is more diffuse. Although in *Princess*, the journey is initially focalized by the heroine, this later gives way to shifts in focalization between Irene and Curdie. In *Triumphs*, certain aspects of the journey are focalized through Serena, but a large proportion of the underground landscape and its inhabitants are presented directly by the narrator to the implied reader. Overall then, female katabasis is, to adopt Hourihan's phrase, much less exclusively *her* story, than male katabasis is *his*.

Another notable difference is that while men of all ages undertake katabases, only little girls or very young women are free to enter the underground. As in the

FIG. 3.4. Alice looking very small in Wonderland
John Tenniel, 1865

adventure stories this serves to further align protagonist and targeted reader. Like Télémaque, Alphonse and Axel, Serena has just reached the point of putting away childish things, having 'enter'd those important years, / [...] When nobler toys the female heart trepan, / And dolls rejected, yield their place to Man' (I, 27). All of the other travellers are, like Rémi, clearly distanced from adulthood. Irene is 'about eight years old' when *Princess* begins (2), and the narrator/protagonist of 'La Fée Poussière' an unspecified 'jeune' (394) [young]. Tangle is ten years old when she sets out on her journey and although she is described as having 'wrinkles on her forehead' as she crosses the plain of shadows (41) and is, thus, presumably an old woman by the time she undertakes her katabasis, Maurice Sendak's 1967 image of her in the underground nevertheless presents her as a young girl. The age prohibition is particularly clear in *Wonderland* where Alice, who is seven and a half in *Looking-Glass*, leaves her older sister behind on the surface (Fig. 3.4). The underground remains as unsuitable for grown women in these texts as in the adventure stories; if these female protagonists venture below, it is because they are so young that issues of purity and chastity have not yet entered the equation.

As opposed to the other works for young readers, but like the pre-texts, the female katabases are always solitary rather than group undertakings. Opportunities for the interaction and solidarity apparent in the adventure stories are therefore much more limited. Similarly, whereas male travellers in works for young readers decide upon the journey themselves, the female travellers set out almost always in accordance with instructions received from others. In *Princess*, Irene enters the underground by dutifully following her grandmother's instructions and it is under the direction of their fairy guides that Serena and the narrator/protagonist of 'La Fée Poussière' embark upon their descents.

That the journey's impetus comes from elsewhere is very much in line with the general nature and behaviour of the central protagonists. MacDonald's heroines undertake the descent with as much purposefulness as their male counterparts (when presented with the passage leading to the Old Man of Fire, Tangle 'threw herself headlong into the hole' (58)), but in other texts the intentional undertaking of the journey is quickly called into question. In 'La Fée Poussière', the active 'je m'enfonçai sous terre' [my trans: I plunged under the ground] is immediately followed by the passive 'sans pouvoir m'en défendre' (397) [without being able to resist]. Likewise, Alice actively follows the White Rabbit into the rabbit hole, but she soon 'found herself falling' (26) which conveys a double element of passivity: not only does she 'find herself' doing something rather than actively choosing it, but that something, i.e. falling, is an essentially passive experience.

In the course of the journey, these travellers also frequently find themselves in situations, and find things happening to them, rather than making decisions for themselves. Serena 'found / Her soft foot press upon the solid ground' (51), while Tangle 'found herself in a glimmering cave' (55) and 'found herself gliding down fast and deep' (58). Similarly, the narrator/protagonist of 'La Fée Poussière' does not actively go from place to place but repeatedly finds herself in the various locations: 'je me trouvai dans un lieu terrible / dans les ténèbres / au milieu d'un grand bal / dans un champ' (397, 398, 404) [I [...] found myself in a terrible place / in darkness / in the midst of a grand ball in a field]; 'je me retrouvai dans mon lit' (405) [I found myself in my bed]. As the frequent use of the 'elle me fit ...' [she made me] construction, as well as phrases such as 'je fus transportée' (395) [I was transported] and 'elle me conduisit' (396) [she led me], make clear, it is very much the fairy who acts, while the narrator/protagonist is acted upon. Coulloux argues that the heroine remains a 'spectatrice' [spectator] throughout, and one who is, furthermore, utterly 'impuissante' [helpless].[36]

Indeed, as opposed to male katabases, passivity tends to be the constant rather than temporary condition of the female travellers. Instead of making autonomous decisions, they tend to do as they are told, and are thus characterized much more by their compliance than by their sense of initiative. Serena, referred to as 'the obedient Nymph' or maid (III, 46, 174), is 'convey'd' into (III, 46) and 'led' around the underground by Sophrosyne (III, 70, 333, 405, 501). As opposed to the active participation of Dante the pilgrim who constantly interrogates both his guide and the underworld inhabitants, Serena asks only two questions in the course of the entire descent (III, 73–74, 129–34). Irene's journey, the trajectory and purpose of which are unknown to the heroine beforehand, takes place entirely under the direction of her grandmother. Irene is then to some extent an obedient instrument manipulated by her grandmother rather than a free agent.

For her part, Alice demonstrates a much greater degree of initiative than the other female travellers. As opposed to the encounters of Aeneas and Dante the pilgrim with Cerberus, Alice faces the 'enormous puppy' alone, and it is she herself who successfully manages to abate the hound. She gradually learns to manage her own height through a process of experimentation, is capable of making independent decisions and of formulating — though not executing — plans:

> 'The first thing I've got to do [...] is to grow to my right size again; and the second thing is to find my way into that lovely garden. I think that will be the best plan.'
>
>   It sounded an excellent plan, no doubt, and very neatly and simply arranged: the only difficulty was that she had not the smallest idea how to set about it [...] (64)

Yet several critics see Alice as fundamentally non-active and indeed this is borne out by the various points in the narrative when she seems totally unable to control what happens to her.[37] She feels that she has '*been changed* several times' since getting up (67) and the words she means to say evaporate while other words are spoken through her: following her rendition of 'You are old Father William', Alice herself recognizes that 'some of the words *have got altered*' (72, my emphases — note the use of the passive construction in both phrases). The majority of Tenniel's twenty-three illustrations featuring the heroine present a largely static, passive Alice who, whether standing or sitting, merely gazes at her various interlocutors (e.g. Fig 2.4).

Here, as in *Triumphs* and 'La Fée Poussière', this impotency and lack of control can be attributed to the fact that the journey takes place within a dream. Strictly speaking, these narratives recount the mental rather than physical meanderings of the protagonists.[38] If in male katabasis the threat of women can be embodied in the female protagonists and/or the feminized landscape, the majority of the female katabatic travellers are, at least technically, disembodied. In 'La Fée Poussière', the traveller's incorporality is commented upon explicitly: the narrator/protagonist is informed by the fairy that in the underground she is 'un esprit débarassé de cette carapace qu'on appelle un corps. Tu as laissé le tien dans ton lit et ton esprit seul est avec moi' (398) [a mind disencumbered of the shell called a body. You have left yours in your bed, and your mind alone is with me]. That Tangle's recuperative bath in the home of the Old Man of the Sea is the point at which she in fact dies, also logically implies a departure from her body.

Yet each heroine nevertheless retains a more or less marked physicality via reference to sensory perception or physical activities. One of the key qualities of the traditional classical and medieval shades who, as we saw in the previous chapter, are disembodied yet retain a physical presence, is thus transferred to the female traveller. Serena, for example, explicitly enters the underground 'with her body bent' (54), and, as we have already seen, drags her weary feet through it. In 'La Fée Poussière', the principal advantage of incorporality is, according to the dust

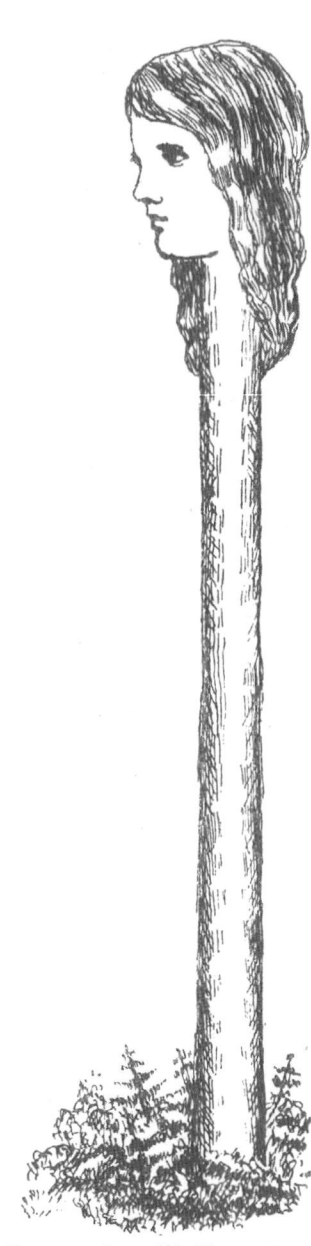

fairy, the very physical ability to *'toucher et brasser la matière première'* (398, my emphasis) [*touch and clutch* primary matter]. Similarly, although Tangle undergoes the ultimate disembodiment of death, she nevertheless retains a strong physical presence and one of the principal benefits of the bath is the improvement to her sensory (i.e. physical) perception. Although Tangle does do rather a lot of immobile contemplation, there are also points at which her motion is stressed: as she passes from the cave of the Old Man of the Fire to that of the Old Man of the Earth, she glides 'down fast and deep' and 'went sweeping on' (58). Similarly, Carroll's heroine, described by Rackin as 'the kinetic, manifestly physical Alice', runs across the field after the White Rabbit and, having fallen lengthily down the well, immediately picks herself up and continues to pursue him 'like the wind' (29).[39] Although, like Tangle, Alice is often stationary as she conducts her various conversations, she also moves energetically from location to location: she runs from the White Rabbit's house into the wood 'as hard as she could' (64), from the puppy 'till she was quite tired and out of breath' (66) and 'panted as she ran' towards the trial (142).

In addition to her general mobility, a further way in which Alice's physical presence is emphasized, and which deserves particular attention because of the highly negative connotations it carries in male katabases, is via her physical metamorphoses. Alice undergoes no less than twelve distinct changes which substantially alter her size and/or the proportions of her body.[40] A quality which, in *Paradis* and the *Inferno*, is an attribute of the inhabitants of the underworld is here transferred to the traveller. Profoundly unsettling for the heroine, these shifts at times bear the traditional negative connotations of female metamorphosis, and, according to Carpenter, serve to alienate her from the Wonderland inhabitants.[41] The massive extension of Alice's neck leads the pigeon to mistake her for a snake, thus aligning the heroine with the sinful serpentine residents of *Paradis*. Clear sexual connotations are also apparent in Carroll's highly phallic illustration in the original manuscript (Fig. 3.5). (Tenniel chose not to illustrate this particular episode).

FIG. 3.5. Carroll's illustration of one of Alice's many metamorphoses.
Lewis Carroll, 1864; by courtesy of Special Collections, University of Birmingham

Yet Alice's various shifts also align her with inhabitants such as the baby who transforms into a pig, the Cheshire cat and the caterpillar. They also enable Alice to integrate herself more easily with her surroundings and its residents, as is clear in her actions as she approaches the house of the Duchess:

> she came suddenly upon an open place, with a little house in it about four feet high. 'Whoever lives there,' thought Alice, 'it'll never do to come upon them *this* size: why I should frighten them out of their wits!' So she began nibbling at the right-hand bit again, and did not venture to go near the house til she had brought herself down to nine inches high. (77–78)

Whereas male travellers are the adversaries of the monolithic, fixed female landscape, Alice's shifting form enables her to become integrated with the shifting environment, without being fully equated with it.

Feminized, or even personified, landscapes may not feature in these texts, but there is nonetheless a significant female presence within their underground locales. There are far more female inhabitants in these undergrounds than in those visited by male protagonists, and again this can be seen as a way of bringing reader and subject matter into proximity. In *Triumphs*, Hayley significantly increases the number of female inhabitants and residents of Dante's underworld. With its female ruler and her many attendants and guardians, the Abode of Spleen seems a peculiarly feminine environment. At one point, Sophrosyne indicates Serena's expectations concerning the gender specificity of certain forms of disagreeable conduct, but does so only to correct her: 'Nor think', she says, 'that Females only fill the cave! / Male Termagents have liv'd, and here they rave' (III, 354). Indeed, in addition to male figures such as Charon, the prime minister Ennui, and Misanthropy, the residents of Hayley's underworld are evenly distributed in terms of their gender. One female and one male inhabitant are particularized in the cells of both the Fierce and the Fretful: Xantippe and the Lord Mayor of London represent the former; the 'vext Nymph' fretting over her freckle and the 'peevish Wit' obsessed by his single bad review the latter (III, 431, 438). Women may occupy a greater (although less sexually oriented role) than in the *Inferno*, but they do not have the monopoly of bad behaviour.

On the other hand, in both *Wonderland* and *Princess*, female inhabitants of the underworld are far more unpleasant than the male, and are at once threatening and impotent, violent and ridiculous. In *Princess*, the numerous goblin population comprises men and women, as well as the non-gender-specific cob's creatures. Of the three members of the royal family, the violent and physically powerful queen receives by far the most attention. Although the family as a whole delights in the prospect of killing Curdie, it is the Queen who captures the young miner and formulates the plan of feeding him to the cob's creatures. Irascible, proud and superior, she dominates her husband, although is nevertheless dependent upon him: she may not shed her granite shoes as he asks, but nor can she persuade him to provide a replacement when one is stolen. It is the grotesque queen who both leads her people into battle, and is the first to beat a retreat. Similarly, it is the female figures who are the most brutal and threatening of the Wonderland inhabitants. The noisy violence and confusion of the Duchess's kitchen is particularly infernal and much of the second half of the text is punctuated by the Queen of Hearts's calls for decapitation. Richard Kelly refers to the Queen as a 'monstruous female' who is 'the most grotesque figure in Wonderland'.[42] In 1887, Carroll stated that in writing the text, he had imagined her as 'a sort of embodiment of ungovernable passion — a blind Fury' who would not be out of place in Hayley's underworld.[43] Yet to an even greater extent than in *Princess*, male intervention — the King's overruling of her orders of decapitation — renders the only superficially powerful female protagonist an impotent and fundamentally ridiculous figure of fun.

Clearly, then, *transexuation* in no way guarantees radical revisioning: female figures may take up the role of katabatic traveller in these texts but the portrayal of femininity is in many ways unchanged. Nevertheless, these narratives do also incorporate aspects which present alternatives to traditional patterns and portrayals and which attempt to rethink standard representations. This becomes apparent in two main areas. Firstly, although the travellers themselves frequently lack the dynamism of their male counterparts, the nature of their guides ensures an active female presence in three of the five texts. In the *Triumphs*, an all-female traveller and guide team journeys to the realm of a female power for the first — but not the last — time. Sophrosyne may be tiny and insubstantial (4) but she has considerable power to influence human behaviour, and it is at her behest and under her direction that the entire journey takes place. Like her classical and medieval predecessors, Sophrosyne plays an integral role in the learning process, fortifying and hurrying, providing detailed commentaries, and directing attention to specific features of the underground. The same configuration of roles is apparent in 'La Fée Poussière' where the fairy guide also offers full responses to the narrator/protagonist's queries and, unprompted, provides a series of lengthy and detailed expositions concerning the evolutionary scene before them. Although Didier argues that the fairy appears in the story 'uniquement comme une voix' [as a voice alone], her physical presence is underlined in similar ways to that of the female travellers.[44] Active and mobile, she, like Alice, undergoes a series of transformations in terms of her age, beauty, and dress. The fairy is initially described as a 'fine et [...] menue' [light and [...] tiny] little old lady who 'portait toujours une vilaine robe grise traînante et une sorte de voile pâle que le moindre vent faisait voltiger autour de sa tête ébouriffée en mèches jaunâtres' (394) [was always dressed in a slatternly trailing grey gown, and a sort of veil which the least breath of wind sent whirling about her head with its yellowish dishevelled locks]. But she also periodically adopts the guise of 'une dame resplendissante de jeunesse et de beauté' [a lady resplendent with youth and beauty], wearing 'de magnifiques habits de fête' (395) [magnificent festal clothes], her physical appearance always carefully attuned to the surrounding environment. As with Alice, the transformations of the fairy, who informs her ward of 'l'activité incessante et suprême' [the incessant and supreme activity] of the natural world (402), align her very much with the underground locale over which she presides. Finally, in *Princess*, Irene enters the mine alone, yet the thread she follows is so much a physical manifestation of her grandmother that it can be considered a form of guide leading her through the underground. Here, as in the rest of the text, the enigmatic grandmother proves herself protective, reliable and authoritative. Sophrosyne, the fée poussière and Irene's grandmother all share the extensive wisdom of Gagool and the Sibyl before her. But they are neither morally ambiguous and replaced nor treacherous and eliminated. These are, instead, assiduous, powerful and highly effective figures.

A further way in which departures are apparent in certain texts is in their focus on, and portrayal of, relations between the sexes. In the *Triumphs*, *Princess* and *The Golden Key* they are of much greater importance than the rather flimsy love interests of the adventure stories. Neither adventure, fame nor riches motivates these descents; Serena's ultimate goal is to secure a good husband ('To love, and be lov'd' was all her prayer' (I, 82)) while Tangle descends so as to reach the higher world, not so much for its own sake but because 'there she hoped to find Mossy again' (48). In MacDonald's works relations between the sexes constitute a real focus of interest and the descents specifically invite comparison between male and female protagonists. In the course of the katabases themselves there is the same lack of complicity and proximity which characterizes male–female relations in the adventures stories and earlier works. In *The Golden Key* as in *Sans Famille* and *Voyage*, male and female protagonist are kept apart, with one remaining on the surface while the other ventures below. Here, however, the traditional schema is reversed: it is Tangle who undertakes the arduous descent while Mossy pursues a much more leisurely over-water journey. In *Princess*, on the other hand, the male and female protagonists are at one point together in the underground. This unusual physical proximity (otherwise apparent only in *King Solomon's Mines* and *Paradis*) means that for Wendy Lesser, *Princess* constitutes an example of underground children's literature which carries a certain sexual undertone.[45] However, if Irene and Curdie are physically close and collaborate in order to return to the surface, they are poles apart, as distant from each other as Dido and Aeneas in terms of their basic outlook and understanding at this point in the text. This is made clear in the description of Irene's account of events and its reception by the hero:

> [...] [Curdie] begged Irene to tell him how it was that she had come to his rescue. So Irene too had to tell a long story, which she did in rather a round-about manner, interrupted by many questions concerning things she had not explained. But her tale, as he did not believe more than half of it, left everything as unaccountable to him as before, and he was nearly as much perplexed as to what he must think of the princess. (167)

Understandably, Irene is somewhat offended when Curdie tells her that she is talking nonsense. Her narrative skills may be somewhat limited, but she nevertheless liberates Curdie and successfully accomplishes her journey. The katabasis of *Princess*, in which a female character performs the role of rescuer to the immobile and impotent hero, clearly valorizes feminine faith, fortitude and duty while at the same time implicitly critiquing the short-sightedness and generally limited outlook which is associated with the initial masculine position. Similarly, although the katabasis of *The Golden Key* has been seen as an implicit denunciation of the feminine, a form of punishment or expiation which Tangle must undergo because as a girl she lacks the phallic key in Mossy's possession, it can more satisfactorily be read as a valorization of the feminine.[46] Tangle's journey, which is narrated first and in considerably more detail than that of Mossy (twelve as opposed to six pages of seventy-eight), can be seen as richer and more fulfilling, because more demanding, than that of Mossy. The heroine acquires a much broader range of experiences and greater insight than the male protagonist. Furthermore, and crucially, Tangle reaches the hall from which they ascend to the land of shadows, *before* Mossy. The female route is, then, better and more rapid than the male. *Princess* and *The Golden Key*, as well as MacDonald's *The Day Boy and the Night Girl* all establish an incontrovertible link between the feminine and the underground. But as opposed to the adventure stories where this also occurs via the feminization of the landscape, MacDonald's texts demonstrate the superiority of female over male. It seems that MacDonald has fallen into the common trap of reversal referred to by Val Plumwood with reference to a strikingly apt katabatic landscape:

> the misty, forbidding passes of the Mountains of Dualism have swallowed many an unwary traveller in their mazes and chasms. In these mountains a well-trodden path leads through a steep defile to the Cavern of Reversal, where travellers fall into an upside-down world which strangely resembles the one they seek to escape.[47]

As Hourihan puts it, more directly, if less evocatively: 'The trouble with a dualism is that if you simply turn it on its head it is still a dualism.'[48] Yet none of the virulence apparent in earlier texts regarding women is here transferred to men. Moreover, in both texts, equality is ultimately achieved. Mossy and Tangle eventually reach the same final destination, even if they get there via very different routes. Curdie later evolves to the point that his understanding equals that of Irene and he reciprocates the heroine's actions by saving her from goblin abduction. While the descents thus promote the feminine, the dangers of reversal are thus avoided in the texts overall.

The undergrounds of these texts frequently reproduce the standard patterns of domination outlined by Margery Hourihan with reference to the hero story. Many works for young readers retain the pattern of the pre-texts, foregrounding and elevating male heroes and masculinity whilst demonstrating hostility towards and/or marginalizing women. Even in texts which bring female protagonists centre stage, many of the underlying elements of traditional katabasis relating to gender remain apparent. Always young and often dreaming, the female travellers are largely passive and their behaviour circumscribed. Nevertheless, to cast female figures in such a role at all is remarkable, and, given that adult literature would lag far behind in this respect, fantasy for young readers can be regarded as a privileged space in which to reconfigure or at least to rethink the gender roles and relations of traditional katabatic narratives. Indeed, in the featuring of powerful and benevolent guide figures, efforts are made in these texts to move away from standard images and portrayals. Moreover, it is in these texts that sustained interrogation of male–female relations takes place, again casting into doubt Genette's assertions concerning the avoidance of such issues in works for young readers. Perhaps what emerges most clearly in attending to the gender dimension of katabasis is in fact the sheer variety of children's literature, and the opportunities it offers rather than the constrictions from which it suffers.

Notes to Chapter 3

1. Hourihan, p. 2.
2. Hourihan, pp. 68–69.
3. Hourihan, pp. 69, 76–88.
4. Hourihan, p. 3.
5. Hourihan, p. 156.
6. Elizabeth Segel, '"As the twig is bent...": Gender and Childhood Reading', in *Gender and Reading: Essays on Readers, Texts and Contexts*, ed. by Elizabeth A. Flynn and Patrocinio P. Schweickart, 2nd edn (Baltimore, MD/London: Johns Hopkins University Press, 1992), pp. 165–86 (p. 170). See also Ottevaere-van Praag, pp. 219–20.
7. Hourihan, p. 38.
8. Hourihan, p. 3.
9. Psyche's story is recounted by a sibylline figure to entertain and console the abducted Charite. Worshipped as a goddess at the beginning of the story and finally made immortal at its close, Psyche is nevertheless mortal when she undertakes the descent.
10. Ovid's narration of Aeneas's descent in *Metamorphoses* XIV foregrounds the Sibyl, who tells her story as she accompanies the hero back to the surface. She serves as guide throughout the journey, yet in this case no mention is made to an earlier descent. Ovid's Sibyl thus gains importance as narrator and guide, but at the expense of her status as a katabatic traveller.
11. Louis Lodge, 'Tales of Adventure', in *Give Them Wings: The Experience of Children's Literature*, ed. by Maurice Saxby and Gordon Winch, 2nd edn (Melbourne: Macmillan, 1991), pp. 151–62 (p. 154).
12. Although Vierne recognizes that Axel is older than other Vernien heroes such as Robert Grant, she nevertheless refers to him as 'un enfant vivant dans le doux cocon de la famille' [a child living in the comfortable cocoon of the family] (Simone Vierne, *Jules Verne et le roman initiatique* (Paris: Éditions du Sirac, 1973), p. 407).
13. In England, the 1842 Mining Act prohibited the employment of children under ten and of all women in the mines, while in France the Child Labour Law of 1874 banned women and children under twelve from working in mines or quarries. Nevertheless, male children over these ages continued to work in the underground. See James Walvin, *A Child's World: A Social History of English Childhood* (Harmondsworth: Penguin, 1984), pp. 64–65; Colin Heywood, *Childhood in Nineteenth-Century France: Work, Health and Education among the 'classes populaires'* (Cambridge: CUP, 1988), pp. 141–42, pp. 299, 303.
14. Samivel, 'Les Surprises de Jules Verne', in *Jules Verne*, ed. by Pierre-André Touttain (Paris: Herne, 1974), pp. 216–21 (p. 220).
15. Anne McClintock, *Imperial Leather: Race, Gender and Sexuality in the Colonial Contest* (New York/London: Routledge, 1995), p. 245.
16. Elaine Showalter, *Sexual Anarchy: Gender and Culture at the 'Fin de Siècle'* (London: Virago Press, 1992), p. 197. Showalter quotes C. F. Marshall, *Syphilology and Venereal Disease* (New York: Wood, 1906).
17. Although Virgil makes no reference to the guide's physical appearance in *Aeneid* VI, in Ovid's version of Aeneas's descent the Sibyl tells the hero: 'tempus erit, cum de tanto me corpore parvam / longa dies faciet, consumptaque membra senecta / ad minimum redigentur onus' [The day will come that length of time shall make my body small / And little of my withered limbs shall leave or nought at all] (*Metamorphoses* XIV, 147). Similarly in Petronius's *Satyricon*, Trimalchio says that he has seen the Cumaen Sibyl so reduced in size that she was 'in ampulla pendere' [suspended in a bottle] (XLVIII).
18. McClintock, p. 246.
19. Extract from the fifth book of Andrea da Barberino's *Guerino, dit le Meschino*, included in *Le Paradis*, pp. 81–103 (p. 98).
20. Rebecca Stott, '"Scaping the Body: Of Cannibal Mothers and Colonial Landscapes', in *The New Woman in Fiction and in Fact: Fin-de-Siècle Feminisms*, ed. by Angelique Richardson and Chris Willis (Basingstoke: Palgrave Macmillan, 2002), pp. 150–66 (p. 151). Bunn describes the

almost systematic feminization and eroticization of exotic otherworlds — 'virgin' lands waiting passively to be 'inscribed by masculine colonizing zeal' — as 'one of the most recurrent enabling metaphors of colonialism'. (David Bunn, 'Embodying Africa: Woman and Romance in Colonial Fiction', *English in Africa*, 15 (1988), 1–28 (p. 11)). See also McClintock, pp. 21–31.

21. McClintock, pp. 1–4 (p. 3).

22. The bracketed section of the quotation was added to the 1905 edition of the text.

23. Rider Haggard, 'Découverte des Mines de Salomon', in *Le Magasin d'Éducation et de Récréation*, 47–48 (1888) (various pages throughout).

24. Rider Haggard, 'Découverte des Mines de Salomon', 47, pp. 188, 44.

25. For more details see Kiera Vaclavik, 'Visibilité variable: la carte au trésor des *Mines du roi Salomon* de Henry Rider Haggard', *Cahiers Robinson* (forthcoming, 2010).

26. Béatrice Didier, 'Images et éclipses de la femme dans les romans de Jules Verne', in *Jules Verne et les sciences humaines*, ed. by François Raymond and Simone Vierne (Saint Armand: Collection 10/18, 1979), pp. 326–57 (p. 344).

27. Lyle Thomas Williams refers to the text's 'blatantly obstetric conclusion', p. 55.

28. Gerald Monsman, 'Of Diamonds and Deities: Social Anthropology in H. Rider Haggard's *King Solomon's Mines*', *English Literature in Transition (1880–1920)*, 43 (2000), 280–97 (p. 289); Stott, p. 155.

29. Andrew Martin, *The Knowledge of Ignorance: From Genesis to Jules Verne* (Cambridge: CUP, 1985), p. 218.

30. Gail Ching-Liang Low, *White Skins/Black Masks: Representation and Colonialism* (London/New York: Routledge, 1996), p. 49.

31. Low, p. 48.

32. William J. Scheick, 'Adolescent Pornography and Imperialism in Haggard's King Solomon's Mines', *English Literature in Transition (1880–1920)*, 34 (1991), 19–30 (p. 26). See also Low who argues that: 'The deliberate gendering of the natural world as female, and all human agency as male, means that women who possess agency in Haggard are inevitably punished for it' (p. 48).

33. Genette, pp. 423–30.

34. Jack Zipes, ed., *Victorian Fairy Tales: The Revolt of the Fairies and Elves* (New York/London: Routledge, 1989), p. 176.

35. Hourihan, pp. 208–09.

36. Monique Coulloux, 'Aspects du merveilleux chez George Sand: *Les Contes d'une Grand-Mère*' (unpublished doctoral dissertation, University of Colorado at Boulder, 1978), pp. 76, 71.

37. Paul Schilder argues that Alice does act at the end of the journey but that until that point she 'remains passive. Things happen to her.' (Paul Schilder, 'Psychoanalytic Remarks on *Alice in Wonderland* and Lewis Carroll', in *Aspects of Alice: Lewis Carroll's Dreamchild as seen through the Critics' Looking-Glasses, 1865–1971*, ed. by Robert Phillips (London: Victor Gollancz, 1972), pp. 283–92 (p. 286)). Likewise, Peter Heath asserts that 'adventures happen to Alice [...] she encounters them passively and cannot be said to seek them out'. (Peter Heath, 'The Philosopher's *Alice*', in *Lewis Carroll*, ed. by Harold Bloom (New York: Chelsea House, 1987), pp. 45–52 (p. 49)).

38. The dream framework itself links these narratives to the katabatic pre-texts. Dante the pilgrim is so 'pien di sonno' (I,11) [full of sleep] that he does not know how he entered the wood, and loss of consciousness recurs throughout the journey. There is also a strong suggestion of the oneiric in Virgil's katabasis due to Aeneas's much-debated departure via the gate of ivory, through which 'false dreams' rather than 'true shades' are sent.

39. Donald Rackin, 'Mind over Matter: Sexuality and where "the body happens to be" in the *Alice* books', in *Textual Bodies: Changing Boundaries of Literary Representation*, ed. by Lori Hope Lefkovitz (New York: State University of New York Press, 1997), pp. 161–83 (p. 170).

40. See Selwyn H. Goodacre, 'On Alice's Changes of Size in Wonderland', *Jabberwocky: The Journal of the Lewis Carroll Society*, 6 (1977), 20–24.

41. Carpenter, p. 66.

42. Kelly, p. 69.

43. Lewis Carroll, '*Alice* on the Stage', in *The Lewis Carroll Picture Book*, ed. by Stuart Dodgson Collingwood (London: Fisher Unwin, 1899), pp. 163–74 (p. 171).

44. Béatrice Didier, 'La Voix de Mère-grand', *Ethnologie Française*, 20 (1990), 293–300 (p. 298).

45. Lesser, pp. 156–57.

46. Robert Lee Wolff, *The Golden Key: A Study of the Fiction of George MacDonald* (New Haven, CT: Yale University Press, 1961), pp. 144–45.

47. Val Plumwood, *Feminism and the Mastery of Nature* (London/New York: Routledge, 1993), p. 3.

48. Hourihan, p. 205.

CHAPTER 4

Didacticism and Diversion

As we have seen in the previous chapters, katabases for young readers call into question Genette's association of children's literature with suppression and sanitization. But in *Palimpsestes*, Genette also argues that particular types of material tend to be inserted into rewritings of adult works for young readers. He refers to the 'effets de moralisation' [moralizing effects] apparent in Charles and Mary Lamb's *Tales from Shakespeare* and *Adventures of Ulysses* and describes *Télémaque* as 'l'édifiante extrapolation fénelonienne' [Fénelon's didactic extrapolation].[1] In the latter text:

> à travers les erreurs, les tentations surmontées, les épreuves, les bons et mauvais exemples et les leçons opportunes de Mentor, Télémaque subit un véritable apprentissage, évidemment destiné, par procuration, au duc de Bourgogne, et dont le principe même (évolution et formation d'un caractère) est tout à fait étranger au fixisme résolu de l'épopée.[2]

> [by way of errors and temptations overcome, tests and trials, good and bad examples, and Mentor's timely lessons, Telemachus is made to go through a real apprenticeship, obviously intended by proxy for the Duke of Burgundy. Its very principle, the evolution and formation of a character, is quite alien to the resolute fixedness of epic psychology.]

Thus, both protagonist and reader undergo a learning experience in the course of a text which injects a didactic dimension absent, in Genette's view, from its principal hypotext. Given the localized didactic contexts from which many of the texts of this corpus emerge, as well as the moral functions of some of the unsuppressed material (i.e. deaths), Genette certainly seems on firmer ground in this respect. But if children's literature serves to educate, it also seeks to entertain, and indeed to educate *by means of* entertainment. Fénelon's 'propos essentiel' [chief objective] in *Télémaque* may be, as Genette states, 'd'ordre pédagogique' [pedagogical], but as we saw in the introduction to this study, the archbishop fully recognized the importance of entertainment in the learning process.[3] As Robert Granderoute makes clear, Fénelon was '[h]ostile à la distinction traditionnelle travail–divertissement, il veut faire du travail un divertissement, du divertissement un travail. Il souhaite réconcilier instruction et joie' [hostile to the traditional work/play distinction, he wanted to make work playful and play constructive. He sought to reconcile study and pleasure].[4] Fénelon's belief in the *dulce utile* would be shared by countless other writers and publishers for young readers.[5] Yet from the second half of the nineteenth century in England in particular, many writers for young readers regarded entertainment not as a means of sugaring the didactic pill, but as an end in itself.

This chapter will explore the katabatic narratives in terms of their capacity to educate and entertain. It will begin by examining whether katabases for young readers are more didactically and moralistically oriented than their classical and medieval predecessors. What is the relative importance of knowledge and of knowledge acquisition in these narratives? What is the relationship between protagonist and audience in this respect? Having examined the katabasis as learning experience in the first part of this chapter, we shall then consider what the narration of this journey offers by way of entertainment for both the traveller and reader, first in the classical and medieval narratives and then in those aimed at young readers specifically. In addition to, or instead of 'effets de moralisation', to what extent do the katabases for young readers demonstrate what may be referred to as 'effets de ludicisation'?

Knowledge and Learning in Classical and Medieval Katabases

In the Platonic cave narrative recounted in book VII of the *Republic*, the underground is the starting point of the journey and is equated with ignorance. With their legs and necks chained, the prisoners of the dark underground perceive only the shadows which play on the wall before them rather than the light entering the cave mouth at their backs. It is by being forced to undertake the difficult and painful journey away from the depths to which the prisoner is accustomed — i.e. an *anabasis* — that knowledge is attained. As he ascends the mountain, the former prisoner is increasingly able to tolerate the light and gradually learns to see the truth. The travellers are then obliged to return to the underground in order to share the knowledge attained on the surface. The parable of the cave thus works on the basis of a series of binary oppositions between depth, darkness, and ignorance on the one hand, and height, enlightenment and knowledge on the other.

Yet a conceptualization of the underground diametrically opposed to the powerful and influential Platonic model is also possible. The idea that knowledge resides down below rather than on the surface has, in fact, long been dominant. In the second chapter of *Notes on the Underground*, Rosalind Williams demonstrates how the journey away from the surface down into the underground underpins the major projects of modern intellectual enquiry as well as informing scientific pursuits such as geology and archaeology. The conviction 'that surface reality can be misleading and that truth is found only by descending to uncharted depths' unites thinkers as varied as Bacon, Marx and Freud, in addition to structuralists and even deconstructionists.[6] Equally, for many Christian thinkers, it is by undertaking a downward journey that a higher realm can be reached: in his *Confessions*, for example, Augustine exhorts his reader to descend so as to ascend to God.[7] The underground may be dark and unpleasant but it offers the opportunity to go beyond the superficial, to access the essential. Descent — whether physical or metaphorical — enables spiritual, intellectual and moral ascent.

Pierre Brunel argues that prophecy — knowledge of the future — is the 'but ultime de toute catabase' [ultimate goal of every katabasis],[8] and it is indeed the acquisition of knowledge which constitutes the principal motivation of the katabatic travellers of both the *Odyssey* and the *Aeneid*. Odysseus ventures into the underground to find out how to return home successfully, while Aeneas undertakes the journey in large part to learn about his new home and people (V, 737). The information sought in both cases is thus of a practical, concrete nature. For his part, Dante the pilgrim embarks upon his journey less in search of specific information or even a particular goal than to avoid the dangerous and frightening situation in which he finds himself.

But as Robert W. Brockway points out, '[w]hatever the purpose or goal, the hero or heroine descends into the depths to emerge wiser than before.'[9] Although Dante the pilgrim does not undertake his descent in search of knowledge, he demonstrates throughout the journey a considerable desire to learn, to understand and experience the underground as fully as possible. In the eighth circle, for example, he states that:

> Pur a la pegola era la mia 'ntesa,
> per veder de la bolgia ogne contegno
> e de la gente ch'entro v'era incesa. (XXII, 16)

> [Intent upon the pitch, I tried to know
> All that I could of the nature of this pouch
> And those who burn in it.]

In each of the texts, the wide-ranging knowledge acquired during journeys which are as harrowing as the anabasis undertaken in the Platonic cave narrative, is all the more valuable for being hard won. It often far exceeds any specific information originally sought, and is extremely diverse in nature: both concrete and abstract, concerning the travellers themselves and others, the future and the past, the surface and the underground. Each of the travellers gains knowledge of their own future and of that of their people more generally. Odysseus learns not only about the difficult journey which awaits him but also of the turbulent situation in Ithaca, and receives an update on the circumstances of his wife, son and father. He learns that once revenge against the suitors is attained, he will again set out on his travels, but will finally experience a gentle, painless death in his own newly pacified and prosperous land (XI, 134–37). Aeneas sees the son who will be born after his own death and, as he surveys a series of illustrious figures, learns of the various sites which will be constructed in the future, and of the foundation and glory, the empire and wars, of Rome. He then learns of his own role in his nation's destiny, the wars he will wage, and the ways to avoid or to bear the trials of the future (VI, 890). Dante the pilgrim learns on two occasions of the future strife of his own city, and acquires somewhat less specific information than that acquired by Odysseus or Aeneas concerning his own destiny. Charon informs him that he will not cross the Styx but

> [...] «Per altra via, per altri porti
> verrai a piaggia, non qui, per passare:
> più lieve legno convien che ti porti». (III, 91)

> ['By other ports, in a lighter boat,' he said,
> 'You will be brought to shore by another way.']

He is later told that although he will meet with opposition and engender several enemies: '«Se tu segui tua stella, / non puoi fallire a glorïoso porto,' ['If you keep navigating by your star / You'll find a glorious port] (XV, 55).

In the course of their journeys, the travellers are also plunged into the past, discovering the fates of specific individuals, and frequently revisiting their own prior acquaintances and experiences. Odysseus learns of Anticleia's death and its cause, as well as that of Agamemnon at the hands of the perfidious Clytemnestra. Aeneas also finds out more about the precise manner of the deaths of his friends, including that of the mutilated Deiphobus as a result of Helen's betrayal. The rumours of Dido's suicide are confirmed. For his part, Dante the pilgrim discovers the sins and punishments of a number of specific, usually Italian, figures, including his former mentor, Brunetto Latini (XV, 22–124).

The pilgrim also learns about the operation of Fortune on the surface, and, as we saw in the previous chapter, all three travellers discover in different ways the dangers of women and of the sexually active woman in particular. The heroes learn too of the nature, organization, operation and physical features of the underground realm. Odysseus discovers the way in which to successfully converse with the dead by allowing them to drink the blood in the trench and about the highly negative condition of death more generally. Aeneas learns of the conditions required in order to cross the Styx, the nature of the criminals and guards residing within the walls of Dis, and the return of certain shades to the surface having passed through the river Lethe. Dante the pilgrim not only discovers the current state of the underground, but also learns about events which have taken place there in the past (the landslide, Christ's own descent and rescue of certain inhabitants) and others which will take place in the future, following the Last Judgement.

The various forms of knowledge are acquired in several ways. Firstly, the traveller learns from what he sees; sight thus playing as important a part in the dark expanses of the underground traversed in the katabasis as it does in the anabasis of the Platonic cave narrative. Odysseus looks on at the punishments of Tityus, Tantalus and Sisyphus; and although Aeneas does his utmost to engage Dido in conversation, he too simply observes the shades who had taken their own lives (VI, 435). In canto XXV, Dante looks on at the series of gruesome fusions and transformations of the thieves. The principal method of knowledge acquisition in the course of these descents is, however, conversation. The travellers are not only attentive listeners but are also adept at posing questions. Aeneas and Dante the pilgrim converse extensively with, and gain considerable information from, their accompanying guide. Although, as we saw in the last chapter, certain embittered shades shun the travellers' attempts to engage them in conversation, each of the travellers also talks at length with various underworld inhabitants, some of whom (e.g. Tiresisas in the *Odyssey* and Ciacco in the *Inferno*) reveal their knowledge of the future during such exchanges.

If the katabatic traveller often acquires knowledge via these conversations, he can also, like the liberated prisoners who return to their former dwelling place in the Platonic cave narrative, *bring* knowledge to the underground and its inhabitants. Each of the travellers is interrogated on at least one occasion by the residents of the underworld. Concerned about their sons, Agamemnon and Achilles ask Odysseus

(XI, 457–60; 492–93) and Cavalcante de' Cavalcanti asks Dante the pilgrim (canto X) for news of their welfare. Aeneas is asked by Deiphobus (VI, 531) and Dante the pilgrim by Brunetto Latini (canto XV) about the nature of their katabatic journeys. Several of the inhabitants of Dante's underworld seek to establish the identity of the traveller, and ask him about the surface and the state of Florence specifically (e.g. canto XVI). The katabatic travellers almost always supply the information requested — Odysseus's rebuffal of Agamemnon being one of the rare occasions when it is withheld (XI, 463–64). Knowledge is, then, exchanged as well as simply retrieved in a one-way process; in however small a way, the traveller has the power to change the underworld as well as being changed by it.

Admittedly, it is not only during the katabasis that Odysseus, Aeneas and Dante the pilgrim acquire knowledge. The underworlds of these texts can nevertheless be regarded as privileged sites of knowledge acquisition, in that what is learnt in the underground is generally unavailable elsewhere. On the point of leaving Troy, Aeneas had learnt of his own future from the ghost of his wife, Creusa: he will undergo a long period of exile before reaching Hesperia where success — a kingdom and bride of royal blood — awaits (book II). Yet the actual identity of this bride, as well as the information concerning the future members of his race and their activities, is disclosed only in the underground. Much of what Odysseus learns from Tiresias about his own future, in addition to more specific details concerning the next stages of his travels, is also imparted by Circe following his descent. But not all of the information which Odysseus receives from the seer concerning his future is repeated by Circe; nor does he learn from Tiresias alone. The knowledge acquired via conversation with a range of inhabitants concerning, for example, his mother's death, the condition of the dead or Agamemnon's fate, is available only in the underground.[10]

If, then, the katabasis furnishes the traveller with a range of privileged information, it also enables a learning experience on the part of the reader. Modes of narration and/or focalization which, as we saw in the previous chapter, foreground the hero, also encourage the reader to identify with the protagonist, and thus '[take] on the protagonist's goals and plans', as well as his experiences, including the acquisition of knowledge.[11] As Karín Lesnik-Oberstein points out, the concept of identification as it is commonly deployed by children's literature critics is actually antithetical to the learning process: widely assumed to work on the basis of a one-to-one correspondence between protagonist and reader, it 'cannot account for reading which is not a perpetual reading of the self [...] it cannot account therefore for other hypothetical processes in reading such as a possible learning of the new, or escapism.'[12] Yet readers not only identify with characters who are *like* them (and may be undergoing learning experiences which can take the reader beyond a mere 'reading of the self'), but also with those who are different to them (whether better or worse) and can therefore be carried beyond the realm of their own everyday experiences. In an article entitled 'Levels of Identification of Hero and Audience', Hans Robert Jauss outlines no less than five different forms of identification: in addition to the 'sympathetic' identification which prevails in children's literature criticism, he also points to associative, admiring, cathartic and ironic identification.[13]

In classical katabasis, the brave and skilful hero, who is infinitely superior to the average reader, prompts an admiring form of identification. In the *Inferno*, a blend of sympathetic and admiring identification is in operation: like any mortal, the pilgrim initially finds himself in difficulty, but his special status is quickly established by the intervention of Beatrice and Virgil. In each of the texts, it is precisely the bravery, skill, and status of the traveller that enables him to enter the underground and thus provide the reader with access to a usually inaccessible world where, as we have seen, various forms of privileged knowledge can be acquired.

Knowledge of various kinds is thus made available to readers in the course of these narratives. They can learn not only about the nature of the underground and its inhabitants, and the largely deplorable condition of death, but also have their attention drawn to aspects of their own world. Indeed, Page argues with reference to the *nekyia* that '[t]he purpose was to relate events above the earth, not below it'.[14] Because of the temporal settings of the katabases (see Chapter 2), the knowledge acquired by the protagonist concerning their own future and that of their people, constitutes, for the reader, a review of *past* events. That which is the most distant future for the hero (e.g. the rule of Augustus) is the most nearly contemporaneous to the reader and vice versa. By taking the reader back to a point at which foundational events had not yet occurred, the katabasis can reinvigorate and defamiliarize the past, reducing the sense of inevitability which it can accrue. In both the *Aeneid* and *Inferno*, this strategy has a clearly political function: while Virgil uses it to praise the glories of Rome and his own emperor, Augustus, it enables Dante to critique the intrigues and political manoeuvrings within the Florentine state. As Clark argues, katabasis thus serves as an 'instrument of national aspiration and social criticism'.[15]

Furthermore, each of the overall texts, and the katabatic narratives specifically, incorporates a pronounced moral and didactic dimension. Genette speaks of the 'fixisme résolu' of the epic form, yet as Granderoute points out, both the *Odyssey* and *Aeneid* are, overall, 'marqués d'un certain mouvement pédagogique' [marked by a certain pedagogical movement]: 'cheminant à travers mille embûches' [negotiating a course through a thousand dangers] the hero 'évolue au contact d'un monde qu'il découvre peu à peu' [evolves through his contact with a world that he discovers little by little].[16] If Fénelon chose the *Odyssey* as his principal pre-text, it was precisely because he too regarded it as an eminently moral and didactic work. In his view:

> L'*Odyssée* renferme de tous côtés mille instructions morales pour tout le détail de la vie, et il ne faut que lire pour voir que le poète n'a peint un homme sage, qui vient à bout de tout par sa sagesse, que pour apprendre à la postérité les fruits que l'on doit attendre de la piété, de la prudence, et des bonnes mœurs.[17]

> [The *Odyssey* contains throughout a thousand moral lessons concerning all aspects of life, and it is immediately apparent that the poet has depicted a wise man, who overcomes everything by his wisdom, solely in order to inform posterity of the fruits that can be expected from piety, prudence and good conduct.]

For his part, Dante has been described by Wallace Fowlie as 'still today the chief moralist poet of the world'.[18] In both the *Inferno* and the *Aeneid*, the didactic process is particularly clear due to the hero–guide pairing — a strategy frequently used in didactic works, in which the protagonist, and through him the reader, is clearly positioned as the recipient of knowledge.[19] In both texts, inhabitants and guides also issue explicit moralizing statements. In *Aeneid* VI, Phylegyas shouts out the cautionary lesson: 'discite iustitiam moniti et non temnere divos' (VI, 620) ['Learn to be just and not to slight the gods. You have been warned']. Likewise, the sight of the squanderers and spendthrifts in the fourth circle is supplemented by Virgil's observation:

> Or puoi, figliuol, veder la corta buffa
> d'i ben che son commessi a la fortuna,
> per che l'umana gente si rabuffa;
>   ché tutto l'oro ch'è sotto la luna
> e che già fu, di quest' anime stanche
> non poterebbe farne posare una». (VII, 61)

> [Now you can see, my son, how ludicrous
> And brief are all the goods in Fortune's ken,
> Which humankind contend for [...]
> [...] all the gold there is beneath the moon,
> Or that there ever was, could not relieve
> One of these weary souls.']

Moral lessons are also clearly conveyed in those cases where both the punishment and the sinful acts which led to them are detailed. The traveller/reader learns not only of the punishment of the shades but, in the case of Tityus in the *nekyia* and of the majority of the shades of both *Aeneid* and *Inferno*, is also informed of the crimes committed. However, the misdeeds of Tantalus and Sisyphus in the *nekyia* go entirely unmentioned. In *Aeneid* VI, the Sibyl can be equally unforthcoming with background details; she merely evokes the presence of the Lapiths, Ixion and Pirithous without expanding on their pasts (VI, 601). In such cases, the audience's familiarity with the crimes committed — which is assumed by the narrator — means that the moral import is no less apparent than in the cases where the sins are detailed. But as familiarity with classical myth gradually diminished over time, the moral content of the narratives, although not eradicated, became considerably more covert. However, modern editors now frequently fill the knowledge gap by providing the background to each of the figures in footnotes and thus reinstate or even increase the moral dimension of the narratives. With reference to the *Inferno*, certain critics have argued that shifts in audience sensibility and outlook may have contributed to the reduction of the narrative's moral import over time. Paraphrased by John Frecerro, Erich Auerbach argues in *Mimesis* that '[o]ver the centuries [...] the sheer force of Dante's verses gradually came to subvert his moralizing intention', heightening a secular reader's empathy with the terrible plight of the damned.[20] Thus, the story of Paolo and Francesca may, as Frecerro points out, have a 'moralizing intent', serving as 'a cautionary tale, warning the suggestible reader about the dangers of romance', but its effect is instead 'to show Dante's mastery of the genre he condemns' and to encourage not condemnation but an even greater degree of pity than that felt by the pilgrim himself.[21]

Despite these attenuating factors, an explicit didactic and moralistic dimension can nevertheless be discerned — or at least recovered — in each of the classical and medieval katabases. The descent into the underground, undertaken in two of the three cases specifically in search of information, constitutes a wide-ranging learning experience both for the protagonist, who acquires information through contemplation and conversation with inhabitants and/or guides, and for the reader, through a process of identification. In the next part of this chapter we shall examine the extent to which the moral and didactic dimension, which is, then, already firmly engrained in traditional katabatic narratives, is further increased in those targeted specifically at young readers.

Knowledge and Learning in Katabases for Young Readers

In what Genette refers to as Fénelon's 'édifiante extrapolation', Télémaque journeys into the underworld, like Odysseus and Aeneas, in search of specific information. This also motivates — entirely or in part — the journeys undertaken in *Triumphs*, *The Golden Key*, and 'La Fée Poussière', while a more general sense of curiosity prompts those of *Paradis*, *Alphonse et Dalinde*, *Sans Famille*, *King Solomon's Mines* and *Wonderland*. But a whole range of other, non-knowledge related factors also motivate or contribute to the motivation of these descents: duty in *Princess*; love in *Triumphs*, *The Golden Key*, *Sans Famille* and *Voyage*; fame and adventure or riches in *Paradis*, *Alphonse et Dalinde*, *Voyage* and *King Solomon's Mines*. It is not, then, by foregrounding the pursuit of knowledge in the motivation of these descents, that the narratives for young readers substantially increase the didactic dimension of the pre-texts.

But what of the outcomes of the journeys? How effective are they in imparting specific information and other forms of knowledge and wisdom, initially sought or otherwise? In *Télémaque*, the hero's initial question is answered — Odysseus is not yet dead — but his journey also generates a whole range of supplementary information and knowledge. Télémaque learns about his personal destiny: he will see Odysseus again and eventually inherit his throne. In addition, much of Télémaque's katabasis teaches him of the rigours of kingship and the nature of (un)just rule, the (ab)uses of power, and the dangers of flattery — all of which is, of course, of personal relevance to the young prince and heir to the throne of Ithaca. As Penny Brown points out, it is the misfortune rather than the glory of Télémaque's future position which is emphasized: he is warned of the disjunction between the opulent appearances and harsh realities of royalty and urged to fear 'une condition si périlleuse' (402) [a condition so perilous].[22] Passing through Tartarus and the Elysian Fields, Télémaque encounters examples of good and bad rulers, and can see for himself the extent to which the former are outweighed by the latter.

Télémaque also acquires more general historical information (concerning, for example, Erichthon, the inventor of money), as well as insights into the perfidious nature of women discussed in the previous chapter. In addition, the young prince gains a range of moral and philosophical information, receiving what Kantizios refers to as an 'audio-visual lesson about virtue and vice'.[23] In a reversal of the Platonic cave narrative, Télémaque also learns of the fundamental disparity between the appearances of the surface and the truths which become apparent only in the depths of the underworld. As Minos tells one sinner:

> Les hommes, ne jugeant des vices et des vertus que par ce qui les choque ou les accommode, sont aveugles et sur le bien et sur le mal: ici, une lumière divine renverse tous leurs jugements superficiels; elle condamne souvent ce qu'ils admirent, et justifie ce qu'ils condamnent. (391–92)

> [Men judge vice and virtue only as they coincide, or not, with their taste and interest, and are blind with respect to both; here a divine light reveals the error of their superficial judgment; for those whom they admired are often condemned; and those whom they condemned, acquitted and justified.]

This principle of reversal is equally apparent in the punishments meted out to certain sinners (e.g. the masters held in chains by their slaves) and it also underpins an existential lesson so important that it is transmitted not once but twice in the course of the journey. The beauty, plenitude and peace of the Elysian Fields prompts Télémaque's realization (reiterated later by Arcésius (410)) that the despair over the curtailment of life experienced just prior to his descent is unwarranted; death should be yearned for rather than feared. The success of the katabasis and indeed the journey overall is jeopardized by this positive presentation, but Télémaque heroically sacrifices the comforts of death and returns to the land of the living.

A lesson broadly akin to one of the insights acquired by Télémaque is also learnt by the German knight of *Paradis*. Not only does the knight acquire an impressive linguistic ability (becoming able to understand all the languages of the world after nine days below ground), but he also learns that which is perhaps implicit in this Babel-esque polyphony, namely that evil lurks in the most beautiful forms. Appearances are shown to be as deceptive as in *Télémaque*, although here the disjunction between the superficial and the real is not split between the deceptions of the surface and the truths of the depths but embodied in the shape-shifting underground inhabitants.

Appearances and prejudices are also re-evaluated as a result of the journey undertaken in 'La Fée Poussière'. The narrator/protagonist learns the value of even the humblest materials ('L'engrais est quelque chose, si ce n'est pas tout' (401) [Manure is something, if it is not everything]), and of past life-forms: the creatures 'qui te paraîtront pauvres, laids ou chétifs seront encore des prodiges d'adaptation' (403) [which appear to you poor, ugly, pitiful, are yet prodigies of adaptation]. If the narrator/protagonist witnesses these creatures of the past, she also learns what the future has in store: constant, natural transformation will eventually bring about a world peopled by 'des fées et des génies qui posséderont la science, la raison et la bonté' (402) [fairies and genii possessing science, reason, and goodness]. She also gains a sense of humanity's relation to these past and present life forms, its place in the overall evolutionary scheme: 'ces premières ébauches de la vie résumée dans l'instinct sont plus près de toi que tu ne l'es de ce que sera, un jour, le règne de l'esprit sur la terre que tu habites' (402) [these first drafts of life, representing simply instinct, are nearer to you than you are to that which will some day be the reign of mind in the earth which you inhabit]. Like Télémaque, the narrator/protagonist learns in the final stages of the journey that death is by no means negative. As the fairy informs her, it is an integral, fundamentally beneficial part of the natural order:

> Je sème la destruction pour faire pousser le germe. Il en est ainsi de toutes
> les poussières, qu'elles aient été plantes, animaux ou personnes. Elles sont la
> mort après avoir été la vie, et cela n'a rien de triste, puisqu'elles recommencent
> toujours, grâce à moi, à être la vie après avoir été la mort. (405)

> [I spread destruction to make the germ spring. It is so of all dusts, whether they
> be plants, animals, or persons. They are death, after having been life, and there
> is nothing sad in it, since, thanks to me, they always begin again to live after
> having been dead.]

Having completed the journey, the narrator/protagonist is able to perceive the true
heterogeneity and richness of the simplest matter.

The same employment of sight as a symbol of learning and intellectual insight,
combined with a positive portrayal of death, is also apparent in the descent of *The
Golden Key*, during which Tangle acquires the ability to see in the darkness. The
journey not only enables her to access the upper world and to rejoin Mossy, but
also furnishes her with fundamental insights. In the course of the descent, she
experiences a true epiphany:

> the moment she stood upright she had a marvellous sense that she was in the
> secret of the earth and all its ways. Everything she had seen, or learned from
> books; all that her grandmother had said or sung to her; all the talk of the beasts,
> birds and fishes; all that had happened to her on her journey with Mossy, and
> since then in the heart of the earth with the old man and the older man — all
> was plain: she understood it all, and saw that everything meant the same thing,
> though she could not have put it into words again. (59)

Although the actual content of what Tangle learns is not made clear, this knowledge
is evidently all-encompassing and allows her to reinterpret the experiences of her
past. Again, as she looks on as the Old Man of the Fire plays with 'balls of various
colours and sizes, which he disposed in strange figures upon the floor beside
him', she receives a series of '[f]lashes of meaning' which are equally impossible to
convey: 'the longer she looked the more an indescribable vague intelligence went
on rousing itself in her mind' (60).

Much more concrete lessons are learnt in other narratives. The travellers of *King
Solomon's Mines* learn about the burial customs of Kukuanaland and the origin of
the diamond in its king's diadem. Although undertaken principally in search of
treasure, the descent brings Quatermain to the realization that 'wealth, which men
spend all their lives in acquiring, is a valueless thing at the last' (287) — the same
lesson delivered by Virgil to Dante the pilgrim in the fourth circle. In *Triumphs*,
Serena does not learn about the nature of life and death, but the ways in which one
should and should not conduct oneself. She discovers the wide range of attitudes
and actions which make life miserable for oneself and for others: railing and
scolding, fretting excessively about minor flaws, drinking, feigning aversion to men
and writing satires are all as much to be avoided as the traditional sin of envy.

The knowledge acquired in the underground by the travellers of other texts is
instead of an immediately practical or scientific nature. The lessons learnt by Alice
enable her to negotiate the situations in which she finds herself. She learns from
previous experience, as when she takes possession of the key before making herself

smaller on returning to the long hall in chapter VII. In the course of his second descent, Alphonse discovers the wonders but also the dangers of the underground. Similarly, Rémi's underground experiences in *Sans Famille* enable him to learn about the geological processes of fossilization, as well as the methods, terminology and hazards of mining, which, he soon realizes, is not his vocation. The narrator/protagonist of 'La Fée Poussière' acquires a range of scientific knowledge concerned principally with evolution in addition to the philosophical lessons learnt. Like her, Axel and Lidenbrock discover the previously unsuspected plenitude of the underground, seeing for themselves not only the intact remains of past life forms but also living and breathing species which had existed on the surface in much earlier periods.

The katabases in texts for young readers thus furnish the travellers with several forms of knowledge, ranging from the philosophical to the behavioural and scientific. As in earlier versions of katabasis, it is the sheer difficulty of the journey which renders it educationally valuable — as Télémaque states in book XII: 'Ceux qui n'ont jamais souffert ne savent rien; ils ne connaissent ni les biens ni les maux; ils ignorent les hommes; ils s'ignorent eux-mêmes' (336) [Those who have never suffered know nothing, neither adversity nor prosperity; they are strangers to men, nay, they are even strangers to themselves]. But in contradistinction to earlier narratives, the lessons learnt by the travellers of these texts tend to be impersonal, concerned with existence in general rather than their own individual lives (past, present or future). Often young and hence unburdened by extensive personal histories, the travellers generally learn about themselves only to the extent of their place in an overall schema, whether scientific or existential. Thus, several of the travellers learn not about their own pasts but about the past — of humanity, the globe — in general. The already extensive temporal parameters of traditional katabasis are thus considerably extended.

There are also important differences between these narratives and their classical and medieval pre-texts in terms of the ways in which knowledge is acquired by the traveller. As before, and as we have already seen, sight often plays an important role in (and serves as metaphor of) the learning process. On the other hand, verbal interaction with underground inhabitants and guides — so important a source of knowledge acquisition in each of the earlier katabases — is much less common in these texts. Where the undergrounds are uninhabited or populated by non-human life-forms conversation is clearly impossible; yet it is also deliberately avoided in situations where it would have been feasible. In *Voyage*, most of the inhabitants are non-human. The single opportunity for conversation, introduced with the insertion of the prehistoric shepherd in the 1867 version of the text, is not taken up. Rather than greeting the shepherd as an (admittedly highly remote) ancestor, Axel and Lidenbrock instead condemn him as 'ce redoutable ennemi' (267) [this redoubtable foe] and, having observed from a distance, flee in terror. In the course of the conversations which do occur, no exchange of information occurs; the travellers can be recipients but never, as in earlier narratives, custodians of knowledge. Moreover, these conversations are not always knowledge-generating and are frequently outweighed by non-verbal methods. Alice's interactions rarely increase her knowledge of herself or the world. Tangle learns in her interactions with the three Old Men, but her 'conversation' with the Old Man of the Earth is explicitly soundless, and her epiphany is (as we have seen) achieved visually rather than verbally. Télémaque conducts extensive conversations through which he gains considerable knowledge and insight, yet he speaks with only a single resident in each of the two realms and much of the knowledge gained is acquired simply by looking on at the inhabitants or listening to the conversations they conduct between themselves. In *Paradis*, the Sibyl Queen converses with her visitor at some length, providing him with detailed explanations. Yet she conceals her demonic nature and that of her court; and it is by what he *sees* that the knight's suspicions are confirmed.

It is by talking with their traveller-wards that certain guides pass on knowledge. Thélismar briefly informs Alphonse about the injustices of mining in the course of the hero's second descent, while Rémi learns about the processes of fossilization from the words and visual aids of the *magister*. Through their speech and actions, Sophrosyne and the dust fairy almost constantly convey a vast range of information to their wards. However, the principal function of guide figures such as Hans, the serpent in *The Golden Key* or the White Rabbit, Queen of Hearts and the Gryphon, is not to supply information but to provide directions or to escort the travellers. In *Voyage*, guidance is largely provided, not via speech, but by gestures, emotions, and through a system of signs. It is striking that, with the exception of the garrulous Lidenbrock, each of the guide figures is characterized by their silence, whether on temperamental and linguistic grounds in the case of Hans, for geographic reasons in that of Graüben, or because, in the case of Saknussemm, he is long dead. In several of these narratives, then, the underground is presented as a place which can be understood and negotiated without assistance or interaction, thus emphasizing the independence and self-reliance of these travellers who must act and observe for themselves rather than relying on others.

In certain texts, the underground is as privileged a site of knowledge acquisition as in earlier katabases. For example, it is only by going underground that Tangle learns the way to the land of the shadows and acquires knowledge which enables her to fully understand all the previous insights she has gained above ground. In *Télémaque*, the underworld constitutes the place of truth and of true life, and is thus elevated over the surface and its deceptions. The knowledge of the 'La Fée Poussière' is much more extensive than that of the so-called *savants* of the narrator/protagonist's world: 'il se passera encore du temps avant que tes professeurs [...] sachent [les grands secrets de la création] eux-mêmes' (398) [there is a long time yet to be passed before your professors themselves will know [the great secrets of creation]]; and the scientific and philosophical information she conveys to her ward is a great privilege: 'Mets à profit ma complaisance pour toi', she tells the narrator/protagonist (403) [profit by my kindness to you].

On the other hand, in several texts the main thrust of the descent is not knowledge acquisition at all. Vital information is often acquired elsewhere: in *King Solomon's Mines*, for example, the travellers discover the fate of Curtis's brother during their journey back home rather than their journey below ground. In

Voyage, the descent undertaken by Lidenbrock and Axel substantiates and validates what these knowledgeable men already know, rather than furnishing them with new insight. Graham Huggan argues that Axel's journey 'does not lead him to any kind of "deeper" knowledge or understanding'.[24] The most important thing brought back from the mines of *Alphonse et Dalinde* and *Princess* is not wisdom but a person (Alphonse's long-lost father and Curdie respectively). Given this Orphic dimension, these undergrounds are less places of knowledge than of action, theatre and melodrama.

Moreover, in the majority of the texts the descents give rise to confusion, obfuscation and mystery. Far from an unambiguous source of knowledge, the undergrounds are frequently associated with ignorance, in the form of more or less fundamental and lengthy problems of comprehension, the existence of unanswered questions, and the actual erosion of knowledge. Even in texts in which the descent clearly generates a learning experience on the part of the traveller, and the underground is thus equated with knowledge, there are moments in the course of the katabasis in which comprehension is difficult, if not impossible. In 'La Fée Poussière', the lowest depths are not only the most frightening but also the most intellectually impenetrable. The underground foregrounds the narrator/protagonist's ignorance: she looks on at the fairy's 'opérations incompréhensibles' [incomprehensible labour] and is obliged to admit that she knows nothing about chemistry (397). The fairy also draws attention to the narrator/protagonist's lack of knowledge:

> Tu ignores la chimie, tu ne sais pas encore de quoi cette matière est faite, ni par quelle opération mystérieuse ce qui apparaît ici sous l'aspect de corps solides provient d'un corps gazeux [...] Tu es une enfant, je ne peux pas t'initier aux grands secrets de la création... (398)

> [You are ignorant of chemistry; you do not yet know of what this matter is made, nor by what mysterious operation what appears here under the aspect of solid bodies come from a gaseous body [...] You are a child; I cannot initiate you into the great secrets of creation...]

It is only as they gradually re-ascend that the narrator/protagonist is able to understand, so that the knowledge-generating upward motion of the cave parable is combined with a subterranean setting.

It is also in the furthest depths of the highly mystical underground of *The Golden Key* that Tangle experiences moments both of utter clarity ('all was plain: she understood it all' (59)), and of total obscurity:

> And now Tangle felt that there was something in her knowledge that was not in her understanding. For she knew there must be an infinite meaning in the change and sequence and individual forms of the figures into which the child arranged the balls, as well as the varied harmonies of their colours, but what it all meant she could not tell. (60)

If at times she receives '[f]lashes of meaning', at others 'all would be not merely obscure, but utterly dark' (60). In the final stages of her journey, as the Old Man of the Fire calls forth the snake which will lead her out of the underground, '[h]e then spoke something Tangle could not understand' (65).

In *Alphonse et Dalinde*, the hero's initial descent is certainly part of a wider learning process, serving as the catalyst to the commencement of his true education. Alphonse is so cowed by Thélimar's critique and apparent omniscience that he will henceforth submit properly to his mentor's advice. But the katabasis takes place in the first place only because of Alphonse's tendency to show off his shaky knowledge instead of listening to others, and it demonstrates the hero's ignorance, vanity and credulity rather than his willingness to learn.

In other texts, the lessons learnt in the underground are transient and go unheeded. Having ascertained the true nature of the underground realm and its inhabitants, the knight of *Paradis*, makes a swift departure and hurries to Rome to attain absolution. But when this is unforthcoming, and being tricked by his squire into believing that it will remain so, the knight returns to the underground, professing his intention to save his body if not his soul. The lure of the underground and its considerable pleasures thus wins out over the immorality which the knight knows it to contain. In *King Solomon's Mines*, Quatermain's epiphanic realization concerning the futility of wealth is also swiftly discarded. Whereas La Sale's knight had at least spent some time trying to assure his salvation before finally going against the lesson learnt in the underground, it takes Quatermain less than a day to decide that he 'may as well pocket a few' diamonds in case they 'ever should get out of this ghastly hole' (292).

Although the travellers of *King Solomon's Mines* do not extract all of the treasure held in the underground, they nevertheless emerge from the underground as rich men. Similarly, in *Voyage*, Lidenbrock and Axel successfully attain the fame and prestige originally sought. But if the katabases of these texts confirm knowledge or generate riches and fame, they also produce mystery and questions. *King Solomon's Mines* sees the eradication of the Sybil-esque embodiment of knowledge, and the travellers emerge from the underground with a great many unanswered questions: how is the stalactite chamber lit? What is the precise nature of its door mechanism? Who stored this treasure? Quatermain owns his ignorance quite openly: 'As for the subterranean river in the bowels of the mountain, Heaven only knows what it was or whence it flows, or whither it goes' (298). The conclusions the travellers do reach are mere speculation. In *Voyage*, while the compass mystery is cleared up on the last page of the text, several questions remain unanswered, confirming Butcher's observation that there are more 'unsolved problems' in Verne's work than his positivistic reputation generally suggests.[25] What is the answer to the temperature issue which is constantly addressed in the course of the text? More fundamentally, can the centre of the earth be reached, and was this ever achieved by Arne Saknussemm?

In *Wonderland*, the underground is simultaneously a place in which practical know-how is acquired and one in which more fundamental forms of knowledge are eroded. The underground witnesses the gradual breakdown of Alice's self-knowledge as well as her rather shaky knowledge of the world. As is clear from the following interior monologue of chapter II, the erosion of both forms of knowledge begins early in the journey:

> 'Dear, dear! How queer everything is today! And yesterday things went on just
> as usual. I wonder if I've been changed in the night? Let me think: *was* I the
> same when I got up this morning? I almost think I can remember feeling a little
> different. But if I'm not the same, the next question is, "Who in the world am
> I?" Ah that's the great puzzle. [Alice begins to review her acquaintances.] I'm
> sure I can't be Mabel, for I know all sorts of things, and she, oh, she knows such
> a very little! Besides, *she's* she, and *I'm* I — oh dear how puzzling it all is! I'll try
> if I know all the things I used to know. Let me see: four times five is twelve, and
> four times six is thirteen, and four times seven is — oh dear! I shall never get to
> twenty at that rate! However the Multiplication Table doesn't signify; let's try
> Geography. London is the capital of Paris, and Paris is the capital of Rome, and
> Rome — no *that's* all wrong, I'm certain! I must have been changed for Mabel!
> I'll try and say *'How doth the little –'*. (37–38)

Needless to say, Alice's recitation is equally unsuccessful, the 'little busy bee' of the
original poem by Isaac Watts becoming the 'little crocodile' of her own version
(38). Likewise, when the Caterpillar later questions her as to her identity, Alice is
still unsure: 'I — I hardly know, Sir, just at present — at least I know who I *was*
when I got up this morning, but I think I must have been changed several times
since then' (67).

Finally, in *Sans Famille*, the underground is initially a place of knowledge but
later becomes a place of ignorance, a place in which knowledge is lost. The miners
lose all sense of the passage of time during their imprisonment since none of their
watches survives the flood (ironically the item stolen by Compayrou but unfor-
tunately hidden under his bed, is none other than a watch). They frequently wonder
what time it is, how long they have spent underground and how long it will take
for them to be rescued:

> Quelle heure était-il? Depuis combien de temps étions-nous dans la remontée?
> On se consulta mais sans tomber d'accord. Pour les uns, il était midi; pour les
> autres, six heures du soir, c'est-à-dire que pour ceux-ci nous étions enfermés
> depuis plus de dix heures et pour ceux-là depuis moins de cinq. (84)
>
> [What o'clock was it? How long had we been in the shed? We consulted each
> other, but without agreeing. According to some it was midday; according to
> others, six in the evening: meaning that to some, we had been shut up for more
> than ten hours; to others, less than five.]

Whereas the imprisonment had lasted some two weeks, their own highest
estimates are a mere five or six days (119). It is this temporal issue which serves
to highlight the fact that although the underground had previously furnished
Rémi with a range of information, it is now the surface which constitutes the
site of knowledge: 'Combien de temps', asks the *magister*, 's'écoulera, avant qu'on
commence notre sauvetage? *Ceux-là seuls qui sont sur la terre peuvent le dire*' (my
emphasis, 75) ['How many hours will go by before they begin our rescue? *Only
those above ground can tell that*']. The importance of the surface is confirmed
by the fact that, in order to 'raconter cette effroyable catastrophe des mines
de la Truyère, telle qu'elle a eu lieu' (89) [recount this frightful catastrophe of
the Truyère mine, just as it happened], the narrative shifts to the overground
rescue attempt.

Overall, then, in terms of the experiences of the protagonists, the undergrounds of the texts for young readers are much less straightforwardly equated with knowledge than those of their classical and medieval predecessors and, in certain texts, the underground is in many ways closer to the Platonic conceptualization of the depths. Although the journey does generate various forms of knowledge in various ways, it does not always constitute a straightforward learning experience on the part of the traveller, but can also confuse, highlight ignorance and raise as many questions as it answers. Only in *Télémaque* and *Triumphs*, the texts most closely modelled on early katabases, is the descent exclusively knowledge-generating for the travellers.

But in order to fully assess the didactic dimension of the undergrounds of these texts, we must consider not only their protagonists but also their young readers. The 'véritable apprentissage' undergone by Télémaque in the course of his travels is, as Genette points out, 'évidemment destiné, par procuration, au duc de Bourgogne'. One of the text's central didactic strategies is the use of the central protagonist as proxy to the reader: Fénelon's hero is in a similar position to his young ward and is endowed with many of his characteristics. Although few of the other texts share this tailor-made quality to such a high extent, they all employ devices which align reader and protagonist and therefore encourage the former to share in any learning experiences undergone by the latter. In *Sans Famille*, *Voyage*, *King Solomon's Mines* and 'La Fée Poussière', first person narratives bring the reader and character into close proximity, while in the third-person narratives of the remaining texts, events are for the most part focalized through the travellers. The young reader's identification with the protagonists of these narratives is further encouraged as a result of the various *translations proximisantes* which, as we saw in the previous chapter, are effected by the texts in terms of both age and gender.

All this maximizes the likelihood of the reader's assimilation of the knowledge acquired by the protagonists, which, as we have seen, ranges from the philosophical and existential to the practical and scientific. In each of the nineteenth-century French texts the incorporation of a wide array of technical and scientific information enables an understanding of the fields of geology, palaeontology and evolutionary theory, as well as their associated terminology. In certain texts, knowledge of a more philosophical, existential nature is also conveyed: *Télémaque*, 'La Fée Poussière' and *The Golden Key* all present death as a positive part of the natural order which should not be feared but embraced. In 'La Fée Poussière', the two forms of knowledge (scientific and existential) are inextricably linked.

The majority of the knowledge gained by the travellers and available to the readers is, as we have seen, impersonal in nature and thus of a wide relevance. The lessons acquired by Télémaque concerning the nature of rule are clearly of greater personal relevance to the young duc de Bourgogne than to other non-royal young readers but they nevertheless provide the latter with more general socio-political information. Although expressly denied by the author, the text as a whole has always been read as a critique of the government and character of Louis XIV and is perhaps most widely read today as a work of political theory. *Télémaque* is, however, the only katabasis for young readers which, like earlier versions of the narrative, explicitly and extensively conveys such lessons. If the young reader is frequently conducted back in time in the course of the narratives, s/he is encouraged to reflect not on the previous experiences or events of an individual or even a race but the pre-historic, pre-human past. Rather than an 'instrument of national aspiration and social criticism', the katabasis for young readers instead serves to convey the reader beyond history, society and nationhood.

But the knowledge made available to the reader in the course of these narratives is by no means limited to that acquired by the traveller. In texts in which the travellers themselves acquire considerable information, didacticism is further extended by direct addresses from narrator to implied reader. In *Triumphs*, for example, it is not Sophrosyne but the narrator who describes Discontent as:

> By dignity debas'd, by blessings curst,
> Who poisons Pleasure with the sourest leaven,
> And makes a Hell of Love's extatic Heaven. (III, 262)

Occurring at a narrative level from which the characters are excluded, such a statement must be aimed at the reader. Likewise, in *Télémaque* the narrator's lengthy exposition concerning the suffering of the kings in Tartarus is directed, as it were, over the hero's head towards the reader (394). The lesson that hypocrisy is the worst of all sins due to the way in which it undermines true virtue is similarly targeted (390).

Similarly positioned above and beyond the consciousness of the characters are the illustrations of these texts. Edouard Riou's illustrations for *Voyage* are particularly didactically oriented, playing a crucial role in the reader's understanding of the general conditions of the underground locale, the nature of its prehistoric flora and fauna, and the various operations or procedures undertaken by the characters. Moreover, as Arthur B. Evans points out, all illustrations serve a didactic purpose with respect to inexperienced, novice readers.[26]

That didacticism is not always tied absolutely to the experiences of the protagonist is particularly apparent in texts in which the travellers themselves do not undergo a straightforward learning experience. Mora-Lebrun claims that the *Paradis* has no 'morale explicite' [explicit moral] and 'n'a rien d'un texte didactique' [is by no means a didactic text], but although the central moral lesson learnt by the knight of *Paradis* goes unheeded, the text is nevertheless permeated with didactically oriented narratorial digressions concerning the death of Pontius Pilate, the dates of various Popes and the identity of classical Sibyls.[27] In *Voyage*, the travellers may not themselves substantially increase their own knowledge in the course of the journey, but their experiences make available for the young reader an extensive range of geological and palaeontological information and terminology. Axel is already familiar with the process of fossilization, the passage of sound through rocks and recent palaeontological discoveries, but the young reader can learn of them via his detailed explanations (in chapters XX, XXVIII and XXXVIII respectively). In *Princess*, the protagonist may herself learn little in the course of her katabasis, apart from the nature of the underground and the fact of Curdie's imprisonment, but her guiding thread nevertheless renders material and immediate for the reader issues of faith and belief, obedience and duty.

As in *Princess*, the katabases frequently offer moral and behavioural lessons not learnt explicitly by the travellers themselves: as we saw in Chapter 2, in *Sans Famille* and *King Solomon's Mines* the evil are punished in the underground, the brave and the good rewarded.[28] Each of the texts demonstrates that even in the direst of straits, hope should not be lost, and that bravery, perseverance and determination ultimately pay off. Furthermore, if katabatic narratives for young readers rarely address political issues, they nevertheless convey, as we saw in the previous chapter, a series of largely covert lessons concerning sexual politics via the allocation and characterization of key roles, as well as the presentation and discussion of relations between the sexes. Such messages were probably not consciously registered by the targeted young readers of these texts. Even the feminization and sexualization of the underground, which now seems so overt and unavoidable a feature of *King Solomon's Mines*, may have been overlooked. Monsman argues that 'Victorian schoolboys probably did not notice any extended patterns of sexual imagery'.[29] It is difficult to know for sure (were opinions on such issues likely to be expressed freely?); but even if such elements were not directly apparent, their operation on a more subliminal level may have rendered them all the more powerful.

Finally, although certain travellers (notably Télémaque) are aware of their katabatic predecessors, few actually learn about earlier journeys in the course of their own travels. Yet as we saw in the first chapter, the intertextual relationships encompassed by the katabases contribute to the cultural education of the young reader by further familiarizing them with, or exposing them to, foundational literary works, as well as providing insights into the nature of textuality more generally.

Whether or not the travellers themselves undergo learning experiences in the underground, a highly tangible didactic and moralizing intent is apparent in several katabatic narratives for young readers: the reader of *Télémaque*, for example, is clearly meant to learn about the art of rule, the deceptions of the surface, and — as in 'La Fée Poussière' and *The Golden Key* — about life and death. The reader of 'La Fée Poussière', *Voyage* and *Sans Famille* is evidently expected to learn about geology and/or evolution. The descent into the Abode of Spleen in *Triumphs* serves as an extended cautionary tale for its 'fair readers'.[30] Yet even in these texts where a didactic dimension is so marked, it is difficult to maintain that it is substantially increased with respect to earlier narratives, if only because didacticism is so firmly engrained in the latter. Furthermore, a moral and/or didactic dimension is not always so readily apparent. As we have seen, knowledge can be lost as well as gained in these underworlds. In the case of *Wonderland*, such issues continue to be the cause of critical debate. Carroll's intentions and the effect of his text are still contested. Certain critics argue that the text sets out to teach and succeeds in doing so; others that the intention was didactic but that the finished work failed to deliver in this respect.[31] Other critics firmly reject both a didactic purpose and effect, and the text's critique of 'edifying' literature, and gentle ridiculing of educational practices in general is certainly much more readily discernible than any moralizing or didactic dimension. Cohen's observation that Carroll 'was more interested in entertaining, in engaging the aesthetic sensibilities and the emotions, than in instructing, preaching, or devising clever meanings', raises the issue which will be examined in the final part of this chapter, namely, the ability of the katabasis to provide pleasure, diversion and entertainment.[32]

Entertainment in Classical and Medieval Katabases

Enlightenment is not the only positive outcome of the katabasis, especially in *Aeneid* VI, where the underground is the land of the blessed as well as the damned. By encountering friends and relatives, a degree of comfort, reassurance or sense of closure can be achieved. But these high-points are often bittersweet, as is most poignantly apparent in the attempted but impossible embraces between travellers and inhabitants. For the most part, the katabatic journey is not so much enjoyed as it is endured. This is made clear in the case of Dante the pilgrim's travels when Virgil tells Chiron that 'necessità 'l ci 'nduce, e non diletto' (XII, 87) [[i]t is necessity, / And not his pleasure, that puts him on this road]. As Wallace Fowlie puts it, the pilgrim's 'descent into Hell will not be a sightseeing tour'.[33] As we saw in the previous chapter, the journey is frightening and emotionally harrowing for each of the travellers, and is also physically demanding for Dante the pilgrim.

Anecdotal evidence suggests that the katabasis can be equally traumatic for the audience. Brunel refers to the tradition that Augustus's sister (the mother of Marcellus) fainted on hearing Virgil read *Aeneid* VI.[34] Yet in general terms, there is no reason why suffering on the part of the protagonist should mitigate against enjoyment on the part of the audience, and this despite the previously outlined process of identification. In his aforementioned article, Jauss observes (with clear disapproval) that admiring identification specifically 'can easily descend from its practical functions, the setting of examples and the institutionalization of proper social behaviour, into false edification or *mere entertainment*' (my emphasis).[35] He also underlines the fact that identification and distance are by no means mutually exclusive.[36] Freud argues that a theatre spectator is protected from the negative experience of the hero 'by the certainty that, firstly, it is someone other than himself who is acting and suffering on the stage, and, secondly, that after all it is only a game, which can threaten no danger to his personal security'.[37] This can equally be applied to the reading process. Thus, if the reader is positioned sufficiently closely to the katabatic hero in order to learn alongside him, s/he nevertheless simultaneously retains a degree of distance and is thus protected from harm. The use of the first person narration in the *nekyia* and *Inferno* may increase the reader's identification with the protagonist, but it also provides reassurance that the traveller will return safely to the surface.

Moreover, if the condition and the at times horrific torments of the dead are rarely satisfying and indeed frequently distressing for the travellers themselves, such spectacles may afford the reader a certain degree of enjoyment. Whereas the bliss of the virtuous in Heaven can seem somewhat dull, the fates of sinners are highly compelling: the *Inferno* has always been more widely read than the other two part of the *Commedia*. Tertullian (c. 155 — c. 230) went so far as to declare that the torments of the underworld are 'things of greater delight [...] than a circus, both kinds of theatre, and any stadium'.[38] Jauss refers to Hans Blumenberg's model which accounts for 'aesthetic enjoyment even in relation to affections which at first glance do not seem "enjoyable," as for example, horror, repugnance or shock' by the fact that they enable the viewer to enjoy 'the pure functioning of his faculties as they are affected by the objects'.[39] This would explain at least in part the mass appeal of horror films and slasher movies. It also suggests that reading about the torture of the dead in katabases, can make us feel alive.

As Alice K. Turner points out in *The History of Hell*, accounts of the underworld can also prompt laughter. 'Alongside solemn eschatology,' she writes, 'there seems always to have been a subversive comic view of the afterlife'.[40] With reference to Aristophanes' satiric *Frogs*, Turner concludes that: 'Merry Hell was fair game to the later Greeks', and argues that in the multiple representations of the Middle Ages the underworld was portrayed with both piety and irreverence.[41] In the katabatic narratives under consideration here, outright comedy is rare but not totally non-existent. Robert Pinsky argues that the *Inferno's* Malebranche 'combine fear and comedy', and that in cantos XXI–XXII Dante simultaneously reaches 'for a moral terrain' and 'anticipates similar scenes of comic tension in classic adventure films'.[42]

If out and out comedy is unusual, these katabases nevertheless provide a privileged glimpse into an unknown, usually inaccessible, otherworld. As Anticleia rightly informs Odysseus: 'It's hard for the living to catch a glimpse of this...' (182). In addition, the prevalence of conversation and dialogue generates animation, and their incorporation of a diverse range of characters, landscapes and events maintains interest. The *Inferno*, in which the travellers encounter a range of obstacles and opponents, is particularly action-packed (cf., for example, the dramatic chase-scene in canto XXIII in which the Malebranche pursue Dante the pilgrim and Virgil). Dante's use of the present tense at various points in the narrative generates a sense of immediacy, (e.g. at the beginning of canto VI: 'I see new torments and tormented ones again / Wherever I step or look. I am in the third / Circle...' (VI, 3)). Furthermore, since the katabatic travellers generally have no inclination to dawdle in the world of death and sin (and when they do, are hurried along by their guide), the narratives acquire a considerable sense of pace and urgency.

Entertainment in Katabases for Young Readers

The travellers do not, on the whole, undertake these journeys in search of diversion, although those who descend in order to satisfy their curiosity or sense of adventure, and especially Alphonse and Alice, can perhaps be regarded less as questers in search of knowledge than as tourists in search of (edifying) amusement.[43] As Alice's rejection of her sister's dull book suggests, her pursuit of the White Rabbit is motivated by a desire for entertainment and diversion rather than knowledge or instruction. In the course of her journey, Alice can at times be amused, especially by the misfortunes of others: she laughs at the frog footmen (80), at the flamingo's puzzled expression (112), and on learning that the Duchess has boxed the Queen's ears (111). The journey can also generate a certain degree of enjoyment and diversion for the travellers and guides of other texts. The pleasures of the underground lead La Sale's knight to repeatedly defer his departure, 'car il jouissait là-bas de tant de plaisirs sans fin qu'un jour lui semblait durer moins d'une heure' (34–35) [for he enjoyed there so many endless pleasures that a day seemed to last less than an hour]. As we saw in Chapter 2, Tangle's experience of the underground is initially positive, her bath making her 'happier and more hopeful than she had been since she lost Mossy' (53), and the underground landscapes of both *Voyage* and *King Solomon's Mines* are highly praised by the travellers. In *King Solomon's Mines* it is above all Gagool who seems to enjoy what she had earlier referred to as 'a merry journey' (254): Quatermain describes her chuckling 'loud and long' before the spectre of Death (266). Likewise, the moral indignation of Sand's narrator/protagonist 'divertit beaucoup la fée Poussière' (401) [highly amused Fairy Dust], and she replies to her ward at one point 'en ricanant' (399) [laughingly].

In general terms, however, the journey is for the most part anything but enjoyable for the travellers, the descents becoming even more arduous than in earlier versions of the narrative. In the case of Alice, for example, her brief moments of amusement are massively outweighed by the difficulties of her journey. The katabasis almost always represents an immense test: as in earlier narratives the most frequent response of the travellers, explicitly stated in each text except *The Golden Key*, is one of fear. As we saw in the previous chapter, for several of the travellers, the journey is not only psychologically and emotionally harrowing but also even more physically demanding than that of Dante the pilgrim.

But to what extent do these narratives provide their targeted young readers with entertainment and enjoyment? Critics of Carroll in particular have argued that *Wonderland* is as upsetting and unpleasant for at least certain child readers as it is for the protagonist herself: Martin Gardner, for example, states that for a modern child reader, the *Alice* books are 'plotless, pointless, unfunny, and more frightening than a monster movie'.[44] Yet, as in earlier narratives, the hardships suffered by the travellers need not mitigate against enjoyment and entertainment on the part of the reader. In addition to the basic protection of fictionality, several texts (including *Wonderland*) provide further reassurance via narrative modes and/or framing devices. As in the *nekyia* and the *Inferno*, *King Solomon's Mines*, *Voyage*, 'La Fée Poussière' and *Sans Famille* all employ first-person narratives which may increase identification and concern but also reassure the reader of the successful completion of the journey. This is further extended in 'La Fée Poussière', and in *Triumphs* and *Wonderland*, by the employment of the dream framework. As Monique Coulloux has shown, Sand disapproved of frightening children, and in 'La Fée Poussière' the dream framework — established, as in *Triumphs*, from the outset — enables children to be entertained 'sans les effrayer ou les inquieter' [without frightening or disturbing them].[45] If in *Wonderland* the dream framework emerges only after the completion of the journey, it nevertheless provides, as Petersen points out, 'an emotionally familiar context in which Alice's adventures need not frighten a child'.[46] But it is worth noting that in the *Nursery Alice*, Carroll's own adaptation of the text for a younger audience, the approach of Sand and Hayley is adopted: the journey's occurrence within a dream is established from the outset and frequently foregrounded in the course of the narrative.[47]

These texts thus offer the young reader varying degrees of protection from harm. But the difficulties undergone by the traveller in many ways contribute to their ability to entertain. The successful completion of the difficult journey with all its obstacles can afford the reader considerable vicarious pleasure. Furthermore, a high degree of tension is frequently apparent — especially in those texts where the life of the travellers is threatened — and there is as much if not more pace and excitement as in earlier katabatic narratives. In *Sans Famille*, *King Solomon's Mines* and especially *Voyage*, time is frequently of the essence: it is raced against, especially by the supremely impatient Lidenbrock, and life-saving events such as the discovery of water in *Voyage*, or the arrival of the rescuers in *Sans Famille*, occur only in the very nick of time when all hope seems lost. As in the *Inferno*, shifts to the present tense in Axel's journal written during the sea crossing in *Voyage* and the account of Gagool's betrayal and death in *King Solomon's Mines* also contribute to the sense of urgency and drama. Guides rush their wards onwards as in earlier katabases, and the travellers themselves are often acutely aware of the pressures of time. In *Princess*, the hero and heroine are both aware of the need to act swiftly: Curdie tells Irene that '[t]here's no time to lose now' (160), while the princess herself is keen to leave 'this horrid place as fast as we can' (161) and encourages the young miner to '[m]ake haste' (414). The disturbance of the goblin rulers and subsequent chase furthers contributes to the tension. Even in *Wonderland*, where the series of conversations sets a rather less urgent, more meandering pace, there are nevertheless moments of rush and hurry. Because Alice is following the harassed White Rabbit, there is 'not a moment to be lost' (29), and he later exhorts her to act quickly: 'Why, Mary Ann, what *are* you doing out here? Run home this moment, and fetch me a pair of gloves and a fan! Quick, now!' (55–56). Alice's search for the garden also generates a degree of forward propulsion.

As this suggests, a great deal happens in the action-packed katabatic narratives for young readers. As well as, or instead of, simply contemplating the underground and conversing with inhabitants or guides, the travellers also fight and kill (*Alphonse et Dalinde*), unexpectedly discover friends or loved ones (*Alphonse et Dalinde*, *Princess*), play games and have tea (*Wonderland*), or get lost (*Voyage*) and imprisoned (*Sans Famille*, *Voyage*, *King Solomon's Mines*). In *Sans Famille*, the shift to the quasi-third-person narration of events on the surface serves to vary the narrative which, because of the imprisonment, is necessarily restricted to a specific, closely circumscribed locale. If, then, there is less dialogue than in earlier narratives, there is considerably more action; interest thus being maintained via the variety of events.

Other elements also serve to vary the narrative and hence militate against lassitude and disengagement. The landscapes through which the travellers pass retain the exoticism of the unknown. Although Thélismar subsequently maintains that there is nothing miraculous about the first underground visited by Alphonse (78), his sober discourse cannot expel the excitement earlier generated. The undergrounds are, moreover, often full of contrasts. In *Télémaque*, the underground encompasses both Tartarus and the Elysian Fields, while in *Voyage*, the claustrophobic, dark, labyrinthine tunnels of the first part of the journey give way to the immense underground cavern. Felicia Miller Frank argues that a reader will only remain interested in 'tunnels and shafts plunging into mysterious depths' for so long, and that it was to combat this potential boredom that Verne included the underground sea in his subterranean landscape.[48] In *Wonderland*, Alice visits various houses in addition to the long hall, wood, seashore, garden and courthouse. In several texts, the underground is endowed with a spectacular, theatrical dimension — the replay of evolution in 'La Fée Poussière' is explicitly compared to 'les actes d'une féerie' (403) [the scenes in a fairy-play] — and indeed Sand, Hayley, Genlis and Verne had all written for the theatre during their careers. In Fénelon's underworld, the mirrors used to torture rulers overly-susceptible to sycophancy and flattery have the distinct air of the theatrical prop, and in *Triumphs* a series of dynamic sets together build what Bishop refers to as the 'pantomime' abode of Spleen.[49] Within these landscapes various fantastic features are clearly designed to amaze and impress the young reader, often as a result of their scale (e.g. the giant mushrooms in *Voyage*). In *King Solomon's Mines*, the effigy of death and the corpse of Twala seem designed to arouse a gothic *frisson*.

Spectacular elements such as these are often rendered visually in the accompanying illustrations of *Voyage*. In each of the illustrated texts, the images play a vital role in maintaining interest and in generating excitement, curiosity and a sense of wonder. The drama and atmosphere of the claustrophobic underground environment is heightened by the dark, character-focused images of *Princess* and *Sans Famille*. Moreover, as Evans argues, all images provide respite from the text, serving as visual breaks in often lengthy narratives.[50]

In terms of characterization, the fact that in the adventure stories several characters rather than a single individual are together in the underground enables opportunities for interaction *between* characters, such as the dealings of the trapped miners with Compayrou in *Sans Famille*. It also provides a range of character traits, for example Lidenbrock's determination which is contrasted with Hans's docility, and different responses to experiences such as Curtis's strength as opposed to the breakdown of Good and Quatermain in the treasure chamber. Furthermore, the underworlds of these texts are peopled by a diverse range of frequently compelling, enigmatic and bizarre inhabitants, including goblins, talking animals and playing cards, animate fossils and snake guides.

Despite the difficulty of the journey, varying degrees of humour are also apparent in these katabases. In the 'kittenish', 'sportive' *Triumphs*,[51] amusement is generated via the typical mock-heroic *décallage* between the lightness of the subject matter and the gravity with which it is presented — Serena, after all, ultimately descends into hell in search of a good husband. In *Sans Famille*, Rémi's naïve insistence on the flood having been caused by a hole opening up in the river above is at once touching and amusing (57, 66, 70). In both *Voyage* and *King Solomon's Mines*, the comedy apparent in other parts of the texts is also carried into the katabases. In *King Solomon's Mines*, the tone is light-hearted at the beginning and more especially at the end of the katabasis, where Good's appearance continues to raise a laugh: he emerges from the exertions of the descent with his trademark eyeglass still firmly in place (299). In *Voyage*, Lidenbrock's Quixoticism, impatience and unswayable optimism provides periodical entertainment throughout, and this is enhanced by the fact that his actions and attitudes are filtered through the eyes of the sardonic Axel.

With reference to *Wonderland*, Gardner argues that much of what he refers to as the 'wit and flavor' of the text has been lost, just as the moralizing import of the *Inferno* has been reduced over time.[52] In the case of *Wonderland*, this is due to both the widening of the text's readership and to the passage of time: 'some of Carroll's jokes could be understood only by residents of Oxford, and other jokes, still more private, could be understood only by the lovely daughters of Dean Liddell' (e.g. the animals who fall into the pool of tears — 'a Duck and a Dodo, a Lory and an Eaglet' — designate the members of the original boating party: the Reverend Duckworth, Carroll, Lorina and Edith Liddell).[53] As in the mythological references concerning the crimes of sinners in classical katabases, editors reinstate such jokes in the notes to modern editions, although Gardner states that those of his *Annotated Alice* are addressed exclusively to adult readers, and he maintains that 'the time is past when a child under fifteen, even in England, can read *Alice* with the same delight as gained from, say, *The Wind in the Willows* or *The Wizard of Oz*'.[54]

Yet much of the extensive wordplay of the text has lost none of its immediacy. If the realm of the Reine Sibylle is multilingual, Wonderland is a place where the slipperiness of language is highlighted. Linguistic complexities, including the multiple meanings of a single word or of similar sounding words, are one of the main sources of Alice's own difficulties and torment. As Gardner points out, children find puns, with which the text is packed, 'very funny' (129): the Mouse tells a dry (dull) tale in order to dry (eliminate the wetness of) the party assembled next to the pool (46–47); Alice confuses the Mouse's next tale with his own tail (50); her innocent reference to the world's axis promptly leads to the Duchess's call for the heroine's decapitation ('Talking of axes...') (84). Moreover, in the course of the text, certain forms of language and terminology are highlighted, deconstructed or recast: a typical, apparently straightforward and innocent formula of polite conversation, i.e. 'I don't think...', is seized upon by the Mad Hatter who tells Alice 'Then you shouldn't talk' (103); and he reacts in the same way to the King's instruction to 'stand down' in the juridical sense: 'I can't go no lower [...] I'm on the floor as it is' (150). As this small number of the many possible examples suggest, the text can still be positioned within the 'merry hell' tradition of underground narratives.

Finally, the intertextual dimension of the katabases with which this study began may fulfil a didactic function, but it can also generate pleasure. If, as we saw in Chapter 1, C. S. Lewis's reading of the *Iliad* is made more enjoyable by the fact that it reminds him of *Sohrab*, familiarity with any of the katabases for young readers may also enhance the enjoyment of a subsequent encounter with an earlier katabatic narrative. Furthermore, should a reader already be familiar with classical and/or medieval katabases, the not inconsiderable pleasures of intertextual recognition are abundantly available in these narratives, as critics have already noted with respect to the narratives of Fénelon and La Sale: Cuche refers to *Télémaque* overall as a work 'qui permet de se livrer à l'infini aux délices de l'intertextualité' [which offers endless opportunities to indulge in intertextual delights], whilst Mora-Lebrun refers to the 'système d'échos' [system of echos] of *Le Paradis* which 'sollicite [...] la culture romanesque du lecteur' [calls on the reader's cultural knowledge] and thus 'accroît son plaisir' [increases his pleasure].[55]

It is not only in their intertextuality that these narratives bring together education and entertainment. The two elements are by no means siphoned off into distinct compartments but instead inter-related and inter-fused. Thus, for example, the limit situations which bring the protagonists to the brink of death simultaneously grip, thrill and excite and instil behavioural lessons about fortitude, faith and perseverance. Illustrations are similarly dual-functioned. As Arthur B. Evans demonstrates with reference to Verne's *Voyages Extraordinaires*, the capacity to successfully educate is strongly dependent on the ability to entertain.[56] The *dulce utile* is apparent not only in Verne's *Voyage* but in different ways in each of the katabases for young readers examined here.

Although these narratives convey a wide range of knowledge, such didacticism is not simply and artificially grafted onto them but instead originates in traditional katabatic narratives. Indeed, at least in terms of the traveller's experience of the underground, katabases for young readers can be *less* didactic than earlier narratives; the underground equated with ignorance and the erosion of knowledge rather a site in which to acquire information. But even if the learning experiences of the travellers are frequently ambiguous, the didactic dimension of the katabatic narrative is nevertheless largely preserved in these texts. Whatever knowledge is acquired by the traveller is also, via a process of identification, made available to the young reader, towards whom a series of additional, frequently covert, lessons, are also directed. Certain differences between the forms of knowledge conveyed in the two groups of texts can be discerned: the knowledge relating to socio-political affairs apparent in early katabatic narratives is largely absent in those targeted at young readers, but a great deal of scientific information drawing on nascent evolutionary discourses and the rapidly developing sciences of geology and palaeontology is introduced. The major difference between traditional versions of katabasis and those targeted at young readers is the greater stress on entertainment. Not only is outright comedy more apparent, but setting and characterization are both more varied, and a higher level of action and drama is incorporated. The journeys are as arduous as ever for the protagonists, but katabases for young readers nevertheless give 'Merry Hell' a new lease of life.

Notes to Chapter 4

1. Genette, pp. 354, 473.
2. Genette, pp. 250–51.
3. Genette, p. 250.
4. Granderoute, p. 48.
5. For Genlis's subscription to this see Introduction, note 39. Hetzel's *Magasin d'Éducation et de Récréation* was founded on the same principles, as the original 'prospectus de lancement' makes clear: 'Il s'agit pour nous de constituer un enseignement de famille dans le vrai sens du mot, un enseignement sérieux et attrayant à la fois, qui plaise aux parents et profite aux enfants. Éducation, récréation — sont à nos yeux deux termes qui se rejoignent. L'instructif doit se présenter sous une forme qui provoque l'intérêt, sans cela il rebute et dégoûte de l'instruction; l'amusant doit cacher une réalité morale, utile, sans cela il passe au futile et vide les têtes au lieu de les remplir' [We aim to create a programme of family education in the true sense of the term, an education both serious and attractive which appeals to parents and benefits children. Education, amusement — for us these two terms are akin. The instructive must be presented in such a way to arouse interest, otherwise it deters and makes instruction distasteful. The entertaining must hide a moral and useful reality, otherwise it becomes futile and empties heads rather than filling them]. (Quoted in Compère, *Jules Verne: Écrivain*, p. 19.)

6. Williams, p. 46.

7. Saint Augustine, *Confessions*, trans by Henry Chadwick (Oxford: OUP, 1998), IV, 12.

8. Brunel, p. 9.

9. Brockway, pp. 37–38.

10. See Clark, pp. 39–48.

11. Keith Oatley, 'Meetings of Minds: Dialogue, Sympathy, and Identification in Reading Fiction', *Poetics*, 26 (1999), 439–54 (p. 445).

12. Karín Lesnik-Oberstein, 'Essentials: What Is Children's Literature? What Is Childhood?', in *Understanding Children's Literature: Key Essays from the 'International Companion Encyclopedia of Children's Literature'*, ed. by Peter Hunt (London/New York: Routledge, 1999), pp. 15–29 (pp. 25–26).

13. Hans Robert Jauss, 'Levels of Identification of Hero and Audience', trans by Benjamin and Helga Bennett, *New Literary History*, 5 (1974), 238–317.

14. Denys Page, *The Homeric Odyssey: The Mary Flexner Lectures*, 2nd edn (Oxford: Clarendon Press, 1966), p. 40.

15. Clark, p. 14.

16. Granderoute, p. 4.

17. Fénelon, 'Dialogues sur l'éloquence', in Fénelon, *Œuvres*, ed. by Le Brun, 1, 3–87 (p. 19).

18. Wallace Fowlie, *A Reading of Dante's 'Inferno'* (Chicago/London: University of Chicago Press, 1981), p. 10.

19. Granderoute, p. 3. Genette also identifies this process.

20. John Freccero, 'Foreword', in Pinsky, pp. xi–xix (p. xiii).

21. Frecerro, note to canto V, p. 385.

22. Penny Brown, *History of French Children's Literature*, 2 vols (New York/London: Routledge, 2008), 1, 49.

23. Ippokratis Kantzios, 'Educating Telemachus: Lessons in Fénelon's Underworld', <http://ablemedia.com/ctcweb/showcase/kantzios1.html> [Consulted 12 December 2009].

24. Graham Huggan, 'Voyages Towards an Absent Centre: Landscape Interpretation and Textual Strategy in Joseph Conrad's *Heart of Darkness* and Jules Verne's *Voyage au centre de la terre*', *The Conradian*, 14 (1989), 19–46 (p. 31).

25. *Journey to the centre of the earth*, trans. by Butcher, p. xxi.

26. Arthur B. Evans, *Jules Verne Rediscovered: Didacticism and the Scientific Novel* (New York: Greenwood Press, 1988), p. 115.

27. Mora-Lebrun, pp. 131, 138.

28. The didactic dimension of *Sans Famille* was capitalized upon and further extended by nineteenth-century publishers. The mining chapters were amongst various episodes of the text published as extracts, supported by a range of pedagogical material. In *Sous Terre. Épisode extrait de 'Sans Famille' par Hector Malot. Livre de lecture courante à l'usage des écoles primaires. Contenant des notes explicatives par L. R. Traitner, Directeur d'école publique à Paris* (Paris: Hachette, 1897), the notes at the bottom of each page test basic comprehension and vocabulary as well as explaining grammatical points and providing background details. They thus seek to actively engage the reader, situate the text within a wider context, and underline its moral/behavioural lessons.

29. Monsman, p. 284.

30. Hayley's memoirs provide evidence of the efficacy of the overall work: the 'sweetest reward he ever received as an author was a cordial declaration from a very good and sensible mother of a large family, that she was truly indebted to the [*Triumphs*], for an absolute and delightful reformation in the conduct and character of her eldest daughter, who, by an ambition to imitate Serena, was metamorphosed from a creature of a most perverse and intractable spirit, into the most docile and dutiful of children.' *Memoirs of the Life and Writings of William Hayley, Esq*, 2 vols (London: Henry Colburn and Co, 1823; repr. Westmead, Hants: Gregg International, 1971), 1, 208.

31. Brockway, p. 42. Heath, p. 50.

32. Cohen, p. 409.

33. Fowlie, p. 21.

34. Brunel, p. 11.

35. Jauss, p. 307.

36. Jauss, p. 286.

37. Sigmund Freud, 'Psychopathic Characters on the Stage', in *The Standard Edition of the Complete Psychological Works of Sigmund Freud*, trans. and ed. by James Strachey, 24 vols (London: Vintage, 2001), VII, 305–10 (p. 306).

38. Quoted in Turner, p. 77.

39. Jauss, p. 286.

40. Turner, p. 3.

41. Turner, pp. 27, 3.

42. Pinsky, notes to canto XXI, p. 407.

43. Early forms of tourism fused education and entertainment much more than those of today. See, for example, Ian Ousby, *The Englishman's England: Taste, Travel and the Rise of Tourism* (Cambridge: CUP, 1990), p. 7.

44. Martin Gardner, 'A Child's Garden of Bewilderment', in *Only Connect: Readings in Children's Literature*, ed. by Sheila Egoff, G. T. Stubbs and L. F. Ashley (Toronto/New York: OUP, 1980), pp. 150–55 (p. 151).

45. Coulloux, pp. 152, 140.

46. Robert C. Petersen, 'To Sleep, Perchance to Dream: Alice Takes a Little Nap', *Jabberwocky: The Journal of the Lewis Carroll Society*, 8 (1979), 27–37 (p. 29).

47. The dream is established in the very first line and reinforced in the second: 'Once upon a time, there was a little girl called Alice: and she had a curious dream. Would you like to hear what it was that she dreamed about?' (Lewis Carroll, *The Nursery Alice* (London: Macmillan, 1890; repr. Ware, Herts: Omega Books, 1985), p. 1).

48. Frank, p. 310.

49. Bishop, p. 131.

50. Evans, *Jules Verne Rediscovered*, p. 121.

51. Bishop, pp. 121, 129.

52. Martin Gardner, 'Introduction', in *The Annotated Alice* (Harmondsworth: Penguin, 1976), pp. 7–16 (p. 7).

53. Gardner, 'Introduction', p. 7.

54. Gardner, 'Introduction', pp. 7–8.

55. François-Xavier Cuche, 'Présentation', *Dix-septième Siècle*, 206 (2000), 3–10 (p. 10); Mora-Lebrun, p. 136.

56. Evans, *Jules Verne Rediscovered*, pp. 141–47.

CONCLUSION

Many significant differences between traditional katabatic narratives and those targeted wholly or in part at young readers have emerged in the preceding chapters. Important departures are discernible in all aspects of the narrative, including setting, character, action, and overall tone and purpose. Rarely, however, are these distinctions in line with Genette's pronouncements about children's literature which together depict it as a conservative, inferior form characterized by sanitization and heavy-handed moralization. Although the narratives are in various ways brought closer to their targeted audience, this process of proximization does not entail the eradication of key elements of traditional katabasis and their replacement with mere fluff or overbearing didacticism. Many of the essential ingredients of classical and medieval katabasis remain very firmly in place. The narratives for young readers continue to incorporate (but do not significantly extend) the already significant moral and didactic dimension of the pre-texts. Moreover, other key elements are not only retained but actually taken further. Thus, death is threatened constantly and occurs repeatedly in the underground locales of these texts. Certain characters like Alphonse, who himself inflicts several deaths in the course of his first descent, are even more combative and active than their predecessors. In some cases, the continuities are largely conservative, serving to bolster the status quo; the continued domination of the narrative by male protagonists and accompanying derogatory portrayal of female figures in the adventure stories is a case in point. Yet other narratives reach towards new positions; fantasy and fairytales for young readers featuring female protagonists certainly fall back on standard portrayals of femininity in many ways, yet they provide opportunities to introduce more dynamic female figures and to interrogate and rethink gender relations. The sheer variety of children's literature (and the difficulty of generalizations about it) is indeed readily apparent in this corpus of eleven texts.

The process of revisioning and interrogation within katabatic narratives for young readers certainly did not stop at the end of the nineteenth century. Pullman's *Amber Spyglass* (2000), the hugely successful and lauded text with which this study began, notoriously reintroduces the element of critique into the katabasis for young readers. The *His Dark Materials* trilogy as a whole has gained an extensive adult as well as child readership, and Pullman has expressed reservations about his classification as a writer for young readers.[1] Yet he has also stressed the superiority of children's literature which, as opposed to contemporary adult fiction, is the only form in which 'the story is taken seriously' and fundamental issues addressed.[2] For Pullman, '[a]fter nourishment, shelter and companionship, stories are the thing we need most in the world', because 'they entertain and they teach', an attitude which places him firmly within the tradition of writers for the young stretching back at least as far as Fénelon.[3] A self-consciously intertextual author, Pullman has frequently reiterated the importance of Homer (as well as writers such as Blake and Milton) in his work, and the katabasis of *The Amber Spyglass* is as high on Genette's scale of explicitness as those of *Télémaque* and the *Triumphs*.[4]

The psychologically and physically harrowing journey is undertaken so that the heroine, Lyra, can make amends to her friend Roger, whom she had unwittingly led to his death, and so that the hero, Will, can speak with his dead father. Having left their daemons (the soul or spirit embodied, in Lyra's case, in animal form) on the shore, the children are rowed across to the desolate underground which houses all the dead, sinners and the virtuous alike. The Christian system of heaven and hell is denounced as a fallacy used by the Church to control humanity. As one shade says: 'The good come here as well as the wicked, and all of us languish in this gloom for ever, with no hope of freedom, or joy, or sleep or rest or peace' (335). Reinstating the classical afterlife system, Pullman manifestly uses the descent as a vehicle for theological *dissent*.

As well as receiving confirmation that the concept of heaven is 'a lie' (35), both travellers acquire precious insights in the course of their journeys: Will's father informs his son about his own life and passes on crucial information. Lyra receives absolution from Roger himself, and learns of the value of life from the shade of another friend: 'Lyra, child, you rest when this is done, you hear? Life is good, and death is over...' (404). But as opposed to protagonists in earlier katabatic narratives for young readers, Will and Lyra bring even more to the underworld than they receive from it: Lyra talks with many of the ghost children about their former daemons, and nourishes them and the harpies with stories of the upper world. Like Dante the pilgrim, she also pledges to carry the experiences of the shades back to the surface. But this is not all. Will and Lyra together succeed in overthrowing the entire system put in place by the Authority in the dim and distant past, releasing the shades from the shackles of death. By cutting into the world of the living with the subtle knife, the vast ranks of the dead are able to pass through the opening where they promptly dissolve, reunited with the universe in a pantheistic vision which recalls that of Sand's 'La Fée Poussière'. The travellers also reappoint the harpies who will henceforth guide the dead through the desolate underground realm in exchange for stories of life on the surface, thus making it incumbent on each individual to live his or her life to the full.

In addition to its theological dimension, Pullman's katabasis is also notable in terms of its presentation of gender roles and relations. As in MacDonald's katabases for young readers, Pullman features both a hero and a heroine in his trilogy. Yet as opposed to Irene and Curdie and particularly Tangle and Mossy, Lyra and Will embark on the katabasis together. As I have argued elsewhere, Pullman fails to fully resolve the gender-related problems grappled with by writers of fantasy and fairytale in the nineteenth century, but he does portray a journey which is very much a shared experience during which there are several moments of intimacy and complicity between Will and Lyra.[5] Indeed, it is made clear that it is in the underworld that the awakening of their love for each other begins. Although action and decisiveness centres around Will, it is Lyra who initiates the journey, enables their access to the land of the dead, and formulates the plan to set free the shades. And it is female figures — the Harpies — upon whom the essential role of guide is bestowed.

Pullman's narrative is perhaps the best-known literary katabasis to have been published in recent years. Yet contemporary katabases specifically targeted at young audiences are by no means limited to literature. In 1975, H. W. Stubbs wrote that katabasis is 'as successful on BBC television as it was in Sumerian cuneiform', but since then it has also been incorporated into various new formats and technologies which nevertheless preserve the traditional dual imperatives of children's literature generally and of katabatic narratives specifically.[6] Philippe Tassel's online text *Un Souterrain d'Enfer* relates the adventures of Chloé and Bérangère who repeatedly enter a series of booby-trapped underground passages in order to find a rare plant with powers to heal the village's elderly outcast.[7] A criminal gang using the tunnels to store toxic waste makes matters more complicated and provides the protagonists with opponents to battle against. As in many of the earlier literary katabases for young readers the travellers themselves learn very little in the course of their action-packed underground adventures. Yet the website serves a clear didactic function. The online version of the novel incorporates italic text which, when touched by the mouse, gives definitions of words, and the speech of the various characters appears in different colours. At the end of the downloadable version of the text a series of comprehension questions place *Un Souterrain d'Enfer* very much in the tradition of nineteenth-century pedagogical adaptations of *Sans Famille*. Another part of the site provides an extensive range of teaching material, including, for example, exercises concerning written expression.[8] A series of links to other internet sites enable children to learn more about the area in which the text is set, the nature of the bird kept by the village outcast, and about environmental issues.

Alongside and in conjunction with this didactic dimension, Tassel's dramatic and action-packed narrative also fulfils the other traditional imperative of children's literature. This is confirmed by the responses of a group of 8 to 10-year-old pupils included on the website: Amandine likes it 'parce qu'il y a plein de mystère et quelquefois ça fait peur' [because there's loads of mystery and sometimes it's scary]; for Guillaume, '[à] la fin du chapitre, on a souvent envie de lire le prochain' [at the end of the chapter you often want to read the next one]; and Andréa states that 'plus il y a de chapitres, plus l'histoire est intéressante et passionante' [the more chapters there are, the more the story is interesting and exciting.][9] But in addition to reading about the katabases of fictional protagonists, visitors to Tassel's website also have the possibility of undertaking their own katabatic journey. One of the site's 'Jeux interactifs' calls on the child to negotiate a virtual underground by making a series of choices made easier by prior reading of the text itself, and thus clearly combining the *dulce* and the *utile*. Children are offered the chance to add their own name to 'la liste des héros du souterrain d'enfer' [the list of heroes of the hellish underground] which, when last consulted, stood at just 389, as opposed to the 2038 having disappeared...[10]

Opportunities for children themselves to perform physical katabases in controlled conditions are also provided by various forms of specifically targeted museum exhibit.

In Manchester's Museum of Science and Industry, for example, the 'Underground Manchester' exhibit allows the visitor to discover the story of the city's water supply, walk through a Victorian sewer, and explore the history of the lavatory! In another Museum of Science and Industry, this time in Chicago, visitors can descend 600 feet underground through a simulated mineshaft. In the same city, situated in the lower level of the Field Museum of Natural History, visitors can venture 'Inside Ancient Egypt' and embark upon an 'Underground Adventure'. Within the former exhibit, visitors descend a spiral staircase leading to a reconstruction of the raided burial chamber of Unis-ankh in which several mummies and burial artefacts are displayed. In the exhibit alongside, the underground is revealed as a place of teeming plenitude, of life rather than of death. A large part of the 'Underground Adventure' exhibit alongside consists of what one of its designers refers to as an 'immersion experience in soil'.[11] The entrance to the exhibit is presented as the 'Base Camp' of the 'Prairie Soil Research Station', and introduces its various different 'facilities' (i.e. the various parts of the exhibition). Pre-recorded short films exhort carefulness and outline the benefits to be gained from the visit. These recordings are interspersed with CCTV clips of the 'Micro Soil Lab' which prepare the visitor for what they are about to experience. In order to enter this part of the exhibit the visitor must pass through the 'Shrink Chamber', an atmospherically lit and sound-tracked room of black and white tiles followed by a mirrored passage. Reduced to a hundredth of their former size — as a gigantic one-cent piece and ruler indicate — the visitor is now free, as the displays inform them, to 'wander through worm tunnels', 'roam through jungles of roots', and 'meet some truly awesome soil critters'. Amongst the sets which combine animatronics with sound and light effects are information columns with headings such as 'Abundance', 'Habitats', 'Connections'. In the 'Reverse Shrinkage Chamber', the visitor is then returned to their former size before entering an area made up of displays and interactive activities relating to subterranean life, including specimens of the insects, roots and plants just encountered in the previous, magnified part of the exhibit. A final room displays large-scale quotes emphasizing the importance of soil from the likes of Walt Whitman, Thomas Jefferson and F. D. Roosevelt. Once the visit is complete, the 'Underground Adventure' can be relived, prolonged and extended by means of the online exhibit on the museum's website.[12]

The purpose of the exhibit is to teach children about soil biodiversity and ecology, and its designers have clearly done their utmost to ensure that the experience is a highly stimulating one: stress is constantly placed on the visit as an adventure, exploration, and process of discovery. The exhibit is frequently 'hands-on', exciting, and even somewhat scary, with its spiders, crayfish and other creatures one hundred times their normal size lurking in the prevailing darkness. The monstrous insects reinvent the underground creatures of 'La Fée Poussière' and *Voyage*, and indeed the whole enterprise of popularizing science and making it accessible for children is very much in the spirit of nineteenth-century French katabases for young readers. Visitors may not undergo Axel's transition from childhood to adulthood within the exhibit's walls, but, like readers at end of Verne's text, they undoubtedly leave the 'Underground Adventure' knowing a great deal more about science and soil than when they entered.

Journeys down into the underground, which, in literary works and other cultural products targeted at the young, frequently remains the land of the dead, are then still very much alive. The recognition of the widespread, longstanding, and continuing presence of katabasis in texts (in the broadest sense of the term) for the young further expands the already extensive intertextual network of katabatic works established by critics whose focus has been largely on canonical works for adult readers. What may be thought of as the critical descent undertaken in this study down into what has been traditionally regarded as a sub-category of literary works, situated far beneath adult literature, has shown that the production of katabatic narratives for young readers specifically entails various shifts in emphasis and transformations of various kinds, but also that many — at times unexpected — aspects of traditional katabases targeted at a general audience remain firmly in place. The differences which do exist by no means constitute marks of inferiority, and thus perhaps one of the principal insights gained by this particular critical trajectory is that, like any examination of children's literature, it has not in fact been a journey down at all, but instead a journey out into a coexistent and equally fertile realm.

Notes to the Conclusion

1. 'If I think of my audience at all, I think of a group that includes adults, children, male, female, old, middle-aged, young, everyone who can read [...] I don't want to shut anyone out'. 'Philip Pullman — Full Interview' <http://www.literacytrust.org.uk/rif/readingstars/full_interviews/full_philip_pullman.htm> [consulted 14 December 2009].
2. Nicholas Tucker, *Darkness Visible: Inside the World of Philip Pullman* (Cambridge: Wizard, 2003), p. 184.
3. 'Philip Pullman — Full Interview'.
4. Pullman cites Homer's *Iliad* and *Odyssey* as books which have 'made a difference' to his life ('Philip Pullman — Full Interview'). In the 'Acknowledgements' at the end of *The Amber Spyglass*, Pullman writes: 'I have stolen ideas from every book I have ever read. My principle in researching a novel is "Read like a butterfly, write like a bee", and if this story contains any honey, it is entirely because of the quality of nectar I found in the work of better writers.' (Philip Pullman, *The Amber Spyglass* (London: Point, 2001), p. 549). Explicit intertextual references within Pullman's katabasis include the evocation of the insubstantial nature of the dead via the traditional leaf metaphor ('the ghosts all turned and fled, even the grown-ups, like dry leaves scattered by a sudden gust of wind' (313)) and the series of impossible embraces, as for example, when Roger 'rushed to embrace' Lyra, but 'passed like cold smoke through her arms' (321–22).
5. Kiera Vaclavik, 'The descent to the underworld retold and regendered in Philip Pullman's *The Amber Spyglass*', *The Journal of Children's Literature Studies*, 5: 2 (July 2008), 37–56.
6. Stubbs, p. 130. See also Soriano who argues that the advent of the printing press did not immediately generate the invention of new paradigms. Instead, the new technology was adapted to existing norms and requirements (p. 337).
7. Philippe Tassel, *Un Souterrain d'Enfer*, 2000 <http://lencrier.net/usde/index.htm> [consulted 14 December 2009].
8. Philippe Tassel, 'Activités pédagogiques' <http://lencrier.net/usde/autour/index.htm> [consulted 14 December 2009].
9. Philippe Tassel, 'Critiques des élèves de cycle 3 de Saint-Fruscien' <http://lencrier.net/usde/autour/fruscien.htm> [consulted 14 December 2009].
10. Philippe Tassel, 'Un Jeu d'Enfer' <http://lencrier.net/usde/autour/jeuinter/jeu.php3> [consulted 14 December 2009].
11. 'Francie Muraski-Stotz', <http://www.fieldmuseum.org/exhibits/exhibit_sites/wis/francie.htm> [consulted 14 December 2009].

12. 'Underground Adventure', <http://www.fieldmuseum.org/undergroundadventure/> [consulted 14 December 2009].

BIBLIOGRAPHY

Primary Sources

AGARD, JOHN and SATOSHI KITAMURA, *The Young Inferno* (London: Frances Lincoln, 2008)

BASSVILLE, NICOLAS-JEAN HUGO DE, *Élémens de mythologie avec l'analyse des poëmes d'Homère et de Virgile, suivie de l'explication allégorique à l'usage des jeunes personnes de l'un et l'autre sexe* (Paris: Laurent, 1784)

BLANCHARD, PIERRE, *Mythologie de la jeunesse* (Paris: Le Prieur, 1801)

BONNARD, ANDRÉ, *L'Odyssée Adaptée pour la jeunesse* (Paris: Nouvelles Presses Françaises, 1948)

CARROLL, LEWIS, 'Alice on the Stage', in *The Lewis Carroll Picture Book*, ed. by Stuart Dodgson Collingwood (London: Fisher Unwin, 1899), pp. 163–74

—— *Alice's Adventures in Wonderland and Through the Looking Glass*, ed. by Roger Lancelyn Green (London: OUP, 1971)

—— *The Annotated Alice*, ed. by Martin Gardner (Harmondsworth: Penguin, 1976)

—— *The Nursery Alice* (London: Macmillan, 1890; repr. Ware, Herts.: Omega Books, 1985)

CHURCH, ALFRED J., *The Children's Odyssey, told from Homer in simple language* (London: Seeley, 1907)

—— *The Children's Aeneid. Told from Virgil in simple language* (London: Seeley, 1909)

—— *L'Odyssée contée aux enfants. Le récit d'Homère simplifié par A. J. Church*, trans. by J.-R. Lugné Philipon (Paris: Vuibert, 1923)

DANTE, *The Inferno*, trans. by Robert Pinsky (London: Dent, 1997)

DEROUX, BLANDINE, *Le Pèlerinage (ou, 'La Divine Comédie' de Dante dei Aligheri racontée aux enfants)* (Paris: Tecdim, 1975)

DU FOSSÉ, PIERRE THOMAS, *Mémoires pour servir à l'histoire de Port-Royal*, 2 vols (Geneva: Slatkine, 1976)

FÉNELON, FRANÇOIS DE, *Aventures de Télémaque*, ed. by Jeanne-Lydie Goré (Paris: Garnier–Flammarion, 1968)

—— *Œuvres*, ed. by Jacques Le Brun, 2 vols (Paris: Gallimard, 1983–97)

—— *Telemachus, son of Ulysses*, ed. and trans. by Patrick Riley (Cambridge: CUP, 1994)

GÉNÉRAL L. M., *L'Énéide racontée à mes petits enfants* (Limoges: Droquet and Ardent, 1935)

GENLIS, STÉPHANIE DE, *Tales of the Castle: or, Stories of Instruction and Delight*, trans. by Thomas Holcroft, 5 vols (London: Robinson, 1785)

—— *Alphonse et Dalinde, ou la féerie de l'art et de la nature, conte moral* (Orléans: Berthevin, 1797–98 [an VI])

—— *Abrégé de mythologie grecque. Arabesques Mythologiques, ou les Attributs de toutes les Divinités de la Fable* (Paris: Barrois, 1810)

—— *Les Veillées du château, ou Cours de morale à l'usage des enfans*, 2 vols (Brussels: Meline and Cans, 1842)

GILES, JOHN ALLEN, *First Lessons in Classical Mythology, adapted to the use of little children* (London: [n.pub.], 1853)

GOUDOT, MARIE, *Enée ou la cité promise* (Paris: L'École de Loisirs, 2005)

HAGGARD, HENRY RIDER, 'Découverte des Mines de Salomon', [no trans.] in *Le Magasin d'Éducation et de Récréation*, 47–48 (1888) (various pages throughout)

——*King Solomon's Mines*, ed. by Dennis Butts (Oxford: OUP, 1998)

HANSON, CHARLES HENRY, *The Siege of Troy and the Wanderings of Ulysses* (London: Nelson, 1887)

HARRISON, ELISABETH, *The Vision of Dante. A story for little children and a talk to their mothers* (Chicago: Chicago Kindergarten College, 1894)

HAYLEY, WILLIAM, *The Triumphs of Temper; a poem in six cantos* (London: Dodsley, 1781)

——*Memoirs of the Life and Writings of William Hayley, Esq*, 2 vols (London: Henry Colburn and Co, 1823; repr. Westmead, Hants.: Gregg International, 1971)

HOMER, *The Odyssey*, trans. by Robert Fagles (London: Penguin, 2001)

HUGO, VICTOR, *Notre-Dame de Paris* (Paris: Livre de Poche, 1972)

KÉRILLIS, HÉLÈNE, *L'Extraordinaire Voyage d'Ulysse* (Paris: Hatier Jeunesse, 2004)

KINGSLEY, CHARLES, *The Heroes, or Greek Fairy Tales For My Children* (London: Macmillan, 1865)

KUPFER, GRACE H., *Legends of Greece and Rome* (London: Heath, 1922)

LA SALE, ANTOINE DE, *Le Paradis de La Reine Sibylle*, trans. by Francine Mora-Lebrun (Paris: Éditions Stock, 1983)

LAMB, CHARLES, *The Adventures of Ulysses* (London: The Juvenile Library, 1808)

LAMÉ FLEURY, JULES-RAYMOND, *Mythologie racontée aux enfants* (Paris: Dufart, 1833)

LANG, JEANIE, *Stories from the Odyssey* (London: Jack, 1906)

LAWRENCE, ROSE, *Cameos from the Antique; or the cabinet of Mythology* (Liverpool: [n.pub.], 1831)

LEWIS, C. S., *Surprised By Joy: The Shape of My Early Life* (London: G. Bles, 1955)

LIVELY, PENELOPE, *In Search of a Homeland: The Story of the Aeneid* (London: Frances Lincoln, 2001)

MACDONALD, GEORGE, *At the Back of the North Wind* (New York: Routledge, 1871; repr. New York/London: Garland, 1976)

—— *The Princess and the Goblin* (London: Puffin, 1996)

—— *The Golden Key* (London/Sydney/Toronto: Bodley Head, 1967)

MACGREGOR, MARY, *Stories from Dante told to the children* (London/New York: Jack/Dutton, 1909)

MALOT, HECTOR, *No Relations*, trans. by May Laffan, 3 vols (London: Bentley, 1880)

——*Sous Terre. Episode extrait de 'Sans Famille'. Livre de lecture courante à l'usage des écoles primaires. Contenant des notes explicatives par L. R. Traitner, Directeur d'école publique à Paris* (Paris: Hachette, 1897)

——*Sans Famille*, 2 vols (Paris: Gallimard, 1997)

MÜLLER, ÉLISABETH, *Mythologie pittoresque. La Fable racontée au jeune âge* (Paris: Bédelet, 1867)

PULLMAN, PHILIP, *The Amber Spyglass* (London: Point, 2001)

SAINT AUGUSTINE, *Confessions*, trans. by Henry Chadwick (Oxford: OUP, 1998)

SAND, GEORGE, 'Fairy Dust: A Story for Children', [no trans.] *The Strand Magazine*, 11 (1891), 536–43

——*Correspondance*, ed. by Georges Lubin, 24 vols (Paris: Garnier, 1964–90)

——*Histoire de ma vie*, ed. by Damien Zanone, 2 vols (Paris: Flammarion, 2001)

——'La Fée Poussière', in *Contes d'une grand-mère*, ed. by Béatrice Didier (Paris: Flammarion, 2004), pp. 394–405

SELFE, ROSE EMILY, *How Dante climbed the mountain. Sunday readings with the children from the Purgatorio* (London: Cassell, 1887)

—— *Selections from the first nine books of the 'Croniche Fiorentine'. Translated for the use of students of Dante and others* (London: Constable, 1896)

—— *With Dante in Paradise — Readings from 'Paradiso'* (London: Cassell, 1900)

SUTCLIFF, ROSEMARY, *The Wanderings of Odysseus: The Story of the Odyssey* (London: Frances Lincoln, 1995)

TASSEL, PHILIPPE, *Un Souterrain d'Enfer*, 2000 <http://lencrier.net/usde/index.htm> [consulted 14 December 2009]

——'Un Jeu d'Enfer' <http://lencrier.net/usde/autour/jeuinter/jeu.php3> [consulted 14 December 2009]

——'Activités pédagogiques' <http://lencrier.net/usde/autour/index.htm> [consulted 14 December 2009]

——'Critiques des élèves de cycle 3 de Saint-Fruscien' <http://lencrier.net/usde/autour/fruscien.htm> [consulted 14 December 2009]

TUSIANI, JOSEPH, *Dante's 'Divine Comedy': As Told for Young People* (Ottowa: Legas, 2001)

VIRGIL, *The Aeneid*, trans. by David West (London: Penguin, 2001)

VERNE, JULES, *Voyage au centre de la terre*, ed. by Jean-Pierre Goldenstein (Paris: Pocket, 1991)

——*Journey to the Centre of the Earth*, trans. by William Butcher, 3rd edn (Oxford/New York: OUP, 2008)

Secondary Sources

ANDERSON, R. D., *Education in France, 1848–1870* (Oxford: Clarendon Press, 1975)

ARCHER, R. L., *Secondary Education in the Nineteenth Century* (London: Cass, 1966)

ARFEUX-VAUCHER, GENEVIÈVE, *La Vieillesse et la mort dans la littérature enfantine de 1880 à nos jours* (Paris: Éditions Imago, 1994)

ATWOOD, MARGARET, *Negotiating with the Dead: A Writer on Writing* (Cambridge: CUP, 2002)

AVERY, GILLIAN, *Nineteenth Century Children: Heroes and Heroines in English Children's Stories, 1780–1900* (London: Hodder and Stoughton, 1965)

BARTHES, ROLAND, *S/Z* (Paris: Seuil, 1970)

——*S/Z*, trans. by Richard Millar (London: Cape, 1975)

BISHOP, MORCHARD, *Blake's Hayley: The Life, Works and Friendships of William Hayley* (London: Victor Gollancz, 1951)

BLANC, ANDRÉ, 'Fonction de la référence mythologique dans le *Télémaque*', *Dix-Septième Siècle*, 125 (1979), 373–88

BOER, WILLIAM DEN, 'Préface', *Les Études classiques aux XIXe et XXe siècles: Leur place dans l'histoire des idées*, ed. by William den Boer (Geneva: Fondation Hardt, 1980), no page numbers

BOLGAR, ROBERT R., 'Latin Literature: A Century of Interpretation', in DEN BOER, ed., *Les Études classiques aux XIXe et XXe siècles*, as previous, pp. 91–126

BRIGGS, JULIA, and DENNIS BUTTS, 'The Emergence of Form (1850–90)', in *Children's Literature: An Illustrated History*, ed. by Peter Hunt (Oxford/New York: OUP, 1995), pp. 130–65

BROCKWAY, ROBERT, 'The *Descensus Ad Inferos* of Lewis Carroll', *Dalhousie Review*, 62 (1982), 36–43

BROGLIE, GABRIEL DE, *Madame de Genlis* (Paris: Librairie Académique Perrin, 1985)

BROWN, PENNY, *History of French Children's Literature*, 2 vols, (New York/London: Routledge, 2008)

BRUNEL, PIERRE, *L'Évocation des morts et la descente aux enfers: Homère, Virgile, Dante, Claudel* (Paris: SEDES, 1974)

BUNN, DAVID, 'Embodying Africa: Woman and Romance in Colonial Fiction', *English in Africa*, 15 (1988), 1–28

BUTLER, CHARLES, 'Introduction', in *Teaching Children's Fiction*, ed. by Charles Butler (Basingstoke: Palgrave Macmillan, 2006), pp. 1–5

BUTOR, MICHEL, 'Suggestion', *L'Arc*, 39 (1969), 99–101

CARADEC, FRANÇOIS, *Histoire de la littérature enfantine en France* (Paris: Albin Michel, 1977)

CARPENTER, HUMPHREY, *Secret Gardens: A Study of the Golden Age of Children's Literature* (London: Allen & Unwin, 1985)

CHANDLER, DANIEL, *Semiotics: The Basics* (London: Routledge, 2002)

CITRON, PIERRE, 'Sur quelques voyages au centre de la terre', in *Nouvelles recherches sur Jules Verne et le voyage I* (Paris: Librairie Minard, 1978)

CLARK, RAYMOND J., *Catabasis: Vergil and the Wisdom-Tradition* (Amsterdam: Grüner, 1979)

CLARKE, M. L., *Classical Education in Britain, 1500–1900* (London/New York: Cambridge University Press, 1959)

CLAYTON, JAY, and ERIC ROTHSTEIN, 'Figures in the Corpus: Theories of Influence and Intertextuality', in *Influence and Intertextuality in Literary History*, ed. by Jay Clayton and Eric Rothstein (Madison: University of Wisconsin Press, 1991), pp. 3–36

COHEN, MORTON N., *Lewis Carroll: A Biography* (London: Macmillan, 1995)

COMPÈRE, DANIEL, *Un voyage imaginaire de Jules Verne: 'Voyage au centre de la terre'* (Paris: Minard, 1977)

——*Jules Verne: Écrivain* (Geneva: Droz, 1991)

COULLOUX, MONIQUE, 'Aspects du merveilleux chez George Sand: *Les Contes d'une Grand-Mère*' (unpublished doctoral dissertation, University of Colorado at Boulder, 1978)

COUNSON, ALBERT, 'Dante en France', *La Revue moderne*, 48 (1904), 232–52

CUCHE, FRANÇOIS-XAVIER, 'Présentation', *Dix-septième Siècle*, 206 (2000), 3–10

CULLER, JONATHAN, *The Pursuit of Signs: Semiotics, Literature, Deconstruction* (London/ Henley: Routledge and Kegan Paul, 1981)

DIDIER, BÉATRICE, 'Images et éclipses de la femme dans les romans de Jules Verne', in *Jules Verne et les sciences humaines*, ed. by François Raymond and Simone Vierne (Saint Armand: Collection 10/18, 1979), pp. 326–57

——'La Voix de Mère-grand', *Ethnologie Française*, 20 (1990), 293–300

DOCHERTY, JOHN, 'Dantean Allusions in Wonderland', *Jabberwocky: The Journal of the Lewis Carroll Society*, 19 (1990), 13–16

——*The Literary Products of the Lewis Carroll–George MacDonald Friendship* (Lewiston, NY/ Queenston, Ont./Lampeter: Edwin Mellen, 1995)

DU FOSSÉ, PIERRE THOMAS, *Mémoires pour servir à l'histoire de Port-Royal*, 2 vols (Geneva: Slatkine, 1976)

DUFOUR, HORTENSE, *George Sand: La Somnambule* (Monaco: Éditions du Rocher, 2002)

EGOFF, SHEILA, 'Precepts, Pleasures and Portents: Changing Emphases in Children's Literature', in *Only Connect: Readings in Children's Literature*, ed. by Sheila Egoff, G. T. Stubbs and L. F. Ashley, 2nd end (Toronto/New York: OUP, 1980), pp. 404–33

EVANS, ARTHUR B., *Jules Verne Rediscovered: Didacticism and the Scientific Novel* (New York: Greenwood Press, 1988)

——'Literary Intertexts in Jules Verne's *Voyages Extraordinaires*', *Science-Fiction Studies*, 23 (1996), 171–87

——'The Illustrators of Jules Verne's *Voyages Extraordinaires*', *Science-Fiction Studies*, 25 (1998), 241–47

——'Jules Verne and the French Literary Canon', in *Jules Verne: Narratives of Modernity*, ed. by Edmund J. Smyth (Liverpool: Liverpool University Press, 2000), pp. 11–39

FALCONER, RACHEL, *Hell in Contemporary Literature: Western Descent Narratives since 1945* (Edinburgh: Edinburgh University Press, 2004)

FLINT, KATE, *The Women Reader, 1837–1914* (Oxford: Clarendon Press, 1993)

FOWLIE, WALLACE, *A Reading of Dante's 'Inferno'* (Chicago/London: University of Chicago Press, 1981)

FRANK, FELICIA MILLER, 'Chateaubriand, Verne, and Méliès: L'Effet d'irréel — Liminal Landscapes and Magic Shows', *Nineteenth Century French Studies*, 23 (1995), 307–15

FREUD, SIGMUND, 'Psychopathic Characters on the Stage', in *The Standard Edition of the Complete Psychological Works of Sigmund Freud*, trans. and ed. by James Strachey, 24 vols (London: Vintage, 2001), VII, 305–10

GARDNER, MARTIN, 'Introduction' in *The Annotated Alice*, ed. by Martin Gardner (Harmondsworth: Penguin, 1976), pp. 7–16

—— 'A Child's Garden of Bewilderment', in *Only Connect: Readings in Children's Literature*, ed. by Sheila Egoff, G. T. Stubbs and L. F. Ashley, 2nd edn (Toronto/New York: OUP, 1980), pp. 150–55

GENETTE, GÉRARD, *Palimpsestes: La Littérature au second degré* (Paris: Seuil, 1982)

——*Palimpsests: Literature in the Second Degree*, trans. by Channa Newman and Claude Doubinsky (Lincoln/London: University of Nebraska Press, 1997)

GONDOLO DELLA RIVA, PIERO, 'George Sand inspiratrice de Jules Verne', in *George Sand et son temps III: Hommage à Annarosa Poli*, ed. by Elio Mosele (Geneva: Slatkine, 1994), pp. 1109–16

GOODACRE, SELWYN H., 'On Alice's Changes of Size in Wonderland', *Jabberwocky: The Journal of the Lewis Carroll Society*, 6 (1977), 20–24

GORÉ, J. L., 'Le Télémaque, périple odysséen ou voyage initiatique?', *Cahiers de l'Association Internationale des Études françaises*, 15 (1963), 59–78

GRANDEROUTE, ROBERT, *Le Roman pédagogique de Fénelon à Rousseau* (Geneva/Paris: Slatkine, 1985)

HARRIS, JOHN R., 'The Katabasis and the Cowboy Film: A Study in Clashing Myths', *Yearbook of Comparative and General Literature*, 47 (1993), 132–48

HAVELY, NICK, 'Introduction: Dante's Afterlife, 1321–1998', in *Dante's Modern Afterlife: Reception and Responses from Blake to Heaney*, ed. by Nick Havely (London: Macmillan, 1998), pp. 1–16

HEATH, PETER, 'The Philosopher's *Alice*', in *Lewis Carroll*, ed. by Harold Bloom (New York: Chelsea House, 1987), pp. 45–52

HEBEL, UDO J., 'Towards a Descriptive Poetics of Allusion', in *Intertextuality*, ed. by Heinrich F. Plett (Berlin/New York: Walter de Gruyter, 1991), pp. 135–64

HEYWOOD, COLIN, *Childhood in Nineteenth-Century France: Work, Health and Education among the 'classes populaires'* (Cambridge: CUP, 1988)

HOLTSMARK, ERLING B., 'The *Katabasis* in Modern Cinema', in *Classical Myth and Culture in the Cinema*, ed. by Martin M. Winkler (Oxford: OUP, 2001), pp. 23–50

HOURIHAN, MARGERY, *Deconstructing the Hero: Literary Theory and Children's Literature* (London/New York: Routledge, 1997)

HUGGAN, GRAHAM, 'Voyages Towards an Absent Centre: Landscape Interpretation and Textual Strategy in Joseph Conrad's *Heart of Darkness* and Jules Verne's *Voyage au centre de la terre*', *The Conradian*, 14 (1989), 19–46

HUNT, PETER, 'What do we lose when we lose allusion? Experience and Understanding Stories', *Signal*, 57 (1988), 212–22

——*An Introduction to Children's Literature* (Oxford: OUP, 1994)

——'"Children's Literature": An Historical/Political/Theoretical Overview', *New Comparison*, 20 (1995), 6–13

—— 'Introduction: The World of Children's Literature Studies', in *Understanding Children's Literature: Key Essays from the 'International Companion Encyclopedia of Children's Literature'*, ed. by Peter Hunt (London/New York: Routledge, 1999), pp. 1–14

JAUSS, HANS ROBERT, 'Levels of Identification of Hero and Audience', trans. by Benjamin and Helga Bennett, *New Literary History*, 5 (1974), 238–317

JENNY, LAURENT, 'La Stratégie de la forme', *Poétique*, 27 (1976), 257–81

JENKYNS, RICHARD, *The Victorians and Ancient Greece* (Cambridge, MA: Harvard University Press, 1980)

KANTZIOS, IPPOKRATIS, 'Educating Telemachus: Lessons in Fénelon's Underworld' <http://ablemedia.com/ctcweb/showcase/kantzios1.html> [Consulted 12 December 2009]

KELLY, RICHARD, "'If you don't know what a Gryphon is': Text and Illustration in *Alice's Adventures in Wonderland*', in *Lewis Carroll, a Celebration: Essays on the Occasion of the 150th*

Anniversary of the Birth of Charles Lutwidge Dodgson, ed. by Edward Guiliano (New York: Potter, 1982), pp. 62–74

KESTNER, JOSEPH A., *Mythology and Misogyny: The Social Discourse of Nineteenth-Century British Classical Subject Painting* (Madison/London: University of Wisconsin Press, 1989)

KRISTEVA, JULIA, Σημειωτιχή: *Recherches pour une semanalyse* (Paris: Seuil, 1969)

——*Desire in Language: A Semiotic Approach to Literature and Art*, trans. by Thomas Gora, Alice Jardine and Leon S. Roudiez (Oxford: Blackwell, 1980)

LESNIK-OBERSTEIN, KARÍN, 'Essentials: What is Children's Literature? What is Childhood?', in *Understanding Children's Literature: Key Essays from the 'International Companion Encyclopedia of Children's Literature'*, ed. by Peter Hunt (London/New York: Routledge, 1999), pp. 15–29

LESSER, WENDY, *The Life Below the Ground: A Study of the Subterranean in Literature and History* (Boston/London: Faber & Faber, 1987)

LODGE, LOUIS, 'Tales of Adventure', in *Give Them Wings: The Experience of Children's Literature*, ed. by Maurice Saxby and Gordon Winch, 2nd edn (Melbourne: Macmillan, 1991), pp. 151–62

LOW, GAIL CHING-LIANG, *White Skins/Black Masks: Representation and Colonialism* (London/New York: Routledge, 1996)

LYONS, MARTYN, 'New Readers in the Nineteenth Century: Women, Children, Workers', in *A History of Reading in the West*, ed. by Guglielmo Cavallo and Roger Chartier (Cambridge: Polity, 2003), pp. 313–44

MACDONALD, RONALD R., *The Burial Places of Memory: Epic Underworlds in Vergil, Dante and Milton* (Amherst: University of Massachusetts Press, 1987)

MARTIN, ANDREW, *The Knowledge of Ignorance: From Genesis to Jules Verne* (Cambridge: CUP, 1985)

McCLINTOCK, ANNE, *Imperial Leather: Race, Gender and Sexuality in the Colonial Contest* (New York/London: Routledge, 1995)

McDOWELL, MYLES, 'Fiction for Children and Adults: Some Essential Differences', in *Writers, Critics, and Children: Articles from 'Children's Literature in Education'*, ed. by Geoff Fox et al. (New York/London: Agathon/Heinemann, 1976), pp. 140–57

McGEORGE, COLIN, 'Death and Violence in Some Victorian School Reading Books', *Children's Literature in Education*, 29: 2 (1998), 109–17

McMORRAN, WILL, 'From Quixote to Caractacus: Influence, Intertextuality, and *Chitty Chitty Bang Bang*', *The Journal of Popular Culture*, 39: 5 (2006), 756–79

MEAKIN, DAVID, 'Jules Verne's Alchemical Journey Short-Circuited', *French Studies*, 45 (1991), 152–65

MEEK, MARGARET, 'Introduction', in *The International Companion Encyclopedia of Children's Literature*, ed. by Peter Hunt (London/New York: Routledge, 1996), pp. 1–13

MILBANK, ALISON, *Dante and the Victorians* (Manchester: Manchester University Press, 1998)

MILLER, OWEN, 'Intertextual Identity', in *Identity of the Literary Text*, ed. by Mario J. Vallès and Owen Miller (Toronto/Buffalo/London: University of Toronto Press, 1985), pp. 19–40

MONSMAN, GERALD, 'Of Diamonds and Deities: Social Anthropology in H. Rider Haggard's *King Solomon's Mines*', *English Literature in Transition (1880–1920)*, 43 (2000), 280–97

MORA-LEBRUN, FRANCINE, 'Postface', in La Sale, *Le Paradis de la Reine Sibylle* (Paris: Éditions Stock, 1983), pp.129–42

MORGAN, THAÏS E., 'Is there an intertext in this text?: Literary and Interdisciplinary Approaches to Intertextuality', *American Journal of Linguistics*, 3 (1985), 1–40

OATLEY, KEITH, 'Meetings of Minds: Dialogue, Sympathy, and Identification in Reading Fiction', *Poetics*, 26 (1999), 439–54

OSBORNE, HUGH, 'Hooked on Classics: Discourses of Allusion in the Mid-Victorian Novel', in *Translation and Nation: Towards a Cultural Politics of Englishness*, ed. by Roger Ellis and Liz Oakley-Brown (Cleveden: Multilingual Matters, 2001), pp. 120–66

OTTEVAERE-VAN PRAAG, GANNA, *La Littérature pour la jeunesse en Europe occidentale (1750–1925)* (Berne: Peter Lang, 1987)

OUSBY, IAN, *The Englishman's England: Taste, Travel and the Rise of Tourism* (Cambridge: CUP, 1990)

PADEL, RUTH, *The Poem and the Journey* (London: Chatto and Windus, 2007)

PAGE, DENYS, *The Homeric Odyssey: The Mary Flexner Lectures*, 2nd edn (Oxford: Clarendon Press, 1966)

PAULSON, RONALD, 'Models and Paradigms: *Joseph Andrews*, Hogarth's *Good Samaritan*, and Fénelon's *Télémaque*', *Modern Language Notes*, 91 (1976), 1186–1207

PETERSEN, ROBERT C., 'To Sleep, Perchance to Dream: Alice Takes a Little Nap', *Jabberwocky: The Journal of the Lewis Carroll Society*, 8 (1979), 27–37

PHILLIPS, RICHARD, *Mapping Men and Empire: A Geography of Adventure* (London: Routledge, 1997)

PIÉGAY-GROS, NATALIE, *Introduction à l'Intertextualité* (Paris: DUNOD, 1996)

PIKE, DAVID L., *Passage Through Hell: Modernist Descents, Medieval Underworlds* (Ithaca, NY/ London: Cornell University Press, 1997)

——*Subterranean Cities: The World Beneath Paris and London, 1800–1945* (Ithaca, NY/London: Cornell University Press, 2005)

——*Metropolis on the Styx: The Underworlds of Modern Urban Culture, 1800–2001* (Ithaca, NY: Cornell University Press, 2007)

PLETT, HEINRICH F., 'Intertextualities', in *Intertextuality*, ed. by Heinrich F. Plett (Berlin/ New York: Walter de Gruyter, 1991), pp. 3–29

PLUMWOOD, VAL, *Feminism and the Mastery of Nature* (London/New York: Routledge, 1993)

PYLES, MARIAN S., *Death and Dying in Children's and Young People's Literature: A Survey and Bibliography* (Jefferson, NC/London: McFarland, 1988)

RABINOVITCH, DINA, 'His bright materials', *The Guardian*, 10 December 2003, section G2, pp. 14–15

RACKIN, DONALD, 'Mind over Matter: Sexuality and where the "body happens to be" in the *Alice* books', in *Textual Bodies: Changing Boundaries of Literary Representation*, ed. by Lori Hope Lefkovitz (New York: State University of New York Press, 1997), pp. 161–83

RAEPER, WILLIAM, *George MacDonald* (Tring: Lion Publishing, 1987)

RIMMON-KENAN, SHLOMITH, *Narrative Fiction: Contemporary Poetics* (London/New York: Routledge, 1999)

ROBIN, CHRISTIAN, 'Avant-Propos', in *Un éditeur et son siècle: Pierre-Jules Hetzel (1814–1886)*, ed. by Christian Robin (Saint-Sébastien: ACL Edition, 1988), pp. 7–11

SAMIVEL, 'Les Surprises de Jules Verne', in *Jules Verne*, ed. by Pierre-André Touttain (Paris: Herne, 1974), pp. 216–21

SCHEICK, WILLIAM J., 'Adolescent Pornography and Imperialism in Haggard's King Solomon's Mines', *English Literature in Transition (1880–1920)*, 34 (1991), 19–30

SCHILDER, PAUL, 'Psychoanalytic Remarks on *Alice in Wonderland* and Lewis Carroll', in *Aspects of Alice: Lewis Carroll's Dreamchild as seen through the Critics' Looking-Glasses, 1865–1971*, ed. by Robert Phillips (London: Victor Gollancz, 1972), pp. 283–92

SEARS, JOHN F., *Sacred Places: American Tourist Attractions in the Nineteenth Century* (Amherst: University of Massachusetts Press, 1998)

SEGEL, ELIZABETH, ' "As the twig is bent...": Gender and Childhood Reading', in *Gender and Reading: Essays on Readers, Texts and Contexts*, ed. by Elizabeth A. Flynn and Patrocinio P. Schweickart, 2nd edn (Baltimore, MD/London: Johns Hopkins University Press, 1992), pp. 165–86

SHABERMAN, RAPHAEL B., *George MacDonald: A Bibliographical Study* (Winchester: St Paul's Bibliographies, 1990)

SHOWALTER, ELAINE, *Sexual Anarchy: Gender and Culture at the 'Fin de Siècle'* (London: Virago Press, 1992)

SIPE, LAWRENCE R., '"Those two gingerbread boys could be brothers": How Children Use Intertextual Connections During Storybook Readalouds', *Children's Literature in Education*, 31 (2000), 73–90

SMITH, EVANS LANSING, *Rape and Revelation: The Descent to the Underworld in Modernism* (Lanham, MD/London: University Press of America, 1990)

—— *The Descent to the Underworld in Literature, Painting and Film, 1895–1950* (Lewiston, NY/ Lampeter: Edwin Mellen Press, 2001)

SMITH, JAMES STEEL, *A Critical Approach to Children's Literature* (New York: McGraw-Hill, 1967)

SØRENSEN, BENT, 'Katabasis in Cormac McCarthy's *Blood Meridian*', *Orbis Litterarum*, 60 (2005), 16–25

SORIANO, MARC, *Guide de littérature pour la jeunesse*, 2nd edn (Paris: Delagrave, 2002)

SPINA, GIORIO [sic], 'The Influence of Dante on George MacDonald', trans. by Paul Priest, *North Wind: The Journal of the George MacDonald Society*, 9 (1990), 15–36

STEPHENS, JOHN, *Language and Ideology in Children's Fiction* (London/New York: Longman, 1992)

—— and ROBYN MCCALLUM, *Retelling Stories, Framing Culture: Traditional Story and Metanarratives in Children's Literature* (London/New York: Garland, 1998)

STOTT, REBECCA, ''Scaping the Body: Of Cannibal Mothers and Colonial Landscapes', in *The New Woman in Fiction and in Fact: Fin-de-Siècle Feminisms*, ed. by Angelique Richardson and Chris Willis (Basingstoke: Palgrave Macmillan, 2002), pp. 150–66

STRAUSS, WALTER, *Descent and Return: The Orphic Theme in Modern Literature* (London: OUP, 1971)

STRAY, CHRISTOPHER, *Classics Transformed: Schools, Universities and Society in England, 1830–1960* (Oxford: Clarendon Press, 1998)

STUBBS, H. W., 'Underworld Themes in Modern Fiction', in *The Journey to the Other World*, ed. by H. R. Ellis Davidson (Cambridge: Brewer, 1975), pp. 130–49

SULEIMAN, SUSAN RUBIN, 'Dialogue and Double Allegiance: Some Contemporary Women Artists and the Historical Avant-Garde', in *Mirror Images: Women, Surrealism and Self-Representation*, ed. by Whitney Chadwick (Cambridge, MA/London: MIT Press, 1998), pp. 128–54

THACKER, DEBORAH COGAN, and JEAN WEBB, *Introducing Children's Literature: From Romanticism to Postmodernism* (London: Routledge, 2002)

TOWNSEND, JOHN ROWE, 'British Children's Literature: A Historical Overview', in *The International Companion Encyclopedia of Children's Literature*, ed. by Peter Hunt (London/ New York: Routledge, 1996), pp. 676–87

TUCKER, NICHOLAS, *Darkness Visible: Inside the World of Philip Pullman* (Cambridge: Wizard, 2003)

TURNER, ALICE, *The History of Hell* (London: Robert Hale, 1995)

VACLAVIK, KIERA, 'George Sand & Jules Verne: A Missing Link', *French Studies Bulletin*, 90 (2004), 8–10

—— 'Death for Beginners: Nineteenth-Century Katabatic Narratives for Young Readers', in *Birth and Death in Nineteenth-Century French Culture*, ed. by Nigel Harkness, Lisa Downing, Sonya Stephens and Timothy Unwin (Amsterdam/New York: Rodopi, 2007), pp. 127–38

—— 'The descent to the underworld retold and regendered in Philip Pullman's *The Amber Spyglass*', *The Journal of Children's Literature Studies*, 5: 2 (July 2008) 37–56

—— 'Visibilité variable: la carte au trésor des *Mines du roi Salomon* de Henry Rider Haggard', *Cahiers Robinson* (forthcoming, 2010)

VANCE, NORMAN, 'Virgil and the Nineteenth Century', in *Virgil and his Influence: Bimillenial Studies*, ed. by Charles Martindale (Exeter: Bristol Classical Press, 1984), pp. 169–92

VIERNE, SIMONE, *Jules Verne et le roman initiatique* (Paris: Éditions du Sirac, 1973)

WALVIN, JAMES, *A Child's World: A Social History of English Childhood* (Harmondsworth: Penguin, 1984)

WEINER, ANDREW D., 'Sidney/Spenser/Shakespeare: Influence/Intertext/Intention', in *Influence and Intertextuality in Literary History*, ed. by Jay Clayton and Eric Rothstein (Madison: University of Wisconsin Press, 1991), pp. 245–70

WILKIE, CHRISTINE, 'Relating Texts: Intertextuality', in *Understanding Children's Literature*, ed. by Peter Hunt (London/New York: Routledge, 1999), pp. 130–37

WILLIAMS, LYLE THOMAS, 'Journeys to the Center of the Earth: Descent and Initiation in Selected Science Fiction' (unpublished doctoral dissertation, University of Indiana, 1983)

WILLIAMS, ROSALIND, *Notes on the Underground: An Essay on Technology, Society, and the Imagination* (Cambridge, MA/London: MIT Press, 1990)

WOLF, DENNIE, and DEBORAH HICKS, 'The Voices within Narratives: The Development of Intertextuality in Young Children's Stories', *Discourse Processes*, 12 (1989), 329–51

WOLFF, ROBERT LEE, *The Golden Key: A Study of the Fiction of George MacDonald* (New Haven, CT: Yale University Press, 1961)

WORTON, MICHAEL, and JUDITH STILL, 'Introduction', in *Intertextuality: Theories and Practices*, ed. by Michael Worton and Judith Still (Manchester/New York: Manchester University Press, 1990), pp. 1–44

ZIPES, JACK, ed., *Victorian Fairy Tales: The Revolt of the Fairies and Elves* (New York/London: Routledge, 1989)

ZELDIN, THEODORE, *France, 1848–1945*, 2 vols (Oxford: Clarendon Press, 1977)

Other Internet Sites Consulted

'Philip Pullman — Full Interview'
    <http://www.literacytrust.org.uk/rif/readingstars/full_interviews/full_philip_pullman.htm>
    [consulted 14 December 2009]

'Francie Muraski-Stotz',
    <http://www.fieldmuseum.org/exhibits/exhibit_sites/wis/francie.htm>
    [consulted 14 December 2009]

'Underground Adventure', <http://www.fieldmuseum.org/undergroundadventure/>
    [consulted 14 December 2009]

INDEX